Wolf Willow

BOOKS BY WALLACE STEGNER
AVAILABLE IN BISON BOOK EDITIONS

All the Little Live Things (BB 709)
*Beyond the Hundredth Meridian: John Wesley Powell
and the Second Opening of the West* (BB 798)
The Big Rock Candy Mountain (BB 855)
Joe Hill (BB 728)
Mormon Country (BB 778)
The Spectator Bird (BB 705)
Wolf Willow (BB 708)
The Women on the Wall (BB 710)

WALLACE STEGNER

Wolf Willow

A History, a Story, and a Memory
of the Last Plains Frontier

University of Nebraska Press ● *Lincoln and London*

"Quiet Earth, Big Sky" and "History Comes to the Great Plains," which appear here in somewhat altered form as "The Question Mark in the Circle" and "The Medicine Line," first appeared in *American Heritage.* "History is a Pontoon Bridge" first appeared in *Horizon.* "The Mounties at Fort Walsh," which makes up part of the chapter entitled "Capital of an Unremembered Past," and "The Town Dump" first appeared in *The Atlantic Monthly.* "Genesis" first appeared in *Contact.* "Carrion Spring" first appeared in *Esquire.* "The Making of Paths," here expanded into the chapter of the same name, first appeared in *The New Yorker.*

First Bison Book printing: 1980
Most recent printing indicated by first digit below:
2   3   4   5   6   7   8   9   10

Library of Congress Cataloging in Publication Data

Stegner, Wallace Earle, 1909–
  Wolf willow.

  "Bison book."
  Reprint of the ed. published by Macmillan, Toronto.
  1. Stegner, Wallace Earle, 1909– —Bibliography—Youth. 2. Frontier and pioneer life—Cypress Hills region, Alta. and Sask. 3. Cypress Hills region, Alta. and Sask.—History. 4. Cypress Hills region, Alta. and Sask.—Fiction. 5. Authors, American—20th century—Biography. I. Title.
  [PS3537.T316Z474 1980]   813'.5'2 [B]   79-18694
  ISBN 0-8032-4109-7
  ISBN 0-8032-9108-6 pbk.

Reprinted by arrangement with the author

Manufactured in the United States of America

This is in memory of my mother

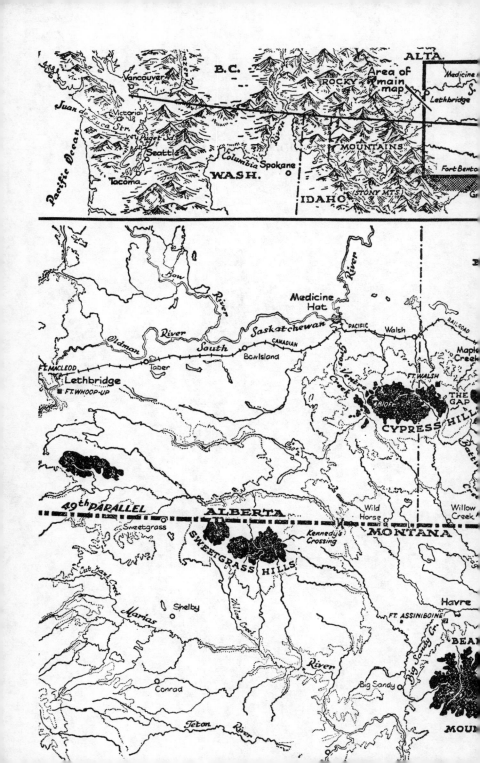

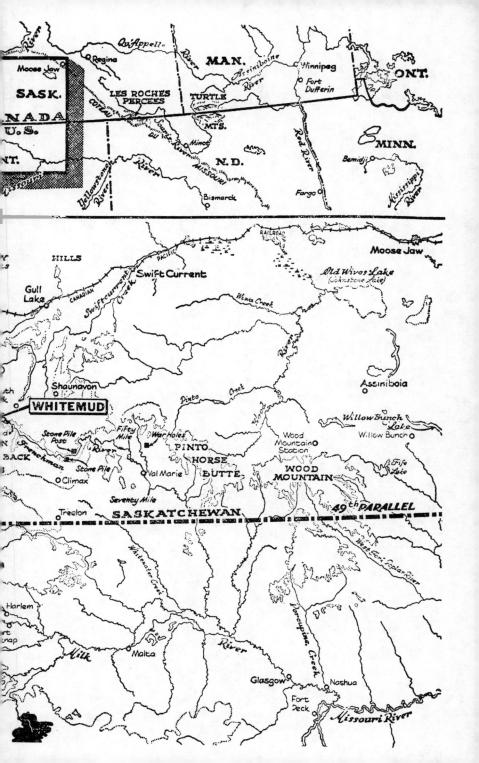

Contents

I THE QUESTION MARK IN THE CIRCLE   1

 1. *The Question Mark in the Circle,* 3
 2. *History Is a Pontoon Bridge,* 21
 3. *The Dump Ground,* 31

II PREPARATION FOR A CIVILIZATION   37

 1. *First Look,* 39
 2. *The Divide,* 44
 3. *Horse and Gun,* 49
 4. *Half World: the* Métis, 57
 5. *Company of Adventurers,* 67
 6. *Last of the Exterminators,* 73
 7. *The Medicine Line,* 81
 8. *Law in a Red Coat,* 100
 9. *Capital of an Unremembered Past,* 111

III THE WHITEMUD RIVER RANGE   125

 1. *Specifications for a Hero,* 127
 2. *Genesis,* 139
 3. *Carrion Spring,* 220

IV TOWN AND COUNTRY   239

    1. The Town Builders, 241
    2. Whitemud, Saskatchewan, 246
    3. The Garden of the World, 254
    4. The Making of Paths, 268

EPILOGUE: FALSE-FRONT ATHENS   285

ACKNOWLEDGMENTS   307

Wolf Willow

I

THE QUESTION MARK IN THE CIRCLE

. . . *whoever even once in his life has caught a perch or seen thrushes migrate in the autumn, when on clear, cool days they sweep in flocks over the village, will never really be a townsman and to the day of his death will have a longing for the open.*

ANTON CHEKHOV, *"Gooseberries"*

1

The Question Mark in the Circle

An ordinary road map of the United States, one that for courtesy's sake includes the first hundred miles on the Canadian side of the Line, will show two roads, graded but not paved, reaching up into western Saskatchewan to link U.S. 2 with Canada 1, the Trans-Canada Highway. One of these little roads leads from Havre, on the Milk River, to Maple Creek; the other from Malta, also on the Milk, to Swift Current. The first, perhaps a hundred and twenty miles long, has no towns on it big enough to show on a map of this scale. The second, fifty miles longer, has two, neither of which would be worth comment except that one of them, Val Marie, is the site of one of the few remaining prairie-dog towns anywhere. The rest of that country is notable primarily for its weather, which is violent and prolonged; its emptiness, which is almost frighteningly total; and its wind, which blows all the time in a way to stiffen your hair and rattle the eyes in your head.

This is no safety valve for the population explosion, no prize in a latter-day land rush. It has had its land rush, and recovered. If you owned it, you might be able to sell certain parts of it at a few dollars an acre; many parts you couldn't give away. Not many cars raise dust along its lonely roads—it is country people do not much want to cross, much less visit. But that block of country between the Milk River and the main line of the Canadian Pacific, and between approximately the Saskatchewan-Alberta line and Wood Mountain, is what this book is about. It is the place where

3

I spent my childhood. It is also the place where the Plains, as an ecology, as a native Indian culture, and as a process of white settlement, came to their climax and their end. Viewed personally and historically, that almost featureless prairie glows with more color than it reveals to the appalled and misdirected tourist. As memory, as experience, those Plains are unforgettable; as history, they have the lurid explosiveness of a prairie fire, quickly dangerous, swiftly over.

I have sometimes been tempted to believe that I grew up on a gun-toting frontier. This temptation I trace to a stagecoach ride in the spring of 1914, and to a cowpuncher named Buck Murphy.

The stagecoach ran from Gull Lake, Saskatchewan, on the main line of the Canadian Pacific, to the town I shall call Whitemud, sixty miles southwest in the valley of the Whitemud or Frenchman River. The grade from Moose Jaw already reached to Whitemud, and steel was being laid, but no trains were yet running when the stage brought in my mother, my brother, and myself, plus a red-faced cowpuncher with a painful deference to ladies and a great affection for little children. I rode the sixty miles on Buck Murphy's lap, half anesthetized by his whiskey breath, and during the ride I confounded both my mother and Murphy by fishing from under his coat a six-shooter half as big as I was.

A little later Murphy was shot and killed by a Mountie in the streets of Shaunavon, up the line. As I heard later, the Mountie was scared and trigger-happy, and would have been in real trouble for an un-Mountie-like killing if Murphy had not been carrying a gun. But instead of visualizing it as it probably was— Murphy coming down the street in a buckboard, the Mountie on the corner, bad blood between them, a suspicious move, a shot, a scared team, a crowd collecting—I have been led by a lifetime of horse opera to imagine that death in standard walk-down detail. For years, growing up in more civilized places, I got a comfortable sense of status out of recalling that in my youth I had been a friend of badmen and an eyewitness to gunfights in wide streets between false-fronted saloons. Not even the streets and saloons, now that I test them, were authentic, for I don't think I was ever in Shaunavon in my boyhood, and I could not have reconstructed an image from Whitemud's streets because at the time of Murphy's death Whitemud didn't have any. It hardly even had houses: we ourselves were living in a derailed dining car.

Actually Murphy was an amiable, drunken, sentimental, perhaps dishonest, and generally harmless Montana cowboy like dozens of others. He may have been in Canada for reasons that would have interested Montana sheriffs, but more likely not; and if he had been, so were plenty of others who never thought of themselves as badmen. The Cypress Hills had always made a comfortable retiring place just a good day's ride north of the Line. Murphy would have carried a six-shooter mainly for reasons of brag; he would have worn it inside his coat because Canadian law forbade the carrying of sidearms. When Montana cattle outfits worked across the Line they learned to leave their guns in their bedrolls. In the American West men came before law, but in Saskatchewan the law was there before settlers, before even cattlemen, and not merely law but law enforcement. It was not characteristic that Buck Murphy should die in a gunfight, but if he had to die by violence it was entirely characteristic that he should be shot by a policeman.

The first settlement in the Cypress Hills country was a village of *métis* winterers, the second was a short-lived Hudson's Bay Company post on Chimney Coulee, the third was the Mounted Police headquarters at Fort Walsh, the fourth was a Mountie outpost erected on the site of the burned Hudson's Bay Company buildings to keep an eye on Sitting Bull and other Indians who congregated in that country in alarming numbers after the big troubles of the 1870's. The Mountie post on Chimney Coulee, later moved down onto the river, was the predecessor of the town of Whitemud. The overgrown foundation stones of its cabins remind a historian why there were no Boot Hills along the Frenchman. The place was too well policed.

So as I have learned more I have had to give up the illusion of a romantic gun-toting past, and it is hardly glamour that brings me back, a middle-aged pilgrim, to the village I last saw in 1920. Neither do I come back with the expectation of returning to a childhood wonderland—or I don't think I do. By most estimates, including most of the estimates of memory, Saskatchewan can be a pretty depressing country.

The Frenchman, a river more American than Canadian since it flows into the Milk and thence into the Missouri, has changed its name since my time to conform with American maps. We always called it the Whitemud, from the stratum of pure white kaolin exposed along its valley. Whitemud or Frenchman, the river is important in my memory, for it conditioned and contained the town. But memory, though vivid, is imprecise, without sure dimensions, and it is as much to test memory against adult observation as for any other reason that I return. What I remember are low bars overgrown with wild roses, cutbank bends, secret paths through the willows, fords across the shallows, swallows in the clay banks, days of indolence and adventure where space was as flexible as the mind's cunning and where time did not exist. That was at the heart of it, the sunken and sanctuary river valley. Out around, stretching in all directions from the benches to become coextensive with the disk of the world, went the uninterrupted prairie.

The geologist who surveyed southern Saskatchewan in the 1870's called it one of the most desolate and forbidding regions on earth. I can remember plenty of times when it seemed so to me and my family. Yet as I poke the car tentatively eastward into it from Medicine Hat, returning to my childhood through a green June, I look for desolation and can find none.

The plain spreads southward below the Trans-Canada Highway, an ocean of wind-troubled grass and grain. It has its remembered textures: winter wheat heavily headed, scoured and shadowed as if schools of fish move in it; spring wheat with its young seed-rows as precise as combings in a boy's wet hair; gray-brown summer fallow with the weeds disked under; and grass, the marvelous curly prairie wool tight to the earth's skin, straining the wind as the wheat does, but in its own way, secretly.

Prairie wool blue-green, spring wheat bright as new lawn, winter wheat gray-green at rest and slaty when the wind flaws it, roadside primroses as shy as prairie flowers are supposed to be, and as gentle to the eye as when in my boyhood we used to call them wild tulips, and by their coming date the beginning of summer.

On that monotonous surface with its occasional ship-like farm, its atolls of shelter-belt trees, its level ring of horizon, there is little to interrupt the eye. Roads run straight between parallel lines of fence until they intersect the circle of the horizon. It is a landscape of circles, radii, perspective exercises—a country of geometry. Across its empty miles pours the pushing and shouldering wind, a thing you tighten into as a trout tightens into fast water. It is a grassy, clean, exciting wind, with the smell of distance in it, and in its search for whatever it is looking for it turns over every wheat blade and head, every pale primrose, even the ground-hugging grass. It blows yellow-headed blackbirds and hawks and prairie sparrows around the air and ruffles the short tails of meadowlarks on fence posts. In collaboration with the light, it makes lovely and changeful what might otherwise be characterless.

It is a long way from characterless; "overpowering" would be a better word. For over the segmented circle of earth is domed the biggest sky anywhere, which on days like this sheds down on range and wheat and summer fallow a light to set a painter wild, a light pure, glareless, and transparent. The horizon a dozen miles away is as clean a line as the nearest fence. There is no haze, neither the woolly gray of humid countries nor the blue atmosphere of the mountain West. Across the immense sky move navies of cumuli, fair-weather clouds, their bottoms as even as if they had scraped themselves flat against the flat earth.

The drama of this landscape is in the sky, pouring with light and always moving. The earth is passive. And yet the beauty I am struck by, both as present fact and as revived memory, is a fusion: this sky would not be so spectacular without this earth to change and glow and darken under it. And whatever the sky may do, however the earth is shaken or darkened, the Euclidean perfection abides. The very scale, the hugeness of simple forms, emphasizes stability. It is not hills and mountains which we should call eternal. Nature abhors an elevation as much as it abhors a vacuum; a hill is no sooner elevated than the forces of erosion begin tearing it down. These prairies are quiescent, close to static; looked at for any length of time, they begin to impose their awful perfection on the observer's mind. Eternity is a peneplain.

In a wet spring such as this, there is almost as much sky on the ground as in the air. The country is dotted with sloughs, every depression is full of water, the roadside ditches are canals. Grass and wheat grow to the water's edge and under it; they seem to grow right under the edges of the sky. In deep sloughs tules have rooted, and every such pond is dignified with mating mallards and the dark little automata that glide after them as if on strings.

The nesting mallards move in my memory, too, pulling after them shadowy, long-forgotten images. The picture of a drake standing on his head with his curly tailfeathers sticking up from a sheet of wind-flawed slough is tangled in my remembering senses with the feel of the grassy edge under my bare feet, the smell of mud, the push of the traveler wind, the weight of the sun, the look of the sky with its level-floored clouds made for the penetration of miraculous Beanstalks.

Desolate? Forbidding? There was never a country that in its good moments was more beautiful. Even in drouth or dust storm or blizzard it is the reverse of monotonous, once you have submitted to it with all the senses. You don't get out of the wind, but learn to lean and squint against it. You don't escape sky and sun, but wear them in your eyeballs and on your back. You become acutely aware of yourself. The world is very large, the sky even larger, and you are very small. But also the world is flat, empty, nearly abstract, and in its flatness you are a challenging upright thing, as sudden as an exclamation mark, as enigmatic as a question mark.

It is a country to breed mystical people, egocentric people, perhaps poetic people. But not humble ones. At noon the total sun pours on your single head; at sunrise or sunset you throw a shadow a hundred yards long. It was not prairie dwellers who invented the indifferent universe or impotent man. Puny you may feel there, and vulnerable, but not unnoticed. This is a land to mark the sparrow's fall.

Our homestead lay south of here, right on the Saskatchewan-Montana border—a place so ambiguous in its affiliations that we felt as uncertain as the drainage about which way to flow. It would be no more than thirty or forty miles out of my way, now, and yet I do not turn south to try to find it, and I know very well why. I am afraid to. In the Dust Bowl years all that country was returned to range by the Provincial Farm Rehabilitation Administration. I can imagine myself bumping across burnouts and cactus clumps, scanning the dehumanized waste for some mark —shack or wind-leaned chickencoop, wagon ruts or abandoned harrow with its teeth full of Russian thistle—to reassure me that people did once live there. Worse, I can imagine actually finding the flat on which our house stood, the coulee that angled up the pasture, the dam behind which the spring thaw created our "rezavoy"—locating the place and standing in it ringed by emptiness and silence, while the wind fingered my face and whispered to itself like an old blind woman, and a burrowing owl, flustered by the unfamiliar visitor, bowed from the dirt mound of its doorstep, saying, "Who? Who?"

I do not want that. I don't want to find, as I know I will if I go down there, that we have vanished without trace like a boat sunk in mid-ocean. I don't want our shack to be gone, as I know it is; I would not enjoy hunting the ground around it for broken crockery and rusty nails and bits of glass. I don't want to know that our protective pasture fence has been pulled down to let the prairie in, or that our field, which stopped at the Line and so defined a sort of identity and difference, now flows southward into Montana without a break as restored grass and burnouts. Once, standing alone under the bell-jar sky gave me the strongest feeling of personal singularity I shall ever have. That was because it was all new, we were taking hold of it to make it ours. But to return hunting relics, to go down there armed only with memory and find every trace of our passage wiped away—that would be to reduce my family, myself, the hard effort of years, to solipsism, to make us as fictive as a dream.

If I say to the owl, "Your great-grandfather lived in my house, and could turn his head clear around and look out between his shoulder blades," I know he will bow, being polite, and then turn *his* head clear around and look out between his shoulder blades, and seeing only unbroken grass, will cough and say, "What house? Whose?" I know the very way the wind will ruffle his feathers as he turns; I can hear the dry silence that will resume as soon as he stops speaking. With the clarity of hallucination I can see my mother's weathered, rueful, half-laughing face, and hear the exact tone, between regretful and indomitable, in which she says the words with which she always met misfortune or failure: "Well," she will say, "better luck next time!"

I had much better let it alone. The town is safer. I turn south only far enough to come up onto the South Bench, and then I follow a dirt road eastward so as to enter Whitemud from the old familiar direction. That much I will risk.

It is a far more prosperous country than I remember, for I return at the crest of a wet cycle. The farms that used to jut bleakly from the prairie are bedded in cottonwoods and yellow-flowering caragana. Here and there the horizontal land is broken by a new verticality more portentous than windmills or elevators —the derricks of oil rigs. Farther north, prosperity rides on the uranium boom. Here it rides on wheat and oil. But though the country is no longer wild, this section within reach of town is even emptier, more thinly lived in, than in our time. Oil crews create no new towns and do not enlarge the old ones more than briefly. Even if they hit oil, they erect a Christmas tree on the well and go away. As for wheat, fewer and fewer farmers produce more and more of it.

To us, a half section was a farm. With modern machinery, a man by himself can plow, seed, and harvest a thousand or twelve hundred acres. The average Saskatchewan farm is at least a section; two sections, or even more, are not uncommon. And that is the good land, not the submarginal land such as ours which has been put back to grass. Even such a duchy of a farm is only a part-time job. A man can seed a hundred acres a day. Once the crop is in there is little to do until harvest. Then a week or two on the combine, a week or two of hauling, a week or two of working the summer fallow and planting winter wheat, and he is all done until May.

This is a strange sort of farming, with its dangers of soil exhaustion, drouth, and wind erosion, and with highly specialized conditions. Only about half of the farmhouses on the prairie are lived in any more, and some of those are lived in only part time, by farmers who spend all but the crop season in town, as we did. Many a farmer miles from town has no farmhouse at all, but commutes to work in a pickup. There is a growing class of trailer farmers, suitcase farmers, many of them from the United

States, who camp for three or four months beside the field and return to Minneapolis or Bismarck when the crop is in.

Hence the look of extensive cultivation and at the same time the emptiness. We see few horses, few cattle. Saskatchewan farmers could go a long way toward supplying the world's bread, but they are less subsistence farmers than we were in 1915. They live in towns that have the essential form and function of medieval towns, or New England country towns, or Mormon villages in irrigated land: clusters of dwellings surrounded by the cultivated fields. But here the fields are a mile or two miles square and may be forty miles from the home of the man who works them.

So it is still quiet earth, big sky. Human intrusions seem as abrupt as the elevators that leap out of the plain to announce every little hamlet and keep it memorable for a few miles. The countryside and the smaller villages empty gradually into the larger centers; in the process of slow adaptation to the terms the land sets, the small towns get smaller, the larger ones larger. Whitemud, based strategically on railroad and river, is one of the ones that will last.

In the fall it was always a moment of pure excitement, after a whole day on the trail, to come to the rim of the South Bench. More likely than not I would be riding with my mother in the wagon while my father had my brother with him in the Ford. The horses would be plodding with their noses nearly to their knees, the colt would be dropping tiredly behind. We would be choked with dust, cranky and headachy with heat, our joints loosened with fifty miles of jolting. Then miraculously the land fell away below us, I would lift my head from my mother's lap and push aside the straw hat that had been protecting my face from the glare, and there below, looped in its green coils of river, snug and protected in its sanctuary valley, lay town.

The land falls away below me now, the suddenness of my childhood town is the old familiar surprise. But I stop, looking, for adult perception has in ten seconds clarified a childhood error. I have always thought of the Whitemud as running its whole course in a deeply sunken valley. Instead, I see that the river has cut deeply only through the uplift of the hills; that off to the southeast, out on the prairie, it crawls disconsolately flat across the land. It is a lesson in how peculiarly limited a child's sight is: he sees only what he can see. Only later does he learn to link what he sees with what he already knows, or has imagined or heard or read, and so come to make perception serve inference. During my childhood I kept hearing about the Cypress Hills, and knew that they were somewhere nearby. Now I see that I grew up in them. Without destroying the intense familiarity, the flooding recognition of the moment, that grown-up understanding throws things a little out of line, and so it is with mixed feelings of intimacy and strangeness that I start down the dugway grade. Things look the same, surprisingly the same, and yet obscurely different. I tick them off, easing watchfully back into the past.

There is the Frenchman's stone barn, westward up the river valley a couple of miles. It looks exactly as it did when we used to go through the farmyard in wagon or buckboard and see the startled kids disappearing around every corner, and peeking out at us from hayloft door and cowshed after we passed. Probably they were *métis*, halfbreeds; to us, who had never heard the word *métis*, they were simply Frenchmen, part of the vague and unknown past that had given our river one of its names. I bless them for their permanence, and creep on past the cemetery, somewhat larger and somewhat better kept than I remember it, but without disconcerting changes. Down below me is the dam, with its wide lake behind it. It takes me a minute to recollect that by the time we left Whitemud Pop Martin's dam had long since washed out. This is a new one, therefore, but in approximately the old place. So far, so good.

The road I bump along is still a dirt road, and it runs where it used to run, but the wildcat oil derrick that used to be visible from the turn at the foot of the grade is not there any longer. I note, coming in toward the edge of town, that the river has changed its course somewhat, swinging closer to the southern hills and pinching the road space. I see a black iron bridge, new, that evidently leads some new road off into the willow bottoms westward, toward the old Carpenter ranch. I cannot see the river, masked in willows and alders, and anyway my attention is taken by the town ahead of me, which all at once reveals one element of the obscure strangeness that has been making me watchful. Trees.

My town used to be as bare as a picked bone, with no tree anywhere around it larger than a ten-foot willow or alder. Now it is a grove. My memory gropes uneasily, trying to establish itself among fifty-foot cottonwoods, lilac and honeysuckle hedges, and flower gardens. Searched for, plenty of familiarities are there: the Pastime Theater, identical with the one that sits across Main Street from the firehouse in my mind; the lumber yard where we used to get cloth caps advertising De Laval Cream Separators; two or three hardware stores (a prairie wheat town specializes in hardware stores), though each one now has a lot full of farm machinery next to it; the hotel, just as it was rebuilt after the fire; the bank, now remodeled into the post office; the Presbyterian church, now United, and the *Leader* office, and the square brick prison of the school, now with three smaller prisons added to it. These are old acquaintances that I can check against their replicas in my head and take satisfaction from. But among them are the evidences of Progress—hospital, Masonic Lodge, at least one new elevator, a big quonset-like skating rink—and all tree-shaded, altered and distorted and made vaguely disturbing by greenery. In the old days we all used to try to grow trees, transplanting them from the Hills or getting them free with any two-dollar purchase from one of the stores, but they always dried up and died. To me, who came expecting a dusty hamlet, the change is charming, but memory has been fixed by time as photographs fix the faces of the dead, and this reality is dreamlike. I cannot find myself or my family or my companions in it.

My progress up Main Street, as wide and empty and dusty as I remember it, has taken me to another iron bridge across the eastern loop of the river, where the flume of Martin's irrigation ditch used to cross, and from the bridge I get a good view of the river. It is disappointing, a quiet creek twenty yards wide, the color of strong tea, its banks a tangle of willow and wild rose. How could adventure ever have inhabited those willows, or wonder, or fear, or the other remembered emotions? Was it along here I shot at the lynx with my brother's .25-.20? And out of what log (there is no possibility of a log in these brakes, but I distinctly remember a log) did my bullet knock chips just under the lynx's bobtail?

A muddy little stream, a village grown unfamiliar with time and trees. I turn around and retrace my way up Main Street and park and have a Coke in the confectionery store. It is run by a Greek, as it used to be, but whether the same Greek or another I would not know. He does not recognize me, nor I him. Only the smell of his place is familiar, syrupy with old delights, as if the ghost of my first banana split had come close to breathe on me. Still in search of something or someone to make the town fully real to me, I get the telephone book off its nail by the wall telephone and run through it, sitting at the counter. There are no more than seventy or eighty names in the Whitemud section. I look for Huffman—none. Bickerton—none. Fetter—none. Orullian—none. Stenhouse—none. Young—one, but not by a first name I remember. There are a few names I do remember—Harold Jones and William Christenson and Nels Sieverud and Jules LaPlante. (That last one startles me. I always thought his name was Jewell.) But all of the names I recognize are those of old-timers, pioneers of the town. Not a name that I went to school with, not a single person who would have shared as a contemporary my own experience of this town in its earliest years, when the river still ran clear and beaver swam in it in the evenings. Who in town remembers Phil Lott, who used to run coyotes with wolfhounds out on the South Bench? Who remembers in the way I do the day he drove up before Leaf's store in his democrat wagon and unloaded from it two dead hounds and the lynx that had killed them when they caught him unwarily exposed out on the flats? Who remembers in *my* way that angry and disgusted scene, and shares my recollection of the stiff, half-disemboweled bodies of the hounds and the bloody grin of the lynx? Who feels it or felt it, as I did and do, as a parable, a moral lesson for the pursuer to respect the pursued?

Because it is not shared, the memory seems fictitious, and so do other memories: the blizzard of 1916 that marooned us in the schoolhouse for a night and a day, the time the ice went out and brought both Martin's dam and the CPR bridge in kindling to our doors, the games of fox-and-geese in the untracked snow of a field that is now a grove, the nights of skating with a great fire leaping from the river ice and reflecting red from the cut-banks. I have used those memories for years as if they really happened, have made stories and novels of them. Now they seem uncorroborated and delusive. Some of the pioneers still in the telephone book would remember, but pioneers' memories are no good to me. Pioneers would remember the making of the town; to me, it was made, complete, timeless. A pioneer's child is what I need now, and in this town the pioneers' children did not stay, but went on, generally to bigger places farther west, where there was more opportunity.

Sitting in the sticky-smelling, nostalgic air of the Greek's confectionery store, I am afflicted with the sense of how many whom I have known are dead, and how little evidence I have that I myself have lived what I remember. It is not quite the same feeling I imagined when I contemplated driving out to the homestead. That would have been absolute denial. This, with its tantalizing glimpses, its hints and survivals, is not denial but only doubt. There is enough left to disturb me, but not to satisfy me. So I will go a little closer. I will walk on down into the west bend and take a look at our house.

In the strange forest of the school yard the boys are friendly, and their universal air of health, openness, and curiosity reassures me. This is still a good town to be a boy in. To see a couple of them on the prowl with air rifles (in my time we would have been carrying .22's or shotguns, but we would have been of the same tribe) forces me to readjust my disappointed estimate of the scrub growth. When one is four feet high, ten-foot willows are a sufficient cover, and ten acres are a wilderness.

By now, circling and more than half unwilling, I have come into the west end of town, have passed Corky Jones's house (put off till later that meeting) and the open field beside Downs's where we used to play run-sheep-run in the evenings, and I stand facing the four-gabled white frame house that my father built. It ought to be explosive with nostalgias and bright with recollections, for this is where we lived for five or six of my most impressionable years, where we all nearly died with the flu in 1918, where my grandmother "went crazy" and had to be taken away by a Mountie to the Provincial asylum because she took to standing silently in the door of the room where my brother and I slept—just hovered there for heaven knows how long before someone discovered her watching and listening in the dark. I try to remember my grandmother's face and cannot; only her stale old-woman's smell after she became incontinent. I can summon up other smells, too—it is the smells that seem to have stayed with me: baking paint and hot tin and lignite smoke behind the parlor heater; frying scrapple, which we called head-cheese, on chilly fall mornings after the slaughtering was done; the rich thick odor of doughnuts frying in a kettle of boiling lard (I always got to eat the "holes"). With effort, I can bring back Christmases, birthdays, Sunday School parties in that house, and I have not forgotten the licking I got when, aged about six, I was caught playing with my father's loaded .30-.30 that hung above the mantel just under the Rosa Bonheur painting of three white horses in a storm. After that licking I lay out behind the chopping block all one afternoon watching my big dark heavy father as he worked at one thing and another, and all the time I lay there I kept aiming an empty cartridge case at him and dreaming murder.

Even the dreams of murder, which were bright enough at the time, have faded; he is long dead, and if not forgiven, at least propitiated. My mother too, who saved me from him so many times, and once missed saving me when he clouted me with a chunk of stove wood and knocked me over the woodbox and broke my collarbone: she too has faded. Standing there looking at the house where our lives entangled themselves in one another, I am infuriated that of that episode I remember less her love and protection and anger than my father's inept contrition. And walking all around the house trying to pump up recollection, I notice principally that the old barn is gone. What I see, though less changed than the town in general, still has power to disturb me; it is all dreamlike, less real than memory, less convincing than the recollected odors.

Whoever lives in the house now is a tidy housekeeper; the yard is neat, the porch swept. The corner where I used to pasture my broken-legged colt is a bed of flowers, the yard where we hopefully watered our baby spruces is a lawn enclosed by a green hedge. The old well with the hand pump is still in the side

yard. For an instant my teeth are on edge with the memory of
the dry screech of that pump before a dipperful of priming
water took hold, and an instant later I feel the old stitch in my
side from an even earlier time, the time when we still carried
water from the river, and I dipped a bucket down into the hole
in the ice and toted it, staggering and with the other arm stuck
stiffly out, up the dugway to the kitchen door.

Those instants of memory are persuasive. I wonder if I should
knock on the door and ask the housewife to let me look around,
go upstairs to our old room in the west gable, examine the ceiling to see if the stains from the fire department's chemicals are
still there. My brother and I used to lie in bed and imagine
scenes and faces among the blotches, giving ourselves inadvert-
ent Rorschach tests. I have a vivid memory, too, of the night
the stains were made, when we came out into the hard cold
from the Pastime Theater and heard the firehouse bell going and
saw the volunteer fire department already on the run, and followed them up the ditch toward the glow of the fire, wondering
whose house, until we got close and it was ours.

It is there, and yet it does not flow as it should, it is all a pump-
ing operation. I half suspect that I am remembering not what
happened but something I have written. I find that I am as unwilling to go inside that house as I was to try to find the old
homestead in its ocean of grass. All the people who once shared
the house with me are dead; strangers would have effaced or
made doubtful the things that might restore them in my mind.

Behind our house there used to be a footbridge across the river,
used by the Carpenters and others who lived in the bottoms,
and by summer swimmers from town. I pass by the opaque and
troubling house to the cutbank. The twin shanties that through
all the town's life have served as men's and women's bath houses
are still there. In winter we used to hang our frozen beef in one
of them. I remember iron evenings when I went out with a lantern and sawed and haggled steaks from a rocklike hind quarter.
But it is still an academic exercise; I only remember it, I do
not feel the numb fingers and the fear that used to move just
beyond the lantern's glow.

Then I walk to the cutbank edge and look down, and in one
step the past comes closer than it has yet been. There is the

gray curving cutbank, not much lower than I remember it when
we dug cave holes in it or tunneled down its drifted cliff on
our sleds. The bar is there at the inner curve of the bend, and
kids are wallowing in a quicksandy mudhole and shrieking on
an otter slide. They chase each other into the river and change
magically from black to white. The water has its old quiet, its
whirlpools spin lazily into deep water. On the footbridge, nearly
exactly where it used to be, two little girls lie staring down into
the water a foot below their noses. Probably they are watching
suckers that lie just as quietly against the bottom. In my time
we used to snare them from the bridge with nooses of copper
wire.

It is with me all at once, what I came hoping to re-establish, an
ancient, unbearable recognition, and it comes partly from the
children and the footbridge and the river's quiet curve, but
much more from the smell. For here, pungent and pervasive, is
the smell that has always meant my childhood. I have never
smelled it anywhere else, and it is as evocative as Proust's made-
leine and tea.

But what is it? Somehow I have always associated it with the
bath house, with wet bathing suits and damp board benches,
heaps of clothing, perhaps even the seldom rinsed corners where
desperate boys had made water. I go into the men's bath house,
and the smell is there, but it does not seem to come from any
single thing. The whole air smells of it, outside as well as in.
Perhaps it is the river water, or the mud, or something about the
float and footbridge. It is the way the old burlap-tipped diving
board used to smell; it used to remain in the head after a sinus-
flooding dive.

I pick up a handful of mud and sniff it. I step over the little
girls and bend my nose to the wet rail of the bridge. I stand
above the water and sniff. On the other side I strip leaves off
wild rose and dogwood. Nothing doing. And yet all around me is
that odor that I have not smelled since I was eleven, but have
never forgotten—have *dreamed*, more than once. Then I pull
myself up the bank by a gray-leafed bush, and I have it. The
tantalizing and ambiguous and wholly native smell is no more
than the shrub we called wolf willow, now blooming with small
yellow flowers.

It is wolf willow, and not the town or anyone in it, that brings me home. For a few minutes, with a handful of leaves to my nose, I look across at the clay bank and the hills beyond where the river loops back on itself, enclosing the old sports and picnic ground, and the present and all the years between are shed like a boy's clothes dumped on the bath-house bench. The perspective is what it used to be, the dimensions are restored, the senses are as clear as if they had not been battered with sensation for forty alien years. And the queer adult compulsion to return to one's beginnings is assuaged. A contact has been made, a mystery touched. For the moment, reality is made exactly equivalent with memory, and a hunger is satisfied. The sensuous little savage that I once was is still intact inside me.

Later, looking from the North Bench hills across my restored town, I can see the river where it shallows and crawls southeastward across the prairie toward the Milk, the Missouri, and the Gulf, and I toy with the notion that a man is like the river or the clouds, that he can be constantly moving and yet steadily renewed. The sensuous little savage, at any rate, has not been rubbed away or dissolved; he is as solid a part of me as my skeleton.

And he has a fixed and suitably arrogant relationship with his universe, a relationship geometrical and symbolic. From his center of sensation and question and memory and challenge, the circle of the world is measured, and in that respect the years of experience I have loaded upon my savage have not altered him. Lying on a hillside where I once sprawled among the crocuses, watching the town herd and snaring May's emerging gophers, I feel how the world still reduces me to a point and then measures itself from me. Perhaps the meadowlark singing from a fence post —a meadowlark whose dialect I recognize—feels the same way. All points on the circumference are equidistant from him; in him all radii begin; all diameters run through him; if he moves, a new geometry creates itself around him.

No wonder he sings. It is a good country that can make anyone feel so.

And it is a fact that once I have, so to speak, recovered myself as I used to be, I can look at the town, whose childhood was exactly contemporary with my own, with more understanding. It turns out to have been a special sort of town—special not only to me, in that it provided the indispensable sanctuary to match the prairie's exposure, but special in its belated concentration of Plains history. The successive stages of the Plains frontier flowed like a pageant through these Hills, and there are men still alive who remember almost the whole of it. My own recollections cover only a fragment; and yet it strikes me that this is *my* history. My disjunct, uprooted, cellular family was more typical than otherwise on the frontier. But more than we knew, we had our place in a human movement. What this town and its surrounding prairie grew from, and what they grew into, is the record of my tribe. If I am native to anything, I am native to this.

2

History Is a Pontoon Bridge

Unless everything in a man's memory of childhood is misleading, there is a time somewhere between the ages of five and twelve which corresponds to the phase ethologists have isolated in the development of birds, when an impression lasting only a few seconds may be imprinted on the young bird for life. This is the way a bird emerging from the darkness of the egg knows itself, the mechanism of its relating to the world. Expose a just-hatched duckling to an alarm clock, or a wooden decoy on rollers, or a man, or any other object that moves and makes a noise, and it will react for life as if that object were its mother. Expose a child to a particular environment at his susceptible time and he will perceive in the shapes of that environment until he dies. The perceptive habits that are like imprintings or like conditioned responses carry their habitual and remembered emotions. Wolf willow is a sample, but things other than smells will do it. I can sing an old Presbyterian Sunday School hymn, "The Fight Is On, Oh Christian Soldiers," and instantly I am seven or eight years old, it is a June day on the homestead, the coulee is full of buttercups, and a flickertail's close-eared head is emerging in jerks from a burrow, the unblinking almond eye watching to see if I move. Only because I must have sung it to myself in that spot, a few bars of that tune can immerse me in the old sun and space, return me to the big geometry of the prairie and the tension of the prairie wind.

I still sometimes dream, occasionally in the most intense and

brilliant shades of green, of a jungly dead bend of the Whitemud
below Martin's dam. Every time I have that dream I am haunted,
on awaking, by a sense of meanings just withheld, and by a profound nostalgic melancholy. Freudian implications suggest themselves, and the brilliant metallic greens of the dream could be
an alarming symptom from my suprarenals. But the Freudian
and endocrine aspects interest me less than the mere fact that
this dead loop of river, known only for a few years, should be
so charged with potency in my unconscious—why around it there
should be other images, almost all from the river valley rather
than from the prairie, that constantly recur in dreams or in the
images I bring up off the typewriter onto the page. They lie
in me like underground water; every well I put down taps them.
If I must have Freudian dreams, and I suppose I must, why does
that early imprinting, rather than all later experience, so often
dictate their form? And if my suprarenals must cut up, why do
the mescalin-vivid colors of my visions have to come, not merely
from childhood but from a fraction of childhood?

I suppose I know, actually. As the prairie taught me identity
by exposing me, the river valley taught me about safety. In a
jumpy and insecure childhood where all masculine elements are
painful or dangerous, sanctuary matters. That sunken bottom
sheltered from the total sky and the untrammeled wind was my
hibernating ground, my place of snugness, and in a country often
blistered and crisped, green became the color of safety. When I
feel the need to return to the womb, this is still the place toward
which my well-conditioned unconscious turns like an old horse
heading for the barn.

Psychological narcissism is interesting enough to the individual
who is indulging in it, but hardly to anyone else. There is something else here, and of a more general bearing. The accident of
being brought up on a belated, almost symbolic frontier has put
me through processes of deculturation, isolation, and intellectual
schizophrenia that until recently have been a most common American experience. The lateness of my frontier and the fact that it
lay in Canada intensified the discrepancy between that part of
me which reflects the folk culture and that part which reflects an
education imported and often irrelevant. The dichotomy between American and European that exists to some extent in all

of us exists most drastically in people reared on frontiers, for frontiers provide not only the rawest forms of deculturation but the most slavish respect for borrowed elegances.

Man, being infinitely adaptable, does not perish of a mere discrepancy. The titanotheres whose fossil bones lie embedded in the Cypress Hills sandstones died off when a climatic change killed the mushy forage for which their chopper teeth were designed, but I shall not lose even sleep or efficiency because of the division in me. I shall only feel half an anachronism in an America that has been industrialized, regimented, bulldozed, and urbanized out of direct contact with the earth.

I may not know who I am, but I know where I am from. I can say to myself that a good part of my private and social character, the kinds of scenery and weather and people and humor I respond to, the prejudices I wear like dishonorable scars, the affections that sometimes waken me from middle-aged sleep with a rush of undiminished love, the virtues I respect and the weaknesses I condemn, the code I try to live by, the special ways I fail at it and the kinds of shame I feel when I do, the models and heroes I follow, the colors and shapes that evoke my deepest pleasure, the way I adjudicate between personal desire and personal responsibility, have been in good part scored into me by that little womb-village and the lovely, lonely, exposed prairie of the homestead. However anachronistic I may be, I am a product of the American earth, and in nothing quite so much as in the contrast between what I knew through the pores and what I was officially taught.

People on a frontier revert quickly, except when they are self-consciously preserving some imported nicety, to folk skills, and some of these are so primitive that they seem to have scarcely any national character at all. In their performance you cannot tell a Norwegian from a Dukhobor, or either one from an Ontario man. It is as if they came down to us from Neanderthal or Cro-Magnon ancestors—our way with simple hand tools, our way with animals, the simpler forms of social organization. On that level, every frontier child knows exactly who he is, and who his mother is, and he loves his alarm clock quite as much as if it had feathers. But then comes something else, a waddling thing with webbed feet, insisting that *it* is his mother, that he is not who he thought he was, but infinitely more, heir to swans and phoenixes. In such a town as Whitemud, school superimposes five thousand years of Mediterranean culture and two thousand years of Europe upon the adapted or rediscovered simplicities of a new continent.

We had our own grain, and our knots as well, but prairie and town did the shaping, and sometimes I have wondered if they did not cut us to a pattern no longer viable. Far more than Henry Adams, I have felt myself entitled to ask whether my needs and my education were not ludicrously out of phase. Not because I was educated for the past instead of the future—most education trains us for the past, as most preparation for war readies us for the war just over—but because I was educated for the wrong place. Education tried, inadequately and hopelessly, to make a European of me.

Once, in a self-pitying frame of mind, I was comparing my background with that of an English novelist friend. Where he had been brought up in London, taken from the age of four onward to the Tate and the National Gallery, sent traveling on the Continent in every school holiday, taught French and German and Italian, given access to bookstores, libraries, and British Museums, made familiar from infancy on with the conversation of the eloquent and the great, I had grown up in this dungheeled sagebrush town on the disappearing edge of nowhere, utterly without painting, without sculpture, without architecture, almost without music or theater, without conversation or languages or travel or stimulating instruction, without libraries or museums or bookstores, almost without books. I was charged with getting in a single lifetime, from scratch, what some people inherit as naturally as they breathe air. And not merely cultural matters. I was nearly twelve before I saw either a bathtub or a water-closet, and when I walked past my first lawn, in Great Falls, Montana, I stooped down and touched its cool nap in awe and unbelief. I think I held my breath—I had not known that people anywhere lived with such grace. Also I had not known until then how much ugliness I myself had lived with. Our homestead yard was as bare as an alkali flat, because my father, observing some folklore fire precaution, insisted on throwing out the soapy wash water until he had killed off every blade of grass or cluster of false mallow inside the fireguard. Our yard in town, though not so littered with feathers and cans and chicken heads as some, was a weed-patch, because our habit of spending the summers on the homestead prevented my mother from growing any flowers except the Wandering Jew and Star of Bethlehem that she carried back and forth in pots.

How, I asked this Englishman, could anyone from so deprived a background ever catch up? How was one expected to compete, as a cultivated man, with people like himself? He looked at me and said dryly, "Perhaps you got something else in place of all that."

He meant, I suppose, that there are certain advantages to growing up a sensuous little savage, and to tell the truth I am not sure I would trade my childhood of freedom and the out-doors and the senses for a childhood of being led by the hand past all the Turners in the National Gallery. And also, he may have meant that anyone starting from deprivation is spared getting bored. You may not get a good start, but you may get up a considerable head of steam. I am reminded of Willa Cather, that bright girl from Nebraska, memorizing long passages from the *Aeneid* and spurning the dust of Red Cloud and Lincoln with her culture-bound feet. She tried, and her education encouraged her, to be a good European. Nevertheless she was a first-rate novelist only when she dealt with what she knew from Red Cloud and the things she had "in place of all that." Nebraska was what she was born to write; the rest of it was got up. Eventually, when education had won and nurture had conquered nature and she had recognized Red Cloud as a vulgar little hole, she embraced the foreign tradition totally and ended by being neither quite a good American nor quite a true European nor quite a whole artist.

Her career is a parable. If there is truth in Lawrence's assertion that America's unconscious wish has always been to destroy Europe, it is also true that from Irving to William Styron, American writers have been tempted toward apostasy and expatriation, toward return and fusion with the parent. It is a painful and sometimes fatal division, and the farther you are from Europe —that is, the farther you are out in the hinterlands of America— the more difficult it is. Contradictory voices tell you who you are.

You grow up speaking one dialect and reading and writing another. During twenty-odd years of education and another thirty of literary practice you may learn to be nimble in the King's English; yet in moments of relaxation, crisis, or surprise you fall back into the corrupted lingo that is your native tongue. Nevertheless all the forces of culture and snobbery are against your *writing* by ear and making contact with your own natural audience. Your natural audience, for one thing, doesn't read—it *isn't* an audience. You grow out of touch with your dialect because learning and literature lead you another way unless you consciously resist. It is only the occasional Mark Twain or Robert Frost who manages to get the authentic American tone of voice into his work. For most of us, the language of literature is to some extent unreal, because school has always been separate from life.

In practice, the deculturation of a frontier means a falling-back on mainly oral traditions, on the things that can be communicated without books: on folklore, on the music and poetry and story easily memorized, on the cookery that comes not from cookbooks but from habit and laziness, on the medicine that is old wives' tales. Before it was more than half assembled from its random parts, the folklore of Whitemud was mine. I knew the going ballads, mainly of cowboy origin and mainly dirty, and because my father had a sticky memory and a knack of improvisation, I knew some that he probably made up on the spur of the moment. I took part and pleasure in the school cantatas and the town jamborees that were our concert stage and our vaudeville. I absorbed by osmosis the local lore, whether it involved the treatment of frostbite or the virtues of sulphur and molasses for "thinning the blood" in the spring. I ate my beef well done because that was the way everyone ate it, and only shame keeps me from eating it that way yet. But I also read whatever books I could lay hands on, and almost everything I got from books was either at odds with what I knew from experience or irrelevant to it or remote from it. Books didn't enlarge me; they dispersed me.

Naturally the books were not exactly what a wise tutor would have prescribed. We were not lucky enough to have in Whitemud one of those eccentric men of learning who brought good libraries to so many earlier frontier towns and who lighted fires under susceptible village boys. The books we saw were the survivors of many moves, accidentally preserved pieces of family impedimenta, or they were a gradual accretion, mainly Christmas presents, ordered sight unseen by the literarily sightless from the catalog of the T. Eaton mail-order house.

Our house contained some novels of George Barr McCutcheon and Gene Stratton-Porter, a set of Shakespeare in marbled bindings with red leather spines and corners, and a massive set of Ridpath's *History of the World*. I handled them all, and I suppose read in them some, uncomprehendingly, from the time I was five. Their exteriors are still vivid to me; their contents have not always stuck. The gray binding and the cover picture of a romance called *The Rock in the Baltic* I recall very well, without recalling anything about the novel or even who wrote it. Until I began to get a few books of my own—Tarzan books, or the Bar-Twenty novels of B. M. Bower, principally—my favorite volumes were the Ridpath histories, because I liked the spidery steel engravings with which they were illustrated. It was my mother's inaccurate boast that I had read clear through Ridpath's volumes by the time I was eight.

Let us say that I had looked at the pictures, and learned a few names, and could parrot a few captions and chapter headings. Much of that random rubbish is still in my head like an impression in wax, and comes out of me now as if memory were a phonograph record. What strikes me about this in recollection is not my precocious or fictitious reading capacity, and not the durability of memory, but the fact that the information I was gaining from literature and from books on geography and history had not the slightest relevance to the geography, history, or life of the place where I lived. Living in the Cypress Hills, I did not even know I lived there, and hadn't the faintest notion of who had lived there before me. But I could have drawn you a crudely approximate map of the Baltic, recited you Tom Moore songs or Joaquin Miller's poem on Columbus, or given you a rudimentary notion of the virtues of the Gracchi or the misfortunes of the Sabine women.

Though my friends and I sometimes planned gaudy canoe expeditions down the Whitemud, we had no notion where such a trip might bring us out, and no notion that there were maps which would tell us. The willow-fringed stream, after it left the Hills, might as well have been on its way to join the Alph. The Hills of which I was an unknowing resident were only a few fixed points: North Bench, South Bench, the sandhills, Chimney Coulee. The world I knew was immediate, not comparative; seen flat, without perspective. Knowledge of place, knowledge of the past, meant to me knowledge of the far and foreign.

I know now that there were some books from which we could have learned a good deal about our own world. Nobody in town, I am sure, knew they existed unless it was Corky Jones, and Corky's interest in history and other matters was never fully comprehended by his fellow townsmen. Certainly school taught us nothing in this line. The closest it came was Frontenac, Montcalm and Wolfe, and the Plains of Abraham. The one relic of the local past that we were all aware of, the line of half-tumbled chimneys where the *métis* village had once stood on the edge of Chimney Coulee, had in our mouths a half-dozen interpretations, all of them wrong. I remember my father's telling us that they were Indian signaling chimneys. He was, in his way, consistently creative. If he lost the verses of a song, he made up new ones; if he was in doubt about the meaning or source of a word, he was fast with a folk etymology; if he was ignorant of the facts, as in the case of the chimneys, he did not let ignorance hamper his imagination.

In general the assumption of all of us, child or adult, was that this was a new country and that a new country had no history. History was something that applied to other places. It would not have seemed reasonable to any of the town's founders to consider any of their activities history, or to look back very far in search of what had preceded them. Time reached back only a few years, to the pre-homestead period of the big cattle ranches. Some ranches had weathered the terrible winter of 1906, and to a child these survivors seemed to have existed forever, floating in an enduring present like the town. For that matter, I never heard of the terrible winter of 1906 until many years later, though it had affected my life for me before I was born.

So the world when I began to know it had neither location

nor time, geography nor history. But it had a wild freedom, a closeness to earth and weather, a familiarity with both tame and wild animals. It had the physical sweetness of a golden age. It was blessedly free of most conventional restrictions, and its very liberation from the perspectives of time and place released our minds for imaginative flights into wonder. Our sensuous and imaginative education was exaggerated, but nobody told us much about what is now sometimes called "vital adjustment."

Under the circumstances it might sound fanciful to suggest that either the geography or the history of the Cypress Hills could have had any substantial part in making the minds and characters of children reared there. Certainly they could have no strong and immediate effect, as they might have upon a child who passes every day the rude bridge where the embattled farmers of Concord precipitated a new age with a volley of musketry; or upon a child who flies his kite in the Saratoga meadow where the bronze boot commemorates the nameless heroism of a traitor. In the world's old places, even the New World's old places, not only books reinforce and illuminate a child's perceptions. The past becomes a thing made palpable in monuments, buildings, historical sites, museums, attics, old trunks, relics of a hundred kinds; and in the legends of grandfathers and great-grandfathers; and in the incised marble and granite and weathered wood of graveyards; and in the murmurings of ghosts. We knew no such history, no such past, no such tradition, no such ghosts. And yet it would be a double error to assume that my childhood had no history, and that I was not influenced by it.

For history is a pontoon bridge. Every man walks and works at its building end, and has come as far as he has over the pontoons laid by others he may never have heard of. Events have a way of making other events inevitable; the actions of men are consecutive and indivisible. The history of the Cypress Hills had almost as definite effects on me as did their geography and weather, though I never knew a scrap of that history until a quarter-century after I left the place. However it may have seemed to the people who founded it, Whitemud was not a beginning, not a new thing, but a stage in a long historical process.

History? Seldom, anywhere, have historical changes occurred

so fast. From grizzlies, buffalo, and Indians still only half possessed of the horse and gun, the historical parabola to Dust Bowl and near-depopulation covered only about sixty years. Here was the Plains frontier in a capsule, condensed into the life of a reasonably long-lived man.

3

The Dump Ground

One aspect of Whitemud's history, and only one, and a fragmentary one, we knew: the town dump. It lay in a draw at the southeast corner of town, just where the river left the Hills and where the old Mounted Police patrol trail (I did not know that that was what it was) made a long, easy, willow-fringed traverse across the bottoms. That stretch of the river was a favorite campsite for passing teamsters, gypsies, sometimes Indians. The very straw scattered around those camps, the ashes of those strangers' campfires, the manure of their teams and saddle horses, were hot with adventurous possibilities. The camps made an extension, a living suburb, of the dump ground itself, and it was for this that we valued them. We scoured them for artifacts of their migrant tenants as if they had been arch-aeological sites potent with the secrets of ancient civilizations. I remember toting around for weeks a broken harness strap a few inches long. Somehow or other its buckle looked as if it had been fashioned in a far place, a place where they were accustomed to flatten the tongues of buckles for reasons that could only be exciting, and where they had a habit of plating the metal with some valuable alloy, probably silver. In places where the silver was worn away, the buckle underneath shone dull yellow: prob-ably gold.

Excitement liked that end of town better than our end. Old Mrs. Gustafson, deeply religious and a little raddled in the head, went over there once with a buckboard full of trash, and as she was driving home along the river she saw a spent catfish, washed in from the Swift Current or some other part of the watershed in the spring flood. He was two feet long, his whiskers hung down, his fins and tail were limp—a kind of fish no one had seen in the Whitemud in the three or four years of the town's life, and a kind that none of us children had ever seen anywhere. Mrs. Gustafson had never seen one like him, either. She perceived at once that he was the devil, and she whipped up the team and reported him, pretty loudly, at Hoffman's elevator.

We could still hear her screeching as we legged it for the river to see for ourselves. Sure enough, there he was, drifting slowly on the surface. He looked very tired, and he made no great effort to get away when we rushed to get an old rowboat, and rowed it frantically down to where our scouts eased along shore beckoning and ducking willows, and sank the boat under him and brought him ashore in it. When he died we fed him experimentally to two half-wild cats, who seemed to suffer no ill effects.

Upstream from the draw that held the dump, the irrigation flume crossed the river. It always seemed to me giddily high when I hung my chin over its plank edge and looked down, but it probably walked no more than twenty feet above the water on its spidery legs. Ordinarily in summer it carried six or eight inches of smooth water, and under the glassy surface of the little boxed stream the planks were coated with deep sun-warmed moss as slick as frogs' eggs. A boy could sit in the flume with the water walling up against his back, and grab a cross-brace above him, and pull, shooting himself sledlike ahead until he could reach the next cross-brace for another pull, and so on across the river in four scoots.

After ten minutes in the flume he would come out wearing a dozen or more limber black leeches, and could sit in the green shade where darning needles flashed blue, and dragonflies hummed and stopped in the air, and skaters dimpled slack and eddy with their delicate transitory footprints, and there pull the leeches off one by one, while their sucking ends clung and clung, until at last, stretched far out, they let go with a tiny wet *puk* and snapped together like rubber bands. The smell of the flume and the low bars of that part of the river was the smell of wolf willow.

But nothing else in the east end of town was as good as the dump ground. Through a historical process that went back to the roots of community sanitation, and that in law dated from the Unincorporated Towns Ordinance of the territorial government, passed in 1888, the dump was the very first community enterprise, the town's first institution.

More than that, it contained relics of every individual who had ever lived there. The bedsprings on which Whitemud's first child was begotten might be out there; the skeleton of a boy's pet colt; books soaked with water and chemicals in a house fire, and thrown out to flap their stained eloquence in the prairie wind. Broken dishes, rusty tinware, spoons that had been used to mix paint; once a box of percussion caps, sign and symbol of the carelessness that most of us had in matters of personal or public safety. My brother and I put some of them on the railroad tracks and were anonymously denounced in the *Leader* for nearly derailing the speeder of a section crew. There were also old iron, old brass, for which we hunted assiduously, by night conning junkmen's catalogs to find out how much wartime value there might be in the geared insides of clocks or in a pound of tea lead carefully wrapped in a ball whose weight astonished and delighted us.

Sometimes the unimaginable world reached out and laid a finger on us because of our activities on the dump. I recall that, aged about seven, I wrote a Toronto junk house asking if they preferred their tea lead and tinfoil wrapped in balls, or whether they would rather have it pressed flat in sheets, and I got back a typewritten letter in a window envelope advising me that they would be happy to have it in any way that was convenient to me. They added that they valued my business and were mine very truly. Dazed, I carried that windowed grandeur around in my pocket until I wore it out.

We hunted old bottles in the dump, bottles caked with filth, half buried, full of cobwebs, and we washed them out at the horse trough by the elevators, putting in a handful of shot along with the water to knock the dirt loose; and when we had shaken them until our arms were tired, we hauled them down in some-body's coaster wagon and turned them in at Bill Christenson's pool hall, where the smell of lemon pop was so sweet on the dark pool-hall air that it sometimes awakens me in the night even yet.

Smashed wheels of wagons and buggies, tangles of rusty barbed wire, the collapsed perambulator that the French wife of one of the town's doctors had once pushed proudly up the plank sidewalks and along the ditchbank paths. A welter of foul-smelling feathers and coyote-scattered carrion, that was all that remained of somebody's dream of a chicken ranch. The chickens had all got some mysterious pip at the same time, and died as one, and the dream lay out there with the rest of the town's short history to rustle to the empty sky on the border of the Hills.

There was melted glass in curious forms, and the half-melted office safe left from the burning of Joe Knight's hotel. On very lucky days we might find a piece of the lead casing that had enclosed the wires of the town's first telephone system. The casing was just the right size for rings, and so soft that it could be whittled with a jackknife. If we had been Indians of fifty years earlier, that bright soft metal could have enlisted our maximum patience and craft, and come out as ring and medal and amulet inscribed with the symbols of our observed world. Perhaps there were too many ready-made alternatives in the local drug, hardware, and general stores; in any case our artistic response was feeble, and resulted in nothing better than crude seal rings with initials or pierced hearts carved in them. They served a purpose in juvenile courtship, but they stopped a good way short of art.

The dump held very little wood, for in that country anything burnable got burned. But it had plenty of old metal, furniture, papers, mattresses that were the delight of field mice, and jugs and demijohns that were sometimes their bane, for they crawled into the necks and drowned in the rainwater or redeye that was inside.

If the history of Whitemud was not exactly written, it was at least hinted, in the dump. I think I had a pretty sound notion even at eight or nine of how significant was that first institution of our forming Canadian civilization. For rummaging through its foul purlieus I had several times been surprised and shocked to find relics of my own life tossed out there to blow away or rot.

Some of the books were volumes of the set of Shakespeare that my father had bought, or been sold, before I was born. They had been carried from Dakota to Seattle, and Seattle to Bellingham, and Bellingham to Redmond, and Redmond back to Iowa, and Iowa to Saskatchewan. One of the Cratchet girls had borrowed them, a hatchet-faced, thin, eager, transplanted Cockney girl with a frenzy for reading. Stained in a fire, they had somehow found the dump rather than come back to us. The lesson they preached was how much is lost, how much thrown aside, how much carelessly or of necessity given up, in the making of a new country. We had so few books that I knew them all; finding those thrown away was like finding my own name on a gravestone.

And yet not the blow that something else was, something that impressed me even more with how closely the dump reflected the town's intimate life. The colt whose picked skeleton lay out there was mine. He had been incurably crippled when dogs chased our mare Daisy the morning after she foaled. I had worked for months to make him well, had fed him by hand, curried him, talked my father into having iron braces made for his front legs. And I had not known that he would have to be destroyed. One weekend I turned him over to the foreman of one of the ranches, presumably so that he could be better cared for. A few days later I found his skinned body, with the braces still on his crippled front legs, lying on the dump. I think I might eventually have accepted the colt's death, and forgiven his killer, if it had not been for that dirty little two-dollar meanness that skinned him.

Not even finding his body cured me of going to the dump, though our parents all forbade us on pain of cholera or worse to do so. The place fascinated us, as it should have. For this was the kitchen midden of all the civilization we knew. It gave us the most tantalizing glimpses into our neighbors' lives and our own; it provided an aesthetic distance from which to know ourselves.

The town dump was our poetry and our history. We took it home with us by the wagonload, bringing back into town the things the town had used and thrown away. Some little part of what we gathered, mainly bottles, we managed to bring back to usefulness, but most of our gleanings we left lying around barn or attic or cellar until in some renewed fury of spring cleanup our families carted them off to the dump again, to be rescued and briefly treasured by some other boy. Occasionally something we really valued with a passion was snatched from us in horror and returned at once. That happened to the mounted head of a white mountain goat, somebody's trophy from old times and the far Rocky Mountains, that I brought home one day. My mother took one look and discovered that his beard was full of moths.

I remember that goat; I regret him yet. Poetry is seldom useful, but always memorable. If I were a sociologist anxious to study in detail the life of any community I would go very early to its refuse piles. For a community may be as well judged by what it throws away—what it has to throw away and what it chooses to—as by any other evidence. For whole civilizations we sometimes have no more of the poetry and little more of the history than this.

It is all *we* had for the civilization we grew up in. Nevertheless there was more, much more. If anyone had known that past, and told us about it, he might have told us something like this:

II

PREPARATION FOR A CIVILIZATION

The old, old maps which the navigators of the sixteenth century framed from the discoveries of Cabot and Cartier, of Varrazanno and Hudson, played strange pranks with the geography of the New World. The coast-line, with the estuaries of large rivers, was tolerably accurate; but the centre of America was represented as a vast inland sea whose shores stretched far into the Polar North; a sea through which lay the much-coveted passage to the long-sought treasures of the old realms of Cathay. Well, the geographers of that period erred only in the description of ocean which they placed in the central continent, for an ocean there is, and an ocean through which men seek the treasures of Cathay, even in our own times. But the ocean is one of grass, and the shores are the crests of the mountain ranges, and the dark pine forests of sub-Arctic regions. The great ocean itself does not present more infinite variety than does this prairie-ocean of which we speak. In winter, a dazzling surface of purest snow; in early summer, a vast expanse of grass and pale pink roses; in autumn too often a wild sea of raging fire. No ocean of water in the world can vie with its gorgeous sunsets; no solitude can equal the loneliness of a night-shadowed prairie: one feels the stillness, and hears the silence, the wail of the prowling wolf makes the voice of solitude audible, the stars look down through infinite silence upon a silence almost as intense. This ocean has no past—time has been nought to it; and men have come and gone, leaving behind them no track, no vestige, of their presence. Some French writer, speaking of these prairies, has said that the sense of this utter negation of life, this complete absence of history, has struck him with a loneliness oppressive and sometimes terrible in its intensity. Perhaps so; but, for my part, the prairies had nothing terrible in their aspect, nothing oppressive in their loneliness. One saw here the world as it had taken shape and form from the hands of the Creator. Nor did the scene look less beautiful because nature alone tilled the earth, and the unaided sun brought forth the flowers.

CAPT. W. F. BUTLER, *The Great Lone Land*

1

First Look

In May, 1805, the six canoes and two pirogues of the Lewis and Clark expedition were working up the Missouri between the mouth of the Yellowstone and the Musselshell. The wooded bottoms and the wide greening plains outside so swarmed with game that "it is now only amusement for Capt. C and myself to kill as much meat as the party can consum." Hardly a day passed that they did not have an encounter with a grizzly —"a verry large and a turrible looking animal, which we found verry hard to kill"—and from morning to night they passed through "great numbers of buffalow, Elk, Deer, antilope, beaver, porcupins, & water fowls . . . such as, Geese, ducks of dift. kinds, and a fiew Swan."

They came watchfully, for they were the first. They came stiffened with resolution and alert with wonder. Beyond the bottoms with their cutbanks and their half-flooded willow-grown bars was the wide disk of the Plains, the same Plains they had known, wintering among the Mandans, but extended and extended beyond expectation and beyond credulity, unknown to every horizon and past it. Every river and creek that came in from south or west brought word of the Stony Mountains and the passes that might lead to the Great South Sea; every stream from north or northwest was a possible trail to the Saskatchewan in Prince Rupert's Land. More and more, as they moved westward, the country that lay between them and these desired goals was not merely unknown, it was unrumored. Lewis and

Clark first crossed it and tested its extent. Things they did not know, and could not discover from their informants the Minnetarees, they guessed at. And they noted everything, for everything was new.

May 8 brought them to the mouth of a large river emptying into the Missouri from the northwest. It looked to be navigable for boats and pirogues, and for canoes perhaps a long way, for it carried a strong flow of milky-white water and seemed to drain a great reach of country to the north. They looked up it with the eye of imagination: like the White Earth and other northern tributaries they had passed, this one intrigued them as a possible way to the Saskatchewan and the fur country of Prince Rupert's Land, bitterly contested by the Hudson's Bay Company and the Northwesters. They mistook the stream for the one the Minnetarees called The-River-That-Scolds-All-the-Others, and so thought themselves farther west than they were, but the name they gave it is the one it is still called by: Milk River. Walking up it several miles, they stood on its bluffy banks and strained their eyes into the characterless country from which it came. One feels that they abandoned it with regret, leaving it unexplored only because of the greater Unexplored that led them westward.

"Capt Clark who walked this morning on the Lard. shore ascended a very high point opposite to the mouth of this river; he informed me that he had a perfect view of this river and the country through which it passed for a great distance probably 50 or 60 Miles, that the river from it's mouth bore N.W. for 12 or 15 Miles when it forked, the one taking a direction nearly North, and the other to the West of N. West."

Standing where he stood, a few miles below the site of modern Fort Peck Dam, Clark was not able to look very far, actually, into that province of the unknown. His fifty or sixty miles of view would have shown him only uninterrupted prairie. The fork that came into the Milk from directly north was a minor creek now called the Porcupine. The Milk itself, if they had chosen to follow it, would have led them not into the north but on to the west, not to the Saskatchewan but to what would some day be Glacier National Park.

Still, they were barely out of sight of the northern divide that they guessed at. To the northwest, up the Milk River valley, lost in the shimmer at the extreme edge of Clark's vision, another tributary did come in from the north, draining the plains that stretched on up across the 49th parallel. Followed, it would have led them through some very rough badlands, across plains that flattened to heat-wrinkled horizons. Along the course of the creek, especially on the north bank where the grass was thin, they would have found the country cut by big rough coulees; out on the level plains they would have found stretches of gravelly unprofitable soil thinly grassed and spotted with round cushions of cactus and with prickly pear and sage. In this gray-brown desolation the ground would have been bitten with burnouts and buffalo wallows, dusty clay depressions where gathering alkali salts had all but prohibited any growth, where wind had blown the powdery dust away and burrowing owls had shrugged their way under the lips overhung with curly grass, and whirlwinds had vacuum-cleaned them into shallow craters. This clay soil they would have found unbelievably sticky in the rain. The grass would have been the short curly variety, extraordinarily nourishing because it cured on the stem, that sometime in the next century would acquire the name of prairie wool.

Out here, far more than in the brushy Missouri bottoms, the explorers would have found a land with no transition between earth and sky: in the heat the horizons melted and ran; on the flats the sky and clouds moved in the reflecting sloughs. This earth was densely peopled with small creatures as with large— prairie dogs, picket-pin gophers, field mice, weasels, ferrets, badgers, coyotes, jackrabbits, burrowing owls. The plains were humped and pimpled with the tailings of their burrows, and across the interminable grasslands, even more homeless and fluid than the clouds that moved from west to east across the immense sky, or the winds that searched the grass and were almost never still, swept the blackness of the buffalo, the red-tawny shadows of antelope bands. In every slough went the mating mallards.

The birds of these prairies—ducks, robins, meadowlarks, sparrows, hawks, shrikes, blackbirds—were birds whose bond with the earth was strong. Their nests lay not in trees, for there were none, but in among the tules of sloughs, or in hidden cups under the curl of the prairie grass, or among the blades of prickly pear. Some of them, like the burrowing owls, went underground and lived like rodents.

This tributary of the Milk whose willowed course groped across the northern plains was later to be called by some the Frenchman, by some the Whitemud. If Lewis and Clark had found and followed it, it would have led them across the 49th parallel and thence northwesterly to a low dome of hills as unknown as the river, and in the hills, 165 beeline miles from the junction with the Milk, to an unknown lake. The hills would later be called Montagne aux Cypres, the Cypress Hills; the lake was Cypress Lake. And from the bench above the unmarked source of the unrecorded stream, on a plateau-like height where oddly arctic vegetation replaced the characteristic vegetation of the Plains, they could have looked on, and still on, north and east and west, and seen only more plains, more antelope, more fleets of clouds running eastward before the constant wind.

But they would have been looking down the imperceptible hill that led to Hudson Bay.

They did not go north, and did not see it. In 1805 nobody had been as close as they, and their brief speculative stare at the southern edge of the region was the last look any white man would give it for more than a half century.

Exploration and the fur trade had consistently fallen short of the Hills or gone far around them. Henry Kelsey, on his doggerel-recorded excursion for the Hudson's Bay Company in 1690 and 1691, had come as far into the prairies as some point between the Saskatchewan and the Assiniboine, and in 1739 the Vérendrye called the Chevalier had penetrated to about the site of Prince Albert, below the junction of the North and South Saskatchewan. Neither Kelsey nor Vérendrye had come within several hundred miles of the Cypress Hills; and the fur trade whose entry into the far Northwest they heralded had followed the route of wood and water along the North Saskatchewan, anchoring itself on a chain of prairie posts: Fort Ellice, Fort Qu'Appelle, Fort Carlton, Fort Edmonton, Rocky Mountain House. Not until the late 1850's would the first white explorer, Palliser, make his way to the high country just north of the 49th parallel; not until the 1860's would *métis* winterers begin to build their shanty villages there; not until the 1870's would it be even partly surveyed; and not until the railroad established it in 1886 would there be a road of passage near it.

As late as 1860, one hundred and fifty years after Kelsey, more than a hundred after Vérendrye, more than fifty after Lewis and Clark, the Cypress Hills and the little river they mothered were lost in an unmapped West as wide as ocean, being saved, perhaps, after all the rehearsals on other frontiers, for the staging of one last drama of white settlement.

But lost as it was, and outside the reach of Lewis's and Clark's vision, the river demonstrated the acuteness of their geographical intuition. Just at the eastern base of the Hills there was then (it has since been drained by the CPR) a shallow pond that in spring released a tiny stream south to join the Frenchman, the Milk, and the Missouri, and another stream north to become the South Fork of the Swift Current, headed for Hudson Bay by way of the South Saskatchewan and Lake Winnipeg. The explorers were close to one of the geographical secrets they were looking for, one of those heights of land which direct the rivers how to flow and so change both politics and history. That little pond in what seemed to be a valley near the modern village of South Fork was balanced like a saucer on the continental divide; the Hills themselves divided the Gulf of Mexico from Hudson Bay.

And they were a divide in more ways than those that concerned the parting of the waters. If William Clark had been a prophet as well as an explorer, and a student of human watersheds as well as a geographer, he might have made some interesting speculations as he stood on the Milk River bluffs looking northward toward the region which would retain longer than any part of the United States, and any but the sub-arctic parts of Canada, the characteristics of the West that he knew in 1805.

2
The Divide

Slight causes often have profound effects. There is a theory held by some archaeologists and historians, for instance, that the absence of cobalt in the soil of northern Jutland resulted in a failure of the cattle to produce Vitamin B-12, which caused abortion sickness, which forced the inhabitants in the 2nd century B.C. southward upon more nutritive grass, which jarred their southern neighbors the Cimbri loose upon still more southerly tribes, which set off the great invasions of the Cimbri and Teutons which shook Rome. It may not be good history but it is an attractive parable, and comforts a student who would like to find specific causes, preferably simple and concrete, for human movements.

A few feet of altitude will do as well as the presence or absence of cobalt in the soil. It is a fact that Denmark's highest hill, about 600 feet high, is called Himmelberg, Heaven Mountain, a name that suggests the people near it must have been strongly influenced by it, though the mountain-bred Norwegians scorn it as a hole in the ground. In Saskatchewan, too, a little height can give distinction. The Cypress Hills, low as they are, are the highest point in Canada between Labrador and the Rockies. Everything about them is special, and everything special about them is explained by the accident of elevation. Their topography, their climate, their plants and animals, their peculiar geographical and zoological lags and survivals, even their human history, are what they are because this uplift has been pushed a thousand to fifteen hundred feet above the plains that apron it. The highest point is at Head of the Mountain, over in Alberta, at 4800 feet; the average of the North Bench, the long narrow plain along the summit, is a little under 4000. The Plains southward are about 3000, those to the north slightly lower. The difference of a thousand feet is at that latitude enough to make the Hills a different world.

If political boundaries were established by topography and logic rather than by expedient and compromise, the North Bench would carry the international boundary, and the lower fifty miles of Saskatchewan would be politically what they are geographically—an uninterrupted part of the American High Plains, separated by the Cypress Hills from Prince Rupert's Land proper, which Charles II's grant of 1670 defined as all the country draining into Hudson Bay.

But the Hills are more than the northern edge of the Missouri watershed. Geologically they are an anomaly, and display in their higher strata rocks that were elsewhere planed away by the ice. Biologically they preserve Rocky Mountain plants and animals far out into the Plains, and southern species far into the north. Wild West longer than anywhere else, last home of buffalo and grizzlies, last sanctuary for the Plains hostiles, last survival of the open-range cattle industry, booby prize in a belated homestead rush, this country saved each stage of the Plains frontier long past its appointed time, and carried 19th-century patterns of culture well into the 20th. All because the Hills are a thousand feet higher than the rest of Saskatchewan.

Being hills, and having been hills since late Eocene or early Oligocene times, they have diverted around themselves various kinds of drainage, beginning with the ice.

In glacial times the climate here was wet and not extraordinarily cold. The ice which blanketed the northern Plains was formed even farther north. It flowed around the Hills and crossed them in what is now called the Gap, where Oxarart Creek comes down to join the Frenchman, but it never entirely covered them. An island eighty or ninety miles square stuck up above the ice sheet, diverted and split the slow flow from the north, and became an Ararat.

Before the ice sheet, many of the flowers, shrubs, and trees that we know as characteristically Rocky Mountain species must have stretched more or less uninterruptedly eastward. The ice plowed between the high points of the mountains and the Cypress Hills and scraped bare a two-hundred-mile interval. But along the ridge of the Hills, spruce and pine and aspen and creeping cedar, wolf willow and mountain orchids, were left as a biological island. They are still there, preserved by their altitude in the first instance and by greater rainfall and a cooler climate since. Possessing wood and water, the Hills made a home for the fur-bearing woods animals, including beaver, and for woods game animals such as elk and bear, and ultimately for the men who pursued the woodland way of life in contradistinction to the Plains life based on the buffalo. This was a woodland biome within the vast Great Plains biome.

And full of survivors of various kinds. To the bench, as the ice came down, the creatures of the country retreated for refuge, stayed treed on the plateau while the ice groaned and ground around the flanks, and crept down again after the ice retreated. That is one explanation, though not necessarily the correct one, why there are now in the Saskatchewan-Montana country scorpions whose nearest relatives are hundreds of miles to the southwest, and horned toads, solpugids, and hog-nosed vipers with no parallels nearer than six hundred miles away in Utah and Nevada.

As if trying to be a laboratory of the unbroken life history of the region, the Hills saved even their fossils when most of the High Plains lost them. In the formations near the summit of the bench lie the petrified bones of saber-toothed cats, camels, titanotheres each of whose great chopping teeth was nearly as big as a teacup, and among them impressions of cinnamon and walnut and redwood leaves, fossilized fruit resembling figs, something like coconuts. These all lie in the Cypress Hills formation of the Oligocene. Two layers below, in the Frenchman formation of the Cretaceous, streams and run-off coulees have exposed the Age of Reptiles, and fossils of Tyrannosaurus and Triceratops record another ancient ecology, meat-eater and grass-eater, hunter and hunted.

Along this wooded, coulee-cut plateau the clouds scrape their bottoms and give up rain. An average of four inches more falls here than falls on the surrounding arid Plains—the luck of elevation, and out of elevation a special economy. The coulees of the high ground have always been an orchard of wild fruit—chokecherries, pin cherries, saskatoons, high bush cranberries, raspberries, gooseberries, buffalo berries, currants both red and black. In the days before settlement the berry patches were a happy hunting ground for bears; and the antelope and on occasion the buffalo, chased in by drouth, fires, or hunters from the Plains, found the benches a perennial hayfield, while the wooded coulees provided winter shelter in the blizzards that came down straight and undeflected from the Pole.

The elevation which created this game sanctuary with its amenities of rainfall, living streams, grass, shelter, berries, and timber served also, partly by a historical freak and partly because it was a visible barrier across otherwise characterless country, to mark a boundary between tribes and kinds of men. It lay between the Canadian fur trade along the Saskatchewan and the American fur trade on the Missouri. It likewise lay between the Cree and Assiniboin pressing west and south from the routes of that trade, and the Piegan, Blood, and Blackfoot of the Blackfoot Confederacy raiding south and east from the foot of the Rockies. Before too long, as the drama of the Plains Indians worked toward its climax, it would be looked upon as a sanctuary by Sioux, Crow, Gros Ventre, and Nez Percé falling back northward before American cavalry, miners, and especially the hide hunters who were systematically destroying the buffalo. Humanity, like the ice and the water, flowed around the edges of this uplift. Technically, in the view of Alexander Henry and others of the fur traders, it was Assiniboin country. Actually it was No Man's Land.

The Cypress Hills came into the knowledge of English topographers in 1859, when Captain John Palliser reported to the Royal Geographical Society on the progress of his British North American Exploring Expedition of 1857-58. But Palliser and his associates were much more interested in passes through the Canadian Rockies than in the arid country that much later would become known as "Palliser's Triangle," which he held to be—with some justice—unfit for settlement. There is only one mention of the Hills: "Although my journey to the western extremity of the boundary line was necessarily a rapid one, I determined on a visit to the 'Cypress Hills.' I was anxious to see this part of the country, in consequence of having heard many reports of its wonderful timber and fine rich soil. I found great tracts of splendid timber wasted by fire; there still remain, however, many valuable pines, and the land is rich, and capable of producing several grain crops in succession without manure."

That is all, from Palliser's quick look in 1858. Henry Youle Hind, who conducted the Canadian Red River Exploring Expedition of 1857 and the Assiniboine and Saskatchewan Exploring Expedition of 1858, did not visit the Hills nor approach near them, though his map, published in 1860, puts them by name in approximately their correct place. The map published with Captain Butler's *Great Lone Land* in 1873 vaguely marks but does not name them, perhaps because Butler too, in his strenuous and often heroic journeyings, missed them by several hundred miles. To most of the Hudson's Bay and Northwest Company traders, as to the mapmakers, they remained for a long time hardly more exact than a rumor, for the fur trade flowed far to the north along the North Saskatchewan, where the Plains and the Northern Woodlands met, and the beaver were plentiful and the Indians interested in hunting them.

Says Isaac Cowie, the first Hudson's Bay trader to come into them, "As far back as the memory and traditions of the Crees then living extended, these Cypress Hills—'me-nach-tah-kak' in Cree—had been neutral ground between many warring tribes, south of the now marked international boundary, as well as the Crees and Blackfeet and their friends. No Indian for hunting purposes ever set foot on those hills, whose wooded coulees and ravines became the undisturbed haunt of all kinds of game, and especially abounded in grizzly bears and the beautifully antlered and magnificent was-cay-sou, known variously by the English as red deer and elk. Only wary and watchful war parties of any tribe ever visited the hills, and so dangerous was it to camp in them that it was customary for such parties to put up barricades about the spots on which they stayed overnight."

That was standard opinion in 1871, and Cowie's experiences during his one winter in the Hills amply corroborated everything the Cree had told him, but that story belongs in a later chapter.

3

Horse and Gun

Indians were a part of our boyhood fantasy, but our image of them was as mixed as our image of most things. Our Indians certainly did not come from life, and we were a little early to get them from the movies. We got them from books, and we did not discriminate among the books from which we got them.

One of our principal sources was Fenimore Cooper, and no Mark Twain had as yet broken in upon us with raucous horse laughs to destroy our faith in Cooper's delicate arts of the forest. We were masters of the lore of the broken twig; we trod the willow bottoms silently, single file, pigeon-toed, like Tuscaroras or Mohicans. Much of our Indian play demonstrated the stubborn persistence of inherited notions, for the Indians we played came mainly out of novels written eighty years before and two thousand miles away, out of the French and Indian wars, out of the darkness of the deep deciduous forests, out of the Noble Savage sentimentalities of Chateaubriand and Thomas Campbell. They came more or less from where our unnaturalized history came from, where our poetry and geography came from—where even our prejudices came from, including the prejudices against real Indians that lay so unconformably upon our literary and sentimental attitudes.

Real Indians we saw perhaps once a year, when a family or two in a rickety democrat wagon came down from somewhere and camped for a few days in the river brush. Probably they were

Cree; undoubtedly they came from some reservation, though it never occurred to us to inquire where it was; probably they were off the reservation without permission. We responded to them as to an invasion or a gypsy visitation. Our fathers sent us out to gather up every tool that had been left lying around, they double-padlocked chickencoops and sheds, they imposed a harsh curfew that haled us in from midsummer twilight unsatisfied and complaining. Their behavior was an explicit reflection of local attitude: that an Indian was a thieving, treacherous, lousy, unreliable, gut-eating vagabond, and that if anything a halfbreed was worse. Most of the townspeople were immigrants from sections of the United States and Canada where Indians were part of a lurid past; they had had hardly more personal contact with them than had the Scandinavians and the Englishmen among us, but they brought fully developed prejudices with them which we inherited without question or thought.

I can remember packs of us hanging wary as coyotes, just out of what we imagined was gunshot, around Indian camps, spying on the dark children, the shapeless women, the heavy-featured men with braids and (we felt) a shiftless mixture of white and Indian clothes. Their ponies were scrawny broomtails and their dogs gaunt and noisy. We watched the whole outfit as we would have watched ugly and perhaps dangerous animals from a blind. The moment an adult emerged from one of the brush shanties we edged back, prepared to scatter. Sometimes we yelled catcalls in their direction, half in derision and half speculatively, to see what would happen. Nothing ever did. With what I now recognize was either helplessness or dignity they ignored us, and any temptation we might have had to go on into the camps and hobnob with their kids was discouraged by the dogs, by our mothers' warnings, and by the smells. We told ourselves we could smell one of those camps a mile away with a clothespin on our noses. When they talked the butcher out of the entrails of a slaughtered beef we knew we could, for they hung their shanties with the red and white guts to dry them in the sun.

Our inherited, irrelevant, ineradicable Indian lore was not modified in the slightest, any more than our humanity was aroused, by these contacts with the real demoralized Cree. We did not pause to reflect that *if* any Indians had made romantic signal smokes from the chimneys on Chimney Coulee, they would have been the grandfathers, or the mortal enemies of the grandfathers, of these people drying guts down in the western bend. Even the elements of our reading which might have tended to correct or amplify or bring distinctions into our view of Indian life remained separate and encysted. Somehow, when we read Zane Grey, it was *The Spirit of the Border,* with its skulking and bloody war in the hardwood forests of Pennsylvania and Ohio, that took our imaginations. That book reinforced our prefabricated notions; other Zane Grey books, including those about the Southwest, somehow entertained us without persuading us that they reflected anything real, and without inciting our imitation.

About the historical Indians of our own region we were not, actually, totally ignorant. We read, and passed eagerly from family to family, *The American Boy,* and in the years between 1914 and 1919 *The American Boy* ran a series of stories by James Willard Schulz, an ex-whiskey trader who had lived with the Blackfoot for a considerable time from the 1870's on, and who spoke with some authority on the life of the northern Plains tribes. We could have answered fairly detailed questions on Blackfoot costume, weapons, beliefs, habits in war and hunting and horse thievery. We could have counted coup on an enemy without too much violating the Blackfoot proprieties, and we would have felt ourselves competent to lead a war party. But what we read did not take root in our play or, really, in our understanding, because we had no comprehension that this Indian lore was local to us. We did not adapt it to ourselves; it occurred to none of us that just such Blackfoot war parties as Schulz wrote of had many times forded the Whitemud, perhaps at the shallows just below the Lazy-S ranch house, and sneaked up the Swift River hill to fall upon an enemy band berrying or hunting or gathering spruce gum in Chimney Coulee.

We might have read, and perhaps did, stories in which Schulz brought the warfare of the Plains to our very doorstep. In his autobiographical *My Life as an Indian,* for example, there is a story told by Rising Wolf:

. . . The Gros Ventre—then at war with the Blackfeet tribes—concluded a treaty with the Crows, and there was a great gathering of them all on the lower Milk River, to celebrate the event. A party of young Gros Ventres returning from a raid against the Cree brought word that they had seen the Piegan camp in the Divide—, or, as the whites called them,—Cypress Hills. This was great news . . . What could the Piegans do against their combined forces? Nothing. They would kill off the men, capture the women, seize the rich and varied property of the camp. So sure were they of success, that they had their women accompany them to sort out and care for the prospective plunder.

From a distant butte the war party had seen the Piegan camp, but had not discovered that just over a hill to the west of it, not half a mile further, the Bloods were encamped in force, some five thousand of them, or in all about one thousand fighting men . . . One morning the Crows and Gros Ventres came trailing leisurely over the Plain toward the Piegan camp all decked out in their war costumes, the plumes of their war bonnets and the eagle fringe of their shields fluttering gaily in the wind. And with them came their women happily chattering, already rejoicing over the vast store of plunder they were going to possess that day. An early hunter from the Piegan camp, going with his woman after some meat he had killed the previous day, discovered the enemy while they were still a mile and more away, and hurried back to give the alarm, sending one of his women on to call out the Bloods. There was a great rush for horses, for weapons; some even managed to put on a war shirt or war bonnet. Luckily it was early in the morning and most of the horse herds, having been driven in to water, were feeding nearby. If a man did not at once see his own band, he roped and mounted the first good animal he came to. And thus it happened that when the attacking party came tearing over the little rise of ground just east of the camp they were met by such an overwhelming force of determined and well-mounted men that they turned and fled, firing but few shots. They were utterly panic-stricken; their only thought was to escape. Better mounted than their women, they left these defenseless ones to the mercy of the enemy, seeking only to escape themselves.

From the point of meeting a fearful slaughter began. Big Lake, Little Dog, Three Suns, and other chiefs kept shouting to their men to spare the women, but a few were killed before they could make their commands known. There was no mercy shown to the fleeing men, however; they were overtaken and shot, or brained with war clubs. So sudden had been the call that many men had found no time to select a swift horse, mounting anything they could rope, and these soon dropped out of the race; but others kept on and on, mile after mile, killing all the men they overtook until their horses could run no more and their clubarms were well-nigh paralyzed from striking so long and frequently. Few of the fleeing party made any resistance whatever, never turned to look backward, but bent forward in the saddle and plied the quirt until they were shot or clubbed from their seats. For miles the trail was strewn with the dead and dying, through which fled their women, shrieking with terror . . . "Let them go," cried Big Lake, laughing. "Let them go! We will do as did the Old Man with the rabbits, leave a few for to breed so that their kind may not become wholly extinct."

That, one would think, was war as bloody and colorful as any in *The Last of the Mohicans,* and from the hints of the terrain it must have happened at the east end of the Hills, within a few miles of our home. Did it affect us? Perhaps our lives, not in the least our imaginations. We lived in the very middle of what had been for generations a bloody Indian battleground and what in the late '70's and '80's became the refuge of the last Plains hostiles. Big Bear, Wandering Spirit, Poundmaker, and Piapot hunted those coulees; Sitting Bull and his Sioux spent five years of exile between the Hills and Wood Mountain after the Battle of the Little Big Horn. Chief Joseph of the Nez Percé, informed by the grapevine that tells hunted animals where they are safe, was headed for the same country with his heroic and battered band when General Nelson A. Miles cornered him in the Bearpaws.

It would all have been news to us. We knew as little of our intense and recent past as if it had been a geological stratum hidden underground. On some frontiers such as Texas, local history and local pride were nurtured together. On ours there was an uncrossable discontinuity. Yet the frontier processes demonstrated by Schulz's Blackfoot, the very Plains Indian culture that limped to its end in Wood Mountain and the Cypress Hills, fulfilled a pattern of which it would have paid us to be aware. The white man literally created the culture of the Plains Indians by bringing them the horse and the gun; and just as surely, by conquest, disease, trade rum, and the destruction of the buffalo, he doomed what he had created.

One indispensable part of the typical nomadic Plains culture began when the first Apache, probably in New Mexico and probably around the year 1630, laid hands on the first escaped Spanish horse. Another part, just as indispensable, became inevitable in 1668, when the ship *Nonsuch* anchored at the mouth of the Rupert River, in James Bay, and Médart Chouart Groseilliers built the first post for the Governor and Company of Adventurers Trading into Hudson's Bay. He called the post first for King Charles; it was later known as Rupert's House. At it and at the later York Factory post, the Cree traded beaver for guns; and as Company middlemen charged with going into the wilderness and bringing back the furs, they spread the need of the gun, if not its possession, all along the canoe routes and out into the Plains and eventually clear into the Mackenzie Basin. But always jealously and penuriously, always in the awareness that any Cree who traded a gun to a rival tribe reduced Cree dominance. Not until the aggressive North-West Company challenged Hudson's Bay Company power by sending white traders into the backlands did a hunter from any of the western tribes have much chance of laying his hands on a musket or on the powder and lead to feed it.

Horse and gun thus moved toward one another from sources almost as remote as the continent could provide. In the Southwest the Spanish controlled the Indian trade so rigidly that few guns fell into Indian hands. But horses were another matter. By war, theft, escape, and trade, the horse spread northward through the Plains until by the middle of the 18th century only the northernmost tribes were still unmounted. The Cree, made powerful by their guns and by Company favor, were still pedestrian; so were the Piegans, Bloods, and Blackfoot of the Blackfoot Confederacy, at that time allies of the Cree. Sometime about 1736-40, according to a story told to Alexander Henry the Younger by a Cree-Blackfoot named Saukamappee, the Blackfoot and their allies for the first time succeeded in defeating the aggressive mounted Snake to the south. The reason was not an equality in horses, but a handful of Cree guns among the Blackfoot bows and warclubs.

That was a significant battle, a turning point. By the second decade of the 19th century the Blackfoot Confederacy had profited from the Hudson's Bay-Nor'westers rivalry to acquire an adequate supply of guns and ammunition. It had also assimilated the horse and the entire military complex that came with it, even to quilted leather armor jackets and shields that had been adapted many miles, many years, and many tribes back from the equipment of Spanish cavalrymen.

The result was double. The previously dominant Snake, the first of the northerly tribes to acquire the horse, now found themselves pinched between the new Blackfoot power on the north and the united mountain tribes, by that time likewise mounted and armed with guns. And the Blackfoot, as they became a major power, began to have differences with the Cree and Assiniboin who had once been their allies against the Snake. A generation after Lewis and Clark passed through the southern borders of their range, the Blackfoot were at war or on bad terms with nearly everybody: with Snake, Gros Ventre, Sioux, Crow, Nez Percé, Salish, and Assiniboin, with both Plains and Woodland Cree, and with at least the American whites. With the coming of the full horse-and-gun culture to the high northern Plains, the excessive advantage that one tribe could achieve by means of either horse or gun was largely nullified. Every tribe had won and could hold a share of the buffalo country. An approximate equality of arms and mobility, plus a balance of power achieved by alliance, brought the shock waves that had begun two centuries before finally jarring to a halt. The stalemate was broken by incessant raiding, and it would last only so long as the buffalo lasted—that is, uneasily, for about a generation and a half. And the place where horse and gun came together, the place where the various forces most clearly canceled one another, was the Cypress Hills, the place truly spoken of by the Gros Ventre as "the divide."

No traders had ever properly "occupied" the Blackfoot country between the Cypress Hills and the Rockies. The North-West Company had established Chesterfield House and Old Bow Fort, but found them too hard to hold; they were abandoned after the North-West-Hudson's Bay merger in 1821. Their closing left the Blackfoot with no fixed trading posts. They had to trade either at Forts Benton, Brule, or Lewis on the Missouri, or at Edmonton or Rocky Mountain House far to the north. Not until the 1860's did free traders, mainly from the Fort Benton area, "open" the Blackfoot country. Throughout the first half of the century, rich in horses and powerful in numbers and fighting qualities, the Blackfoot braced back upon the Rocky Mountains and from their heartland raided a long way, mainly east and south. From the east, both Plains and Woodland Cree, stanch friends of the Company that had made them great, pressed with increasing insistence as the buffalo were cleared from the eastern Plains. Along with them came their allies the Assiniboin and a whole new tribe of French-Indian halfbreeds, the *métis*. From the south, taking long chances and dealing primarily in the cut alcohol that made murderous the Blackfoot whom Henday and Cocking in the 18th century had found kindly and well disposed, came the free traders of the Missouri.

The forces were powerful enough sooner or later to overrun any divide, but for a long time power flowed around the flanks of the Cypress Hills as once ice had. But once history touched the hills, once the stalemate was broken, the stages of the Plains frontier would go through them like fire through prairie grass. As late as 1868, when the American frontier was in its very last phase, it had hardly begun here. The fur trade, already by that year a fading memory south of the border, was just reaching out to this remote tumble of high land. The tribes lay in precarious balance. The *métis* who with luck might have made a mixed-blood nation, a sort of Mexico, in the Canadian West, had not yet made their first rebellious move on the Red River, and their *hivernant* skirmishers had barely felt their way into the dangerous divide.

Within little more than a decade, fur traders, *métis*, and Indians would find their whole world collapsing under them, the buffalo would be all but gone, and law and order in a red coat would be patrolling the coulees where a few years before hardly any man, red or white or halfway between, would have dared go.

4

Half World: the Métis

To give us any understanding of how our remote place of home was brought within the bounds of the semi-civilized world, someone would have had to tell us about the *métis*, the "Frenchmen" from whom our river took one of its names. No one ever did. Our education, that is, did not perform its proper function of giving us distance and understanding by focusing on our life from outside. Instead, it focused on the outside from inside, and we never so much as heard the word *métis*. Nevertheless there were two kinds of them around us. Some of the "Indians" who camped in the willows undoubtedly bore names such as La-Barge, Quesnelle, or Laveillé. And some of the children I played with during our earliest years in the town, boys whom I knew, and who knew themselves, as Henry and Midge and Jewell, had been christened Henri and Michel and Jules. No serious prejudice affected them. Certainly we ourselves made no distinctions, and our mothers did not forbid or discourage our playing with those dark and lank-haired and toughly competent kids: they only combed us out somewhat fiercely with fine-combs when we came inside. But to all intents and purposes the families of Henri and Michel and Jules had gone white, as the campers in the west bend had gone Indian. As a race, a tribe, a possibility, the *métis* had ceased to exist.

They might have developed into a people and a nation, with a life and land of their own. Or they might, if American annexationists had had their way, have become a vast northern extension of

57

the United States. There was a time in 1869 and 1870 when a sober gambler betting on eventual annexation of western Canada by the United States would not have demanded very long odds. The cards fell otherwise. What turned up for the halfbreeds was neither independence nor domination from the south, but domination from the east. The infant Dominion of Canada, whose first Parliament did not meet until November 7, 1867, in the next twenty years generated enough force to take over and hold Rupert's Land and the North-West Territories, bring British Columbia and Prince Edward Island into the federation, and drive a railroad from sea to sea and so consolidate itself as a continental nation. In doing so, it suppressed the *métis* twice: once in 1870, on the Red River, and again in 1885, on the North Saskatchewan. In effect, Sir John Macdonald, Col. Garnet Wolseley, the Royal North-West Mounted Police, and the Canadian militia completed what General Wolfe had died for on the Plains of Abraham. The *métis*, allied to the French by faith and language, and to the Indians by the character of their economic and social life, were double losers, for they lost not only their chance of independence but their chance of identity. Like the Plains Indian culture, the *métis* were a white creation; ethnically and culturally they were the product of the meeting of white and Indian, the spark struck out by the contact between industrial civilization and the stone age. And like the Plains culture, they were obliterated eventually by what had made them.

In March, 1869, Hudson's Bay Company and Canadian delegates agreed on the terms of the transfer of Rupert's Land to Canada. Canadian authority would take over when the pact had been formally signed and the Queen had approved the transfer in a royal proclamation. Sir John Macdonald hoped the proclamation would come by December 1, so that Canada could take over control from the company. But in July William MacDougall, as Minister of Public Works, ordered Col. John Stoughton Dennis to "proceed without delay to Fort Garry, Red River, for the purpose . . . of selecting the most suitable localities for the survey of townships for immediate settlement . . . The American system of survey is that which appears best suited to the country, except as to the area of the section. The first emigrants, and the most desirable, will probably go from Canada, and it will therefore be advisable to offer them lots of a size to which they have become accustomed. This will require you to make the section 800 acres instead of 640, as on the American plan."

There were a number of things wrong with those orders. For one thing, Rupert's Land had not yet been transferred, and was still in effect a foreign country where no Canadian surveyor had any business. For another, MacDougall was both arrogant and politically obtuse in assuming that the "most desirable" settlers would come from Canada. By Canada he meant Ontario, clearly, since only in Ontario had settlers become accustomed to the rectangular surveys he described. And Ontario was strongly Protestant and Anglo-Saxon. In giving preference to settlers of that persuasion, MacDougall was gratuitously insulting the people already resident in the Red River settlements, of whom there were twelve thousand and of whom only about fifteen hundred were of unmixed white blood. MacDougall's orders, that is, derived from the same attitude of contempt that had moved Colin Robertson to refer to the *métis* as "blacks," and helped bring on the Seven Oaks Massacre in 1816, when the *métis* temporarily drove Lord Selkirk's farmers from the Red River settlements.

Almost as exasperating as MacDougall's arrogance was his disregard of the rights of the existing settlers. The rectangular surveys he ordered would cut across the little farms that the *métis* had established on the Assiniboine, the Red, and the other rivers: long strip farms, each with a frontage on the river which gave not only a canoe landing but an access to water for the irrigation of gardens. The strips ran far back and were combined in common pastures like the *ejidos* of Spanish New Mexico, and on these pastures the *métis'* stock could run freely while people were off on the annual hunts. That is to say, the processes of adaptation to Plains life and to the uncertain rainfall had led the *métis* to an economy not unlike that of the Apache after the acquisition of the horse. They were half horticultural, half nomadic, and their system of land division was appropriate to their life. As a matter of fact, it was far better adapted to the arid and semi-arid Plains than the rectangular surveys were, but nobody in Canada or the United States understood that. North Americans would not understand the inadequacy of the rectangular surveys to arid land until deep in the 20th century, and the Canadian government was so far from understanding the reasons for the *métis'* objections that it imposed the same rigid grid on them again in 1885, and brought on a second rebellion.

That second one came later, after the Dominion had consolidated its power, and it was as desperate for the *métis* as for the Cree of Big Bear and Wandering Spirit who joined them. But the one in 1869 had a chance. When MacDougall, newly appointed Governor of the North-West Territories, arrived at the international border at Pembina, he was met by a *métis'* note forbidding him to cross. His lieutenants were turned back and his orders disregarded, and the so-called "Red River Rebellion" was on.

It was a strange rebellion, for though it protested Canadian political action, Canada had as yet no jurisdiction in Rupert's Land. The Hudson's Bay Company, which did, was not a government, and many of its employees were sympathetic to the *métis*. Annexationists and Fenians below the border watched with a wolfish and acquisitive gleam in their eyes as Louis Riel, a *métis* educated as a priest, established the Provisional Government of Rupert's Land and ran up its flag, a gold fleur-de-lis on a white ground.

It flew ten months. Then Col. Wolseley and twelve hundred Imperial and Canadian troops floundered through from Toronto along the impossible woods and quagmires of the Dawson Road, and Riel elected not to fight them. He fled, Fort Garry capitulated without a fight, some *métis* were hunted down and killed in reprisal for Riel's execution of the rabid Orangeman Thomas Scott, and the first act was over.

Joseph Kinsey Howard, in by far the best book on the *métis* as a cultural and political possibility, speaks of playing *métis* rebel in cops-and-robbers games when he was a boy in Alberta. Those were the same years when I was a boy in Saskatchewan, but nobody had told me enough to induce in me any such loyalties or inspire any such play. I had heard of Louis Riel, as a sort of booger-man, but that was all. Yet he and his rebellious nation came closer to my life, probably, than to Howard's. The first non-Indian hunters in the Cypress Hills were *métis* winterers; after the collapse of Riel's Provisional Government in Fort Garry in 1870, many of the more settled *métis* moved west, some of them as authentic refugees, and during the last decade of the buffalo,

Wood Mountain and the Cypress Hills were bases from which the hunts went out. It was the vanishing of the buffalo, in conjunction with renewed political squabbling with Ottawa, that brought them to their final desperate outbreak in 1885.

They were a Plains tribe, but a very special one, for they combined the adaptive virtues of two races and they did not lose their woods skills when they crossed into the Plains. According to Howard, there were halfbreeds, product of Quebec Frenchmen and Huron or Algonquin women, around Sault Ste. Marie as early as 1654, and they made a rendezvous at Mackinac before 1670. The fur trade encouraged racial mixture: the sons of *engagés* and Indian women were literally born into the company, and bound to it as no European would ever be. After the mid-18th century they increased rapidly, and a hundred years after the fall of New France in 1763 there were at least thirty thousand of them west of the Great Lakes on both sides of the border.

They were the wanderers of the wilderness—the best boatmen, best guides, hunters, trappers and traders. They devised a system of freight transport for the Plains which established a new industry and made St. Paul the capital of Minnesota and the commercial center of the Northwestern frontier. Their knowledge of the country—much of it instinctive and thus inexplicable to white men—made them indispensable in development of the West, as did the fact that most of the Indians welcomed them as relatives and friends.

Heirs to the horse-and-gun culture based on the buffalo as well as to the Woodlands culture based on beaver, they were a more formidable people, man for man, than any of the tribes with which they traded, and probably than most whites. Though some lapsed into an Indianism as savage as that of the most unregenerate Blackfoot, many could draw strength from both sides of their inheritance. Multilingual and bi-cultural, they formed an indispensable buffer race, often as traders and middlemen, sometimes as peacemakers, sometimes as fighters, generally on the white side. When they turned their guns against the Canadians in 1885, a scattered and half-organized handful under Gabriel Dumont made even the splendidly disciplined Mounted Police look bad, and might have hurt them a great deal worse if Riel's hysterical vacillation had not tied Dumont's hands.

Of Gabriel Dumont the world has never heard enough. Skilled, strong, brave, gentle to weakness, durable as rawhide, inflexibly faithful to his people and to Riel, whom he worshiped, he not only saw more plainly than most the desperate situation of the *métis*, but he was their most capable leader and their most redoubtable champion. It was Dumont who rode a round trip of 700 miles from the North Saskatchewan to Fort Benton to visit Riel and ask his aid in the fight against Ottawa's implacable stupidities. It was Dumont who, as commander-in-chief of the *métis* sharpshooters, harassed Commissioner Irvine and his Mounted Police and General Middleton and his militia, beat the Mounties at Duck Lake, forced the abandonment of Fort Carlton, whipped Middleton's column at Fish Creek, disabled the steamer *Northcote* that was coming downriver to the aid of the militia besieging Batoche, and finally, against heavy odds and the overwhelming firepower of repeating rifles, 7-pounders, and one of the new Gatling guns graciously donated on a test basis by the United States, was driven out of Batoche and into hiding in the Birch Hills.

Riel, mentally ill and in despair, surrendered, but the search for Dumont threshed all the bushes along the North Saskatchewan in vain. He made his way out of the very middle of them and rode southward, striking far around through the shelter of the Cypress Hills and so into Montana to safety. His career in exile was bizarre, rather sad. A few years after his escape from Batoche he was riding a bronc in the show ring of Buffalo Bill's Wild West Show and shooting glass balls out of the air for the gratification and astonishment of crowds in Great Britain, France, Italy, Germany. When he finally took advantage of amnesty and returned to the North Saskatchewan, the grass-grown rifle pits and the mounds and tilted headboards above his dead companions at Batoche must have seemed to him to mark the grave of his race. As for Riel, the unstable and brilliant Moses of this people, a vindictive volunteer hangman had adjusted the noose around his neck in Regina on November 16, 1885, ending forever the hope of an ethnic or national identity for the *métis*. They buried the last memory of that hope when they carried Gabriel Dumont to his grave in Batoche, a ragged and shuffling remnant, muttering, *"Gabriel Dumont est mort. Pauvre Gabriel!"*

Pauvre Gabriel. Pauvres métis. But none of this had happened, the end was nearly twenty years off, when they first turned their shrieking, dry-axled Red River carts up the slopes of the Montagne aux Cypres, and in those years after 1868 they were no shuffling remnant. They were as colorful a crowd as ever hit the Plains—and the Plains, perhaps because of their own tawny monotony, have specialized in colorful people.

Their invention and their trademark was the Red River cart, which did for the Plains what the York boats and canoes did for the river routes of the fur trade. In 1801 Alexander Henry the Younger wrote in his journal, "Men now go again for meat, with small carts, the wheels of which are one solid piece, sawed off the ends of trees whose diameter is three feet," and in 1803 he remarked that "This invention is worth four horses to us, as it would require five horses to carry as much on their backs as one will drag in each of these large carts." The saving in horses became proportionately greater as the design of the carts improved. The later models, with dished spoked wheels instead of sections of trees, would carry a load of five hundred pounds, and a single pony could haul one fifty miles a day. They were generally hooped like a covered wagon, and covered with canvas or summer bearskins. The wheels were so large in the developed form of the cart that even in a runaway the thing could hardly tip over; a photograph taken of some *métis* traders by the Boundary Survey party in 1874 shows the wheels as high as a man's head, the rims even at that late date still bound with shrunken rawhide. It was in every way a triumph of adaptation to the conditions of the Plains. It was light, strong, durable, and being made entirely of wood and skins, could be easily mended and even made by men a long way from civilization. When there was a river to be crossed, the wheels could be taken off and lashed under the box and the whole thing floated or towed. In a very real way it was a symbol of the *métis'* ingenuity in utilizing whatever they needed from two cultures. To the Indian travois they added the Quebec cart, and without losing mobility, gained carrying capacity.

They also gained something else: noise. The axles were unpeeled poplar or cottonwood logs, and the wheels could not be greased because grease would have collected dust and frozen the hubs to the axles. The shriek of a single Red River cart was enough to set tenderfoot visitors writing home: it was an experience of an excruciating kind. But when they went out a hundred or two hundred at a time, as they did on the annual Red River buffalo hunts, the uproar was beyond imagination. They came like ten thousand devils filing saws, like the Gadarene swine in their frenzy, like the shrieking damned; and they came accompanied by barking dogs, yelling riders, youths shooting off guns—a crawling caravan with a busy cloud of extra horses, oxen, riders swinging wide to stay out of the dust. This was what carried supplies from St. Paul and Pembina to the more northerly posts; this was what went out after robes and pemmican, year by year following the herds farther west. As Howard says, "The Red River cart brigades never sneaked up on anybody. On a still day you could hear them coming for miles, and see the great cloud of yellow dust they raised; and if the buffalo of the plains did finally flee into holes in the ground as the Indians believed—well, it was no wonder."

They were the noisiest and most efficient thing on the prairies for more than three quarters of a century, from their first introduction sometime around 1800 to the coming of the railroads and the ending of the buffalo, the two events that did them in. Every year, as the brigade made its ear-splitting way back toward the District of Assiniboia, loaded with robes and meat and hundred-pound skin sacks of pemmican, some of the *métis* stayed behind and scattered in small bands or family groups like Woods Indians, to spend the winter trapping and hunting. High ground, with its wood and water, was essential to them, and as the whole economy was pulled westward by the diminishing buffalo, *métis* winterers made themselves at home in Turtle Mountain, the wooded banks of the Qu'Appelle Fork, the Touchwood Hills, Wood Mountain, the Cypress Hills, the Sweetgrass Hills, the Bearpaws and Little Rockies.

These *hivernants* were the most Indian of the *métis;* unlike their settled compatriots in Assiniboia, they were unlikely to settle in permanent cabins, grow gardens, or in other ways temper their nomadism. Their villages in the remote hills were only semi-settlements, trading posts dealing mainly in whiskey. The communities that formed in autumn disintegrated, as often as not, in spring. It was probably just as well, for a cabin, being immovable, collected more dirt and more vermin than a skin lodge whose location frequently changed. The *hivernant* villages were undoubtedly crawling and filthy, and the moral excesses of a people with few social restrictions were likely to sadden the traveling priests who went as missionaries along the remote frontier, doing their best to bring these savage ones back to civilization by solemnizing marriages, baptizing children, and burning tallow dips for the dead. Drunkenness, whenever there was whiskey to be had, was universal, and from all accounts often appalling in its violence. The more Indian the *métis*, the more insatiable their desire for drink. On the other hand, there were amenities: they were a dancing and singing people, generally gay and volatile. In any gathering there was likely to be a fiddler. Unwashed and barbarous and infested as it was, this was the germ of a culture that could have come to something in its own special terms if history had been kind.

There is no telling exactly where the first village of *métis* in the Cypress Hills was located, except that it was somewhere along the Whitemud, which the winterers called the Rivière Blanche. Unless this earliest village occupied the Chimney Coulee site that later buildings pre-empted, there is not a trace of it except the reports of Father Lestanc, a missionary priest, to his Bishop in St. Boniface, eight hundred miles back toward civilization on the Red River. The winterers evidently came in 1868, fifteen families of them, and they seem to have been the first. Their settlement, unless its foundation stones are mingled with later foundations on Chimney Coulee, was hardly more permanent than the camps of the war parties in the Hills.

But once they began coming, they came in increasing numbers, and after 1870 they were reinforced by political refugees from the Red River. The least Indian of the *métis* were likely to settle in communities along the North Saskatchewan, reconstituting, far from Canadian interference, the kinds of farms and villages they had had on the Assiniboine and the Red. The more Indian ones became winterers and whiskey traders. In the Cypress Hills they found a sanctuary nearly idyllic. Game was as plentiful as any had ever seen it—more plentiful than any would ever see it again. As late as 1873 a party spent seven days, riding twenty to thirty miles a day, south of the Hills, and all that time they were riding through one placidly grazing buffalo herd. A Mountie the next year estimated eighty thousand animals in a single group as he rode from the Hills to Fort Benton, and that same year a member of the American Boundary Commission looked around him from a hill and could not see the end of the herd in any direction. The coulees of the Hills themselves were opulent with elk and bear, the antelope moved across the aprons of the hills like cloud shadows, the Rivière Blanche and the smaller streams were full of unhunted beaver, mink, otter, ermine, and muskrat.

Beaver heaven, elk heaven, bear heaven, buffalo heaven. Yet the coming of the winterers was the beginning of something ominous and inescapable, for within hardly more than a decade of their arrival these Hills, surviving wilderness, last refuge, would be stripped like the rest of the West, and a way of life would be over. The *métis* themselves would help destroy the world that nourished them. Their bequest to the future would be death and emptiness; they would clear the grasslands and coulees for another sowing.

5

Company of Adventurers

In my boyhood the Hudson's Bay Company meant to me hardly more than a mail-order catalogue—one less commonly used than the T. Eaton and Sears Roebuck catalogs—and the somewhat obscure source of the red point blankets that I slept under. Somebody might have enlarged me by putting in my hands a book called *Company of Adventurers*, by a man named Isaac Cowie.

The son of the Hudson's Bay Company agent in the Shetland Islands, he landed at York Factory for a tour of duty as a junior clerk on August 12, 1867. The ancient and bloody rivalry with the North-West Company was almost two generations past, having been healed by merger in 1821. The Company's unchallenged position in the northwest was also over: since the expiration of its monopoly license in 1859, free trade, in theory at least, had flourished on the Red River and out along the two branches of the Saskatchewan. And on November 19, 1869, when Cowie was at Fort Qu'Appelle, the Company signed the deed of surrender in which it gave up to the new Dominion of Canada the complete legislative, judicial, and executive power it had exercised over Rupert's Land since 1670.

The Governor and Company of Adventurers of England Trading into Hudson's Bay had built their two-hundred-year empire with a slim organization of young Scots and Orkneymen for their clerks and factors, and with so-called "English halfbreeds," possessing varying mixtures of Scot and Swampy Cree blood, as menials. Isaac Cowie, though he served in the late twilight of the

Company's great period, was of the authentic Orkney breed. He was intelligent, resolute, made of rock or iron. Dispatched to the prairie post at Fort Qu'Appelle, he demonstrated that he was capable of facing down a bunch of drunk and murderous Indians, and of controlling the independent *métis* traders who undercut the Company's no-liquor policy, and of keeping the loyalty of an isolated and polyglot band of Company servants. During the smallpox epidemic which began in 1869, Cowie took lymph from the arm of a recently vaccinated daughter of Pascal Breland, one of the *métis* leaders, and from it made vaccine that stopped the disease in its tracks around Swan River, though elsewhere on the Plains, that year and the next, it so decimated and demoralized the tribes, especially the Blackfoot, that they never fully regained their power to make war. Trader, doctor, soldier, judge, explorer, he fulfilled his function as a Company agent, and was one of those who steered the Saskatchewan country through the transition years from wild to half tamed. Also he was nearly the beginning of recorded knowledge with respect to the Cypress Hills. Except for the brief notices of Palliser and Hind, and the letters of Father Lestanc to the Bishop of St. Boniface, Cowie's information about the Hills was the first. In many ways it was not encouraging.

On an October day, such a day as that in 1871 when Cowie and his party came across from Fort Qu'Appelle to establish a winter post, the Hills would have been visible from far out on the prairie, a humped arch across the west mellow with autumn. Even from the Big Sandy Hills, twenty miles to the northeast, where they camped next to a big Indian gathering, they should have been able to see dark blotches of timber on the bench, the jackpine that the *métis* called *cypre*. They might have seen still unshaken tatters of golden aspen tonguing down the coulees. The smells on that October prairie, once one got upwind from the Indian encampment, would have been the smell of curly grass cured on the stem, of smoke from *bois de vache* fires, the ammoniac odor of horse herds. The sky would have been brassy, the wind clean. If it was from the west, which it should have been, Cowie's men might have imagined on it the tang of autumnal berry patches and the coolness of living streams.

Or the odor of death. For out of this big camp of Cree and

Saulteaux and Assiniboin that had been called together for a sun dance and for the purpose of letting the unmolested buffalo herds find their way back to the eastward without being harassed by small bands of hunters, a vainglorious crowd of sixty young Cree had on the day before gone over to the Hills to collect spruce gum. They wanted to please their girls, they wanted to show off their courage on the edge of the Blackfoot country; and their confidence was increased by the fact that the Blackfoot had been so damaged by the smallpox for the past two winters that they had lost the heart for war. Still, there was the adventurous chance that some might be around. Because the Cree did not have even yet as many horses as the Blackfoot, they did not go to war mounted, though, as Cowie says, they hoped to return that way. Now they went afoot to the Hills for their spruce gum, half hoping that there might be a war party of the enemy around that could be induced to start something.

They got both their gum and their wish. Eyes watched them as they stripped pitch from the trees, eyes watched them as they started back across the plain toward the big camp. And when they were well out on the prairie, totally exposed, with not even burnouts for cover, they looked back and saw the boiling dust of a great Blackfoot war party racing to intercept and surround them. The Cree did not run, like the Gros Ventre and the Crow of Rising Wolf's story, who had been shot and clubbed from their horses only a few miles south. Being afoot, the Cree could not have run if they had chosen to. They fought it out in a dust-hazed circle of death, and they lay out there now, all sixty of them, scalped and mutilated and quilled with arrows, victims of a historical process of displacement, and a testimonial to the truth that for Plains warfare an adequate supply of horses might over-power an adequate supply of guns, but that an adequate supply of both was incomparably better than either. The main Cree camp when Cowie's men came into it was loud with the wailing of relatives, with threats of vengeance against the Blackfoot, and with mutterings of discontent against the British, who according to the Indian view subsisted entirely on pemmican and thus forced poor Indians out into territory where they had to risk death from their enemies in order to kill the buffalo demanded by insatiable British appetites.

It was the hope of bringing together the Blackfoot from the west and the Cree, Saulteaux, and Assiniboin from the east and south, and of pacifying them through the mutual benefits of trade, that had brought Cowie to the Montagne aux Cypre. If a post in the Cypress Hills proved successful—and the first *métis* villages, plus the taming effect of the smallpox, seemed to suggest that it might—the Company proposed to build a permanent post somewhere on the upper South Saskatchewan specifically for the Blackfoot trade, thus restoring the situation that had obtained when the Nor'westers had Chesterfield House and Old Bow Fort on the flank of the Rockies. The Blackfoot gave Cowie an object lesson in the difficulties of his task before he ever arrived.

Nevertheless, he built his post on a shelf at the east end of the Hills, overlooking the sweep of prairie where the sixty Cree had died; he was right above the little pond which sent its rills to two oceans. Below the single line of the post buildings was a second line of cabins put up by freemen and independent *métis* traders. Together, they were a strong enough party so that they did not bother to fortify or build a stockade, though the wooded coulee to the north and the high timbered bench to the west provided cover from which they knew they were often watched.

Their efforts to woo the suspicious Blackfoot got nowhere, but the trade, during that winter when frequent chinooks kept the snow melted off the hills and their horses grew fat on the curly grass, was tremendous. Many hands were against Cowie; the independents, some of them armed with the whiskey which Company policy forbade him to dispense, cut heavily into his operations. Yet his share of the trade for that one winter included 750 grizzly bear skins and 1500 elk hides, plus hundreds of the smaller and more valuable furs. He estimated that the independents got as many more. Many of the bear skins, some as big as thirteen feet from nose to tail, were unprime summer hides got when Indians or *métis* caught bears out on the flats and killed them in a running fight from horseback. This, presumably, was sport. It is a reliable index to the life they lived. If riding in on a bear that stands a dozen feet high on his hind legs, with claws five or six inches long and arms that can break the neck of a horse or the back of a man with one cuff, can be called sport, the serious business of life has a wonderfully rugged sound. Those summer hides were not even worth much. The men who risked their lives to get them usually used them as cart covers.

By spring the Blackfoot were still suspicious. The attempt to establish a post where the Qu'Appelle Indians and their traditional enemies might meet was obviously a failure, however profitable the single winter's trade, and as casually as an *hivernant* village the post broke up. And on that frontier where every ounce of lead, every broken saw or file, every piece of metal or glass, had value, there was much in the breaking-up of a post to interest the hangers-on. As the *métis* and the Company servants cleared out the cabins and packed the carts there were nine Assiniboin under their feet and at their elbows, inflamed with lust for the stray bullet to be scrabbled from a crack in the floor, or the old hat or the piece of cloth tossed in a corner. When the carts were starting down the hill toward the Big Sandy, Cowie and one of his men named Birston told the Assiniboin they could have the fresh meat that was left, and also warned them to keep their eye on the bench. There were renewed signs of Blackfoot around.

The Assiniboin joyfully prowling the abandoned buildings were not worried. Cowie and Birston mounted and rode on after the last of the screeching carts. They were barely a quarter mile down the long hill slope when the shooting started, and by the time they caught up with the carts on the edge of the plain they could see the smoke of burning buildings rising over the tender green of the Hills. In June, hunting *métis* found the nine Assiniboin bodies scattered among the ashes of what had been the post.

So the first fur-trading post in the Cypress Hills lasted only a few months. Its going, like its coming, was commemorated with mass murder, and its monuments did not survive its business life by more than a half hour. The ancient stalemate within the Cypress Hills proper, however, was broken; the presence of *métis* and Cree hunters and of Blackfoot war parties made the wooded coulees at once more populous and more truly dangerous. The activities of the independent traders whose currency was a barrel of water-cut alcohol on a Red River cart would go on, though Cowie and the Company departed, and the brisk trade in skins that the winter of 1871-72 witnessed was a prophecy of the extinction of the grizzlies and the elk, and the decimation of the smaller game.

Already the valley of the Whitemud was becoming one of the favored stops on the nomadic circuit of the *hivernants*. It was only a day's journey from the Fourche des Gros Ventres (the South Saskatchewan), and around the Hills during these years was to be found one of the largest divisions of the northern buffalo herd. No one was going to stay away, under the circumstances. Moreover, the experience of Cowie on the shelf by what would later be called Chimney Coulee was instructive: dare the Hills in small numbers and the Blackfoot, smallpox or no smallpox, would exterminate you; inhabit them in force and they were yours.

6

The Last of the Exterminators

One effect of the coming of the horse to any tribe was to make the horse indispensable to that tribe's neighbors, especially to its enemies. The horse very early became the prime objective in inter-tribal raiding, more coveted than captives and all other forms of booty. The immediate cultural effect of this economic and military necessity was that horse-stealing became one of the most honorable of Indian activities. At one stroke the theft of a horse weakened and humiliated the enemy, strengthened the thief's tribe, and glorified the thief. As Paul Sharp remarks in *Whoop-Up Country*, the story of the whiskey forts along the border above Fort Benton, Plains Indians generally regarded the theft of a horse from someone outside the tribe the way Americans regard the theft of home base.

But the white man, painfully aware of the disadvantage of being set afoot in so big and dangerous a country, operated on quite another basis. The semi-mythical cowboy West—which after all both reflected and helped to form the values of the real West —established firmly the convention that the proper response to a horse theft was a hanging. Here was a conflict of values, one of many, sure to provide repeated provocations to hostility between white and Indian. South of the international border that hostility was more easily aroused, and bloodier, for the American attitude was more impatient and more violent than the Canadian, and the circumstances of the American West gave freer play to the instincts of self-reliant and often criminal men. No one who has studied western history can cling to the belief that the Nazis invented genocide. Extermination was a doctrine accepted widely, both unofficially and officially, in the western United States after the Civil War. It was a doctrine all the more plausible since in most of the American West the first of our great raids against natural resources had cleaned away the fur and eliminated any small function that the Indians might have retained in the trade. The changing of fashion from beaver hats to silk only corroborated what would have happened anyway.

North of the border Indians had for generations occupied a useful and established position as middlemen in the fur trade and the pemmican trade, and the very existence of the *métis* as a buffer race helped to cushion the conflict between cultures there. Probably, too, the near-monopolistic control which the Hudson's Bay Company exercised after 1821 over all the vast domain of Rupert's Land meant a degree of responsibility unknown among the American traders. In Canada, the fur trade lasted much longer; settlement came later. Rupert's Land lay so empty of the squatters, miners, and cowboys of the American West that the chances of irritation were minimized. Not until independent American traders from Fort Benton, abetted by *métis* from both sides of the Line, worked up into the Saskatchewan and Alberta Plains in the 1860's, did the Canadian West begin to resemble, in its murderous violence, the American. It is historically appropriate that the most famous conflict between Indian and white in the Cypress Hills country should have started south of the Line; that it should have involved a group of independent traders and wolfers, part of the nervous force working up the Missouri; and that it should have begun with a theft of horses. What is more significant, the episode which became known as the Cypress Hills Massacre was one of the very last acts of a long border drama, one of the final outrages of the literally lawless West. It came at the end of a decade of contact, along that practical and symbolic divide, between the Canadian system of monopoly trading and the American system of competition, whiskey, bullets, exploitation, and extermination. The massacre, with its immediate sequel, brought the American intrusion to an abrupt stop. So far as Canada was concerned, gun-law, self-administered, came to its end at Abe Farwell's whiskey post on Battle Creek in the Cypress Hills.

The band of wolfers that camped on the Teton River a few miles out of Fort Benton in the beginning of May, 1873, was probably, for that country, an ordinary group. Some were veterans of the Civil War, some had been Indian fighters, all were experienced plainsmen. The ferocious virtues that had been necessary for survival on the American frontier were theirs: they were men who lived freely, wastefully, independently, and they lived by killing—animals as a rule, men if necessary. If any of them were thoughtful men, which is not likely, they may have conceived of themselves as the advancing fringe of civilization, an indispensable broom sweeping clean the Plains for white occupation. As a class, the wolfers were particularly disliked by the Indians, for their practice of poisoning buffalo carcasses killed off Indian dogs as well as wolves. In the Indian view, they tainted the whole prairie, they were cousins to the smallpox. On the other hand, in the wolfers' view the Indians were cousins to the wolf, at least as dangerous and with the additional disadvantage of being horse thieves. That was why, when they arose in the morning in their camp on the Teton and found their horses missing, they started without a moment's hesitation into Fort Benton and there they swiftly got together an expedition aimed at recovery and vengeance.

It was not an especially roughneck or outlaw crowd; of them all, only Thomas Hardwick, the "Green River renegade," was considered a hard case. And as Paul Sharp points out, by no means all of those who rode north on the trail of the stolen ponies were Americans. Three of the group that participated in the Cypress Hills fight, including the one who was accused of starting it and the one who died in it, were Anglo-Canadians, and there were several Canadian *métis* as well. The recognized leader was John Evans, a wolfer said to be an ally of the I. G. Baker trading company of Fort Benton; the year before he had been prominent in the "Spitzee Cavalry" that had tried by threat and force to prevent a rival company, the T. C. Power outfit, from selling firearms to the Blackfoot in the Fort Whoop-Up country in Alberta.

That affiliation would introduce trade rivalries into the situation, just as the partly American composition of the avenging party would introduce international suspicions, hysterias, accusations, and legal proceedings.

Perhaps knowingly, perhaps not, the party of revengers rode northward into a hornet's nest. Not that they feared any Indian attack, as they might have done a few years before. They were armed to a man with new Henry repeating rifles, and they would rather have welcomed trouble from Indians using the old Hudson's Bay "fukes," often sawed off short for buffalo hunting, that had been the favorite trade gun on the horse frontier for generations. But in fact the Cypress Hills, in the space of one short year since Isaac Cowie's retreat from Chimney Coulee, had been tamed with unprecedented speed. Reduced by smallpox and impoverished and undermined by the whiskey for which they would trade anything, wife or horse or gun, the Blackfoot were not the aggressive and belligerent alliance they had been. *Métis* villages had spread through the Hills, and made things safer for Cree and Assiniboin and Saulteaux, and in 1872 four posts had been built to tap the trade there. Two of these, both owned by I. G. Baker, had been abandoned at the end of the winter's trading, early in the spring of 1873, but two others remained, one a Power Company post run by Abe Farwell and one an independent owned by Moses Solomon, just across Battle Creek from Farwell's. Very nearby were a *métis* village and a big camp of Assiniboin under Chief Little Soldier.

Both Moses Solomon and Abe Farwell had been selling whiskey, and the Assiniboin oscillated restlessly from drunken belligerence to the sullen anger of a hangover. They especially hated Solomon; for a month they had been telling the *métis* to stay out of the way so they didn't get hurt when the Assiniboin cleaned out Solomon's nest. Unknown Indians had already killed one trader named Rivers earlier in the spring, and that example had inflamed Assiniboin hatreds. Just before the wolfers arrived on their horse hunt, an Assiniboin had stolen a horse from George Hammond, a wolfer friend of John Evans, while he was staying with Farwell.

Hammond had already got his horse back, and the episode had been smoothed over as a sort of joke, when Evans and his party rode in. No one at Farwell's had seen anything of the missing horses of the Fort Benton men; Farwell said he didn't think the Assiniboin of Little Soldier's band could have been the thieves. That might have settled the matter, so far as the Cypress Hills were concerned, except for three circumstances: the wolfers stopped off to do a little Sunday drinking before riding back to Fort Benton; the Assiniboin were energetically engaged in the same way; and in the middle of the festivities George Hammond discovered that his horse had been stolen for the second time.

This is about the point where the evidence begins to fray out in the self-exculpation of individuals, trading jealousies, international relations, Fenian rhetoric, Canadian suspicion, and other forms of obscurity. Pretty surely Evans' excursion had nothing in it of the annexationist provocation that Canadian public opinion later suspected; pretty surely the initial impulse was simply to get the stolen horses back. But what exactly happened at Farwell's post was never very clearly established. Apparently Hammond in a fury grabbed up a gun and started for Little Soldier's camp. He was probably doubly sore because on the occasion of the first theft he had paid the Indian who brought the horse back, though there was every likelihood that he who returned the pony had also carried it off. Now there was every likelihood that the same Indian had so liked the little deal he had worked out that he was trying it all over again. Farwell went along with Hammond, perhaps in the hope of preserving peace. But as his interpreter Alexis Lebompard later testified, Farwell was not competent in the Assiniboin tongue. More than that, Little Soldier was too drunk to hear or speak sense even if Farwell could have handled the language. Farwell may have been an incompetent interpreter, and Little Soldier was certainly drunk; but it is doubtful that either at his best could have dealt with Hammond's provocative rage or with the provocative insolence of the young Assiniboin warriors. Much of Farwell's testimony about what happened was aimed at proving that the American (that is, I. G. Baker's) traders started the fight, and so may have been commercially tainted. He at first blamed the Assiniboin, and then later, after consulting with his anti-Baker employers in Fort Benton, changed his story and said that Little Soldier offered two horses to compensate Hammond. It does not much matter whether Little Soldier actually made that offer, or whether Farwell could have understood him if he did. Considering the exacerbation of feelings and the cumulative distrust and hatred which the whiskey traders' activities had engendered along that border, only the subtlest of diplomats and peacemakers—not exactly numerous in that time and place—could have averted trouble.

During the argument the Benton men had come up behind Hammond and Farwell to back them up, and now they began to grow alarmed at the threatening manner of the Assiniboin, and when the young warriors began to throw off their clothes and the women scurried for the woods, the wolfers took cover in the abrupt gully between Farwell's and the Indian camp. Thomas Hardwick either did or did not yell at Farwell to get out of the way so that the whites could shoot. Farwell either did or did not go on urging the Indians to stay back out of trouble, and either did or did not return to the gully to argue with the angry Benton men. George Hammond either fired at the Indians, as Farwell said in one phase of his testimony, or the Benton men replied to random Indian shots, as *métis* eyewitnesses Joseph Laverdure and Joseph Vital Turcotte testified. The true cause, even the true provocative stimulus, of a little battle like this is about as hard to establish as the true cause of a major war. Fear and anger face each other in a parley; a knight draws his sword to kill an adder that has stung his heel, and the whole Round Table comes down.

Rumor somewhat exaggerated the casualties of this particular quarrel, some stories building the number of dead Assiniboin up to two hundred. Cowie, reporting the incident, said eighty. He also reported that the body of Little Soldier, killed in the midst of his big drunk, was impaled on a lodge pole and left as a warning to all insolent Indians. Farwell in a toothsome modification testified that Little Soldier was found dead drunk in his lodge at the end of the battle, and that his head was cut off and stuck up on a stake.

None of this seems to be true, though Cowie's report of a great sobering of Assiniboin belligerence afterward was probably based on observation. For it is certainly true that a relatively small group of whites (more than the six that Cowie reported, but precisely how many it is impossible to say) inflicted a terrible defeat on the Assiniboin. From the coulee, which was gullied three to eight feet deep and ran along the front of the Indian camp within fifty yards, the wolfers poured a catastrophic fire into the charging warriors. Three times, according to the testimony of John Duval, a *métis*, the Assiniboin rallied with great bravery to rush the coulee; three times the firepower of the repeating Henrys drove them back. Balked in a frontal attack, they withdrew to another coulee to snipe at long range. Flanked by Evans and Hardwick and raked from a hilltop, they flanked the two wolfers in turn and all but had them when the other white men charged to the rescue. In that charge the one white casualty, Ed Grace, received his death, and the wolfers retreated to Farwell's fort with his body. From there they covered the Assiniboin camp until nightfall, when the Indians scattered, leaving their dead behind. There were anything from fifteen to thirty-six of them, depending upon which witness one accepts, when the wolfers next morning pulled down the camp on top of them and set the whole place afire. The body of Ed Grace, to prevent its being found and mutilated, they buried under the floor of Solomon's fort. Then they sloshed kerosene on the log cabin and burned it to ashes, and rode off toward Fort Whoop-Up to see if by any chance the Bloods in that direction had their horses.

And so the trading settlement on Battle Creek, like its predecessor on Chimney Coulee, went up in smoke and the smell of cremated bodies dead by violence. The Indian policy of the American side of the frontier, pushed northward precisely to the divide that separated the Missouri watershed from that of Hudson Bay, came to its logical and many times repeated result of cultural and ethnic conflict culminating in bloodshed. It is impossible to estimate the degrees or shades of blame that attach to individuals involved. The Power interests seem to have taken every opportunity to embarrass the Baker people who took part. At the same time, the massacre blew up much Canadian dislike of the United States, a dislike that had been stimulated by annexationist pressures, by the Fenian invasions, and by the not always ingenuous sympathy in American quarters for Louis Riel and his "rebellious" *métis*. Once charge and counter-charge had begun, American opinion in general gathered in support of the wolfers, feeling that they were being victimized by Hudson's Bay Company pressure. Canadian opinion held the wolfers to be a band of Missouri River gunmen. It seems safe to believe that the traders and wolfers, though violent and bloody enough, true offspring of the violent frontier that had bred them, were less ruffianly than some of the testimony and most Canadian opinion suggested.

But one thing must be said and triply underlined: the solution which Canada almost immediately found for such eruptions of violence in its North-West Territories was better than any the Americans had found in all the generations of their frontier history. When the exaggerated and lurid story of the Cypress Hills fight, getting dirtier as it went, like a summer whirlwind, reached Ottawa, it stirred up a fury of public feeling against Americans at large and against whiskey traders in particular. Already before the Canadian Parliament was a bill by which it was proposed to create a police force charged with maintaining—or rather, establishing—law and order on the western Plains. The Cypress Hills Massacre made it certain that the bill would pass and the force be created. But before it reached the Cypress Hills there would be another development that even before the arrival of official law would bring the outlines of law and history to the border country.

7

The Medicine Line

. . . that a line drawn from the most northwestern point of the Lake of the Woods, along the forty-ninth parallel of north latitude, or, if the said point shall not be in the forty-ninth parallel of north latitude, then that a line drawn from the said point due north or south as the case may be, until the said line shall intersect the said parallel of north latitude, and from the point of such intersection due west along and with the said parallel, shall be the line of demarcation between the territories of the United States, and those of His Britannic Majesty, and that the said line shall form the northern boundary of the said territories of the United States, and the southern boundary of the territories of His Britannic Majesty, from the Lake of the Woods to the Stony Mountains.

Article 2, *Convention of London,*
Oct. 20, 1818

The 49th parallel ran directly through my childhood, dividing me in two. In winter, in the town on the Whitemud, we were almost totally Canadian. The textbooks we used in school were published in Toronto and made by Canadians or Englishmen; the geography we studied was focused on the Empire and the Dominion, though like our history it never came far enough west, and was about as useless to us as the occasional Canadian poem that was inserted patriotically into our curriculum. Somehow those poems seemed to run to warnings of disaster and fear of the dark and cold in snowy eastern woods. My mind is still inclined at inopportune moments to quote me Tom Moore's "Canadian Boat Song" (Row, brothers, row, the stream runs fast/ The rapids are near and the daylight's past) or tell me, out of Charles Dawson Shanley,

> Speed on, speed on, good Master!
> The camp lies far away;
> We must cross the haunted valley
> Before the close of day.

The songs we sang were "Tipperary" and "We'll Never Let the Old Flag Fall" and "The Maple Leaf Forever" and "God Save the King"; the flag we saluted was the Union Jack, the heroes we most revered belonged to the Canadian regiment called the Princess Pats, the clothes and the Christmas gifts we bought by mail came from the T. Eaton mail-order house. The businesses whose names we knew and whose products we saw advertised were Ltd., not Inc., the games we played were ice hockey and rounders, the movie serials that drew us to the Pastime Theater on Tuesdays and Saturdays were likely to retail the deeds of Mounted Policemen amid the Yukon snows. Our holidays, apart from Thanksgiving and Christmas, which were international, were Dominion Day, Victoria Day, the King's birthday. Even the clothes we wore had a provincial flavor, and I never knew till I moved to Montana and was taught by the laughter of Montana kids that turtle-necked sweaters and shoepacs were not standard winter costume everywhere.

But if winter and town made Canadians of us, summer and the homestead restored us to something nearly, if not quite, American. We could not be remarkably impressed with the physical differences between Canada and the United States, for our lives slopped over the international boundary every summer day. Our plowshares bit into Montana sod every time we made the turn at the south end of the field. We collected stones from our fields and stoneboated them down into Montana to dump them. I trapped Saskatchewan and Montana flickertails indiscriminately, and spread strychnine-soaked wheat without prejudice over two nations.

The people we neighbored with were all in Montana, half our disk of earth and half our bowl of sky acknowledged another flag than ours, the circle of darkness after the prairie night came down was half American, and the few lights that assured us we were not alone were all across the Line. The mountains whose peaks drew my wistful eyes on July days were the Bearpaws, down below the Milk River. For all my eyes could tell me, no Line existed, for the obelisk of black iron that marked our south-eastern corner was only a somewhat larger version of the survey stakes (the Montana ones had blue tops, the Canadian not) that divided our world into uniform squares. It never occurred to us to walk along the border from obelisk to obelisk—an act that might have given us a notion of the boundary as an endless, very open fence, with posts a mile apart. And if we had walked along it, we would have found only more plains, more burnouts, more gopher holes, more cactus, more stinkweed and primroses, more hawk shadows slipping over the scabby flats, more shallow cou-lees down which the drainage from the Old-Man-on-His-Back hills crept into Montana toward the Milk. The nearest custom house was clear over in Alberta, and all the summers we spent on the farm we never saw an officer, Canadian or American. We bought supplies in Harlem or Chinook and got our mail at Hydro, all in Montana. In the fall we hauled our wheat, if we had made any, freely and I suppose illegally across to the Milk River towns and sold it where it was handiest to sell it. Even yet, between Willow Creek and Treelon, a degree and a half of lon-gitude, there is not a single settlement or a custom station.

We ignored the international boundary in ways and to degrees that would have been impossible if it had not been a line almost completely artificial. And yet our summer world was a different world from the Canadian world of town. The magazines to which we now subscribed were American magazines, the newspapers we read were published in Havre, Great Falls, even Minneapolis. The funny paper characters to whom I devoted charmed after-noons were Happy Hooligan, the Katzenjammer Kids, Hair-breadth Harry, Alphonse and Gaston—all made in the U.S.A. Our summer holidays were the Fourth of July and Labor Day, and the *pièce de résistance* of a holiday get-together was a ball-game. In summer, when we bought anything by mail, we bought it not from T. Eaton but from the lavish and cosmopolitan catalogs of Sears Roebuck and Montgomery Ward. We learned in summer to call a McLaughlin a Buick.

Undistinguishable and ignored as it was, artificially as it split a country that was topographically and climatically one, the international boundary marked a divide in our affiliations, expectations, loyalties. Like the pond at the east end of the Cypress Hills, we could flow into either watershed, or into both simultaneously, but we never confused the two. Winter and summer were at odds in us. We were Americans without the education and indoctrination that would have made us confident of our identity, we were Canadians in everything but our sentimental and patriotic commitment. Whatever was being done to us by our exposure to Canadian attitudes, traditions, and prejudices—an exposure intensified by the strains and shortages of the war in which Canada was a belligerent through four of my six years there—we never thought of ourselves as anything but American. Since we could not explain why the United States was "too cowardly to get into the fight" against Germany, and since we were secretly afraid it was, we sometimes came to blows with the uncomplicatedly Canadian boys. It used to agonize me, wondering whether or not the Canadians really did defeat the Americans at the Battle of Lundy's Lane during the War of 1812. It did not seem possible or likely, and yet there it was in the history book. Perhaps I reached the beginning of wisdom, of a sort, when I discovered that Lundy's Lane, which loomed like Waterloo or Tours in the Canadian textbooks and in my anxious imagination, was dismissed as a frontier skirmish by histories written in the United States. The importance of that battle depended entirely on which side of the frontier you viewed it from.

That was the way the 49th parallel, though outwardly ignored, divided us. It exerted uncomprehended pressures upon affiliation and belief, custom and costume. It offered us subtle choices even in language (we stooked our wheat; across the Line they shocked it), and it lay among our loyalties as disturbing as a hair in butter. Considering how much I saw of it and how many kinds of influence it brought to bear on me, it might have done me good to learn something of how it came there. I never did until much later, and when I began to look it up I discovered that practically nobody else knew how it had come there either. While I lived on it, I accepted it as I accepted Orion in the winter sky. I did not know that this line of iron posts was one outward evidence of the coming of history to the unhistoried Plains, one of the strings by which dead men and the unguessed past directed our lives. In actual fact, the boundary which Joseph Kinsey Howard has called artificial and ridiculous was more potent in the lives of people like us than the natural divide of the Cypress Hills had ever been upon the tribes it held apart. For the 49th parallel was an agreement, a rule, a limitation, a fiction perhaps but a legal one, acknowledged by both sides; and the coming of law, even such limited law as this, was the beginning of civilization in what had been a lawless wilderness. Civilization is built on a tripod of geography, history, and law, and it is made up largely of limitations.

John Evans' angry wolfers, following the tracks of their stolen ponies northward, undoubtedly knew that they were carrying their gun-law in Canada, but the fact would not have troubled them. For one thing, Canada was still only a name, hardly a force; it had as yet made hardly a move to carry its authority into the North-West Territories. For another, there was enough Fenian sentiment and enough Manifest Destinarianism around Fort Benton to persuade most of its citizens that the northern Plains were a natural and inevitable extension of the United States. For a third, the boundary was less a boundary than a zone. There was no telling where the precise line lay: wolfers and traders did not carry astronomical instruments. Even such prominent landmarks as Wood Mountain and the Sweetgrass Hills might lie in either nation, and though the Convention of London in 1818 had established the 49th parallel as the boundary from the Lake of the Woods to the Rockies, and the Oregon Treaty of 1846 had extended that line to the Pacific, neither the Indians who stole the horses nor the wolfers who pursued them recognized any dividing line short of the Cypress Hills—a line which had nothing to do with international agreements, but had been established by tradition, topography, and a balance of tribal force.

But even while the wolfers were riding northward across the unsurveyed boundary zone, the first line of the geometry of law was starting west from the Red River settlements. By October,

1873, it would be at Wood Mountain; by the end of the following summer it would reach to the crest of the Rockies, to connect with the line that had been run that far eastward from the Pacific in 1861. Only a little more than a year after John Evans' men poured their murderous fire into Little Soldier's charging Assiniboin, the cairn-marked line of the border would be drawn accusingly across their track, making very clear the international implications of their raid. The series of trials and extraditions by which Canada would attempt for two years to convict and punish the raiders would so publicize the boundary that thereafter no one could cross it, for any purpose, in ignorance.

Surveyors are not heroic figures. They come later than the explorers, they douse with system what was once the incandescent excitement of danger and the unknown. They conquer nothing but ignorance, and if they are surveying a boundary they are so compelled by astronomical and geodetic compulsions that they might as well run on rails. Among the instruments of their profession there is none that lifts the imagination and achieves grace or weight as a symbol. The mythic light in which we have bathed our frontier times, when decision was for the individual will and a man tested himself against wild weathers, wild beasts, or wild men, and so knew himself a man—that light does not shine on the surveyor as it shines on trapper, trader, scout, cowboy, or Indian fighter. Surveyors do not even acquire the more pedestrian glamour of the farming pioneer, though they make him possible, and though their work is basic not merely to his conquering of the frontier, but to some of the mistakes he has made in trying to break it.

Among the chronicles of long Canadian marches, it is the march of Col. Garnet Wolseley from Toronto to Fort Garry in 1870, and that of the Mounted Police from Fort Dufferin to Fort Macleod in 1874, that have become folklore. But when the used-up Mounted Police stopped, 590 miles out of Dufferin, to repair equipment and shoe horses and oxen and to rest men and animals in a burned-over dreary plain within sight of the Cypress Hills, the surveyors were there ahead of them, having made, with practically no fanfare, practically the same march. It was from the survey depot at Willow Bunch, on Wood Mountain. that Assistant Commissioner Macleod begged surplus oats and provisions for his tired command. By that time the surveyors were close to completing a journey that might have been called epic if it had not been so well planned, so successful, and so utilitarian.

They may as well all be nameless: there were no heroes among them. And they do not need to be separated by nationality, for it was of the essence of their work that it was international, cooperative, mutual. But they need credit and remembrance for a job finished swiftly and efficiently—a job of immense importance. And though they have never struck anybody as glamorous enough to be written up in western story, a young man in search of excitement in 1872 could have done worse than enlist with them.

Until the transfer of sovereignty over Rupert's Land to the Dominion government there had been little need for defining the boundary established in 1818. The scare which Louis Riel threw into both Canada and Great Britain in 1869-70 hastened the inevitable. The actual transfer took place in November, 1869, while the Riel situation was waiting for the spring weather that would let Wolseley's expedition start west to settle it. But the suppression of the Red River *métis* could not by itself solve much, for there was nearly a thousand miles of unmarked and unwatched border where trouble could erupt. The Dominion government, no matter what local difficulties might arise, was clearly committed to a swift survey to fix the bounds of its jurisdiction and deter the raids and excursions, unofficial and semi-official, from the United States. The initiating cause for the survey might have been almost anything; in fact, it was a hasty American claim that the Hudson's Bay post at Pembina, on Red River, was actually on American soil.

It took two years and a half, political action being what it is, for agreement to be reached between the United States and Great Britain on the terms of a boundary survey. An American Boundary Commission was authorized, with a customarily inadequate appropriation, by an act of March 19, 1872. The British commission, composed of a commissioner and five officers and forty-four men of the Royal Engineers, augmented by a Canadian party made up of a geologist, surgeon, veterinarian, and a group of surveyors, was organized in June. By September the

British outfit had made its way to Duluth and thence across Minnesota by rail to St. Paul. On September 18 they met at Pembina an American party made up of the commissioner, four officers from the Corps of Engineers, a body of civilian surveyors, and Company K of the 20th Infantry as escort. There their first act was to determine just where the 49th parallel did cross the Red River. The disputed Hudson's Bay post was demonstrated to be a few hundred feet north of the line, but the Canadian custom house was south of it. When the American and British surveyors came up with a discrepancy of thirty-two feet in locating the line, the Joint Commission set a precedent in international relations by amicably halving it.

Not all problems could be solved by dichotomy. After being baptized by an equinoctial snowstorm immediately on arrival, they had a month of fine Indian Summer weather in which to survey the line through the almost impossible terrain from the northwest corner of Lake of the Woods, where the 1826 survey had ended, to the 49th parallel. There they encountered difficulties both political and topographical. The earlier negotiators, confused by an imprecise map, had allowed the border to drift a long way north of the 49th parallel, and it was clear now that to run a straight line south to that parallel would leave an isolated peninsula of American territory deep in Canada. Captain D. R. Cameron of the Royal Artillery, the British Commissioner, had orders not to recognize the northwest angle monument left by the 1826 survey, since the British hoped to eliminate the angle by further negotiation, but he did consent to having a sight line cut from it due south, in order to expedite the rest of the work. But the terrain almost rendered their political agreeableness an empty gesture, for they found that any land which was not soggy with water was under water, and they had a bad time even locating the monument that Cameron's orders forbade him to accept. Finally they did find it—a post surrounded by a crib of logs—several feet under water in a swamp, and started hewing their southward line. Indian axemen labored in water above their knees, surveyors floundered across bogs whose mossy surface gave way to let them down to their waists in cold slime, supplies came in on men's backs, the camps were dreary quagmires. Sixteen miles of that, continuous swamp heavily grown with birch and tamarack, before they cut off the disputed American peninsula; then ten miles across the open lake, where they located the 49th parallel on the ice. From that corner they turned west, marking the first station on solid ground just at the west shore of Lake of the Woods. Again the instruments could not agree as readily as the commissioners; an overlap of twenty-nine feet in the observations was halved. As for direction, once they turned the corner on the ice they would not need to deviate again: straight west would serve them all the way. They were almost at the eastern edge of the Plains; across that oceanic land a boundary line could run as straight as an equator or a tropic, serene, almost abstract.

After the establishment of the joint astronomical station on the shore of the lake, the American party was forced by its inadequate budget to retire to St. Paul and fold up for the winter. It left to the British, on a shared-cost basis, the hewing of a thirty-foot swath through ninety miles of swamps, timber, and prairie to the Red River. The British crews, finding the work easier after the freeze-up, decided to go on with their astronomical and chaining work through the winter; the American party would not finish its share of that stretch until 1874.

The experiences of the British party in 1872-73, and those of the American party a year later, differ only in degree, though it seems likely that no American officer ever served his country under more severe conditions or with more devotion and endurance than Lt. Greene of the Corps of Engineers when he completed the American surveying between Lake of the Woods and Red River. If he was not an explorer, he had all the discomforts, difficulties, and dangers of one; and the life of the British group was comparable. All of them, here at the ecological boundary between Woods and Plains, were in process of becoming plainsmen while having to retain many of the skills of the woods. With modifications, they were in the position that the Saulteaux, Cree, and *métis* had all found themselves in, and the machinery of their daily lives was a bizarre mixture of two cultures. They alternated between mules and dogteams, carts and sleds, skin lodges and brush shelters. Broken up into small parties for maximum efficiency, they were caught out in blizzards that neither horse nor dog would drive against, and fought their way in after days of exposure, half starved, half frozen, and undismayed. Along with the boundaries of their countries they surveyed the limits of endurance. Sometimes in the still cold their spirit thermometers dropped to forty-five, fifty, fifty-one below. In their icy camps they lay and heard the gunshot reports of willows bursting as the sap froze, and on those nights of windless cold they saw the Northern Lights in their greatest splendor, "vapour-like and yet perfectly transparent, so that even the small stars could be distinctly seen through the illuminated mist," or spreading in bands and streamers so bright they lighted the sky like dawn. They learned how eyelashes could freeze together on a trail, and how a muffler moistened by breathing could freeze fast to a man's beard and threaten to smother him. They learned to be wary about turning a tangent screw with the bare fingers, for the brass burned as if it had been white hot; if the hand that touched it was moist, the metal froze fast and could only be removed with the skin. Tenderfeet who made the mistake of drinking out of unwarmed metal cups in the morning left the skin of their lips on the rim. The eyes of all the surveyors were painful from the constant dangerous contact with the eyepieces of their instruments, whose lurking frost could seize an eyelid and hold it fast, "as experienced by Russian officers in Siberia." After long exposure the eye would leak tears that froze instantly into beaded ice on the lashes, "and gave the face a comical look, somewhat like that in children's pictures of Jack Frost."

It was not a game for children. They had cause for pride in their work when they brought the line out of the Woods and into the Red River valley. Now before them lay the Plains, through which they were to sight a beeline for eight hundred miles.

April and part of May, during the spring breakup, were not surveying weather. The British commission spent six weeks under roofs at Red River planning for the season ahead, and they were already in the field when the American party reassembled on June 1, 1873, complete with an escort of one company of the 20th Infantry and two of the Seventh Cavalry under Major Reno. The cavalry would make lurid history three years later when the bankrupt Indian policy of the United States combined with official and unofficial corruption to bring Sitting Bull and Crazy Horse and a thousand Sioux warriors boiling down on Custer's center column on the Little Big Horn. Here, though considered indispensable, they would prove to have no fighting to do. If they had had, the arrangement was that they were to protect without distinction both the American and the British party, though in practice the British and Canadians, beneficiaries of a sounder Indian policy and a less pugnacious history, were undoubtedly less in need of protection than their comrades on the other side of the line.

Working alternate stations, each commission divided into several parties, they closed the line from monument to monument. As far as the western border of Manitoba they would plant eight-foot hollow iron pillars four feet in the ground at mile intervals; in the empty country beyond all settlement their progress would at first be marked every three miles by a cairn of stones or a mound of earth. Ahead of them, thirty *métis* scouts commanded by an engineering officer reconnoitered the country for camp and supply-depot sites in the boundary zone. The measuring worm lengthened out, chaining itself toward buffalo country, toward the Blackfoot country, toward the lost hills where, only a few weeks before, the conflict of cultures had burst into brief and bloody war on Battle Creek.

The climate of the Red River valley is cold, and spring comes slowly, but when it comes, when one warm day is followed by a single night without frost, the whole prairie is misted with sudden green. Out of the same abrupt loosening of winter come mosquitoes in fogs and clouds to drive men and animals wild. The tender skin around the eyes of horses and oxen gathers moving crusts of torment; a rider rubbing a hand across his mount's face brings up a pulpy mass of crushed insects and blood. And horseflies, the savage things called bulldogs: a horse will flinch from the bite of one as if he has been nicked by a knife blade. His dung is full of bots. Even the strongest animals under these conditions are kept thin, and when one is too poor or overworked the constant attacks of the flies and mosquitoes may literally kill him.

Chain by chain, stake by stake, mound by mound, they measured their true-west line, each party surveying as it went a belt five miles wide on its own side. The Red River valley's fertile prairie was back of them, they mounted the ridge known as Pembina Mountain and were on the Second Prairie Steppe, one mighty grassland marked by the skulls and bones and unused wallows of the vanished buffalo, and by the mounded burrows of innumerable badgers. Crocuses gave way to wild roses, but the mosquitoes and flies did not disappear as the summer heat came on. They ceased their biting only for an hour or two during the blaze of noon, and that was precisely the time when work could not go on because "over the whole prairie surface the air was in constant agitation, and in looking through the telescope at a distant flagstaff it was seen to dance with persistent contortions, and no observations on terrestrial objects could be made from point to point with accuracy, except in the early morning or late in the evening." They learned to like cloudy days; they blessed their luck when they were sighting across a valley, for only the lower thirty or forty feet of air did the heat dance.

Seventy miles of plains brought them to Turtle Mountain, straddling the line. Here was relief from heat and glare, plenty of wood for fires and smudges, plenty of water more potable than the sloughs of the prairie. But Turtle Mountain also brought a sharp increase in difficulty of another kind. One group of British axemen and surveyors was all summer cutting a fifteen-foot way through twenty-four miles of Turtle Mountain to meet an American party which worked ten miles in from the other side. In the thirty-four miles of their mutual effort, before they met on opposite shores of a mile-wide lake, they had crossed sixty-five pieces of water, across many of which the line had to be surveyed by triangulation. Also they discovered what havoc a sudden hailstorm, with stones as big as bantam eggs, could create in camp and among the horses. More than once they hunted cover and watched the violent winds that brought these squalls level every tent in camp. Nevertheless, Turtle Mountian was a place they left with some regret, its advantages of wood, water, and shade more than balancing its disadvantages. They established a supply depot there and chained on to catch up with an American party that had set up a depot on the Souris or Mouse River, still farther west.

Now plains again, interrupted by the winding floodplain of the Souris, with good camping and good grass, and past Les Roches Perceés with their badlands erosional forms. For 138 miles the plains swept on without a major lift or break, until after many days the west showed a faint low line of blue. This, which faded almost out of sight as they approached and mounted it, was the Great Coteau of the Missouri, angling southeastward from the Thunder Hills, on the Saskatchewan, to a point east of the Great Bend of the Missouri in what is now North Dakota. This was another distinct step in their measuring-worm march. It brought them to the Third Prairie Steppe, the highest and driest part of the northern Plains, where the flow of streams was uncertain and often alkaline. For many miles west of the Coteau they encountered salt lakes, alkali sinks, creeks that trickled off feebly to one side or other and died in brackish sloughs. They suffered for decent water, and sickened on what they had, and chained on.

Late in September, when the westernmost American party was quitting work at Astronomical Station No. 12, just west of the 106th meridian, 408 miles from Red River, and preparing to start for the Missouri and a steamboat ride to Bismarck and thence home, the British parties were still strung out across 400 miles, and they and their commissariat wagons were caught in various postures of unpreparedness by the first equinoctial snowstorms on September 23. They corralled their wagons into a horseshoe and lashed canvas sheets on the inside and huddled their tents into the frail shelter. For seven days and nights they could do little but stay in their blankets. Their horses, turned loose to graze in the lulls of the storm, came back and stood in the shelter of the wagons and did not eat for a week. That the first storm was almost always followed by several weeks of mild Indian Summer weather did not much console men who had anywhere up to 400 miles to ride, across prairies swept bare of forage by fires, and who had to watch helplessly while their horses turned to scarecrows before their eyes.

A few days after the storm had ended, the most advanced British party was near a fly-by-night whiskey post called Turnay's, on the Frenchman River just below its crossing of the 49th parallel. There was still snow on the ground. They were looking for a *métis* village supposed to be on Wood (or Woody) Mountain. For that matter, they were looking for Wood Mountain, which rumor said lay somewhere near the line. Only the passing of a party of Sioux hunters heading south gave them the clue that let them find it: the Sioux said there was a hunters' camp a long day's journey north. Following the Sioux tracks backward across the snowy plain, the surveyors after 25 miles found the village at what is now Willow Bunch, hidden among the ravines of the high land, with good wood, water, and shelter. A few hours of bright sun let them take a shot with the sextant and determine that the village was actually 22 miles north of the line. Balmy weather made the "rude and desolate huts" of the *hivernants* look attractive enough so that the surveyors selected Willow Bunch as their supply depot for the work of the next season. That was on October 8, 1873. By the end of that month they had ridden, almost casually, all the 450 miles back to Red River and closed up for the year.

The next May the advance commissary train of twenty wagons started west again, accompanied by a road-making and bridge-building party. At the same time a mounted reconnaissance party with Red River carts for its baggage pushed clear on out to Wood Mountain to build depot buildings; when they had those completed, they were to scour the country for a hundred miles to the west to spot water, fuel, and campsites. Two weeks behind the advance groups came the main body, 160 officers and men and 70 wagons, and so efficient had the road-builders been that the main party went 200 miles, clear to the Souris, without a difficulty or an interruption. There the river was in flood. They sank pole cribs loaded with rocks in its channel and in three days built a bridge. At the Great Coteau the astronomical and chaining parties broke off south to follow the boundary track to their stations; the wagons kept on the easier cart track toward Wood Mountain, where they arrived on June 22, thirty-two days out from Red River. At Willow Bunch they found that at least one element of the American frontier system was sound. The trader they had engaged in Fort Benton had already delivered across country sixty tons of oats, bringing them in a train of huge, broad-tired double wagons, each pair drawn by nine yoke of oxen and carrying a payload of eight tons of sacked grain. The British were quite capable of matching American plainsmen in fortitude and more than able to match them in discipline, but in enterprises of this sort Americans would out-perform anybody in the world.

The survey crew had trouble crossing the deep gorge of the Frenchman, and found its water unpalatably salty, and on its plateau in early June they made the acquaintance of the crawling locusts whose swarms, growing wings, would shortly fly east to devastate for the second year in a row the crops of the Red River valley.

And out on the scabby plains beyond the crossing of the Frenchman, out on the flats where exactly forty years later my father would hopefully hunt up the survey stakes marking his half section of land, they met the buffalo for the first time. They chased him and hunted him and blessed his beef and cursed his habit of filling every slough and waterhole with mud and excreta. Once their wagon train, headed for a depot 150 miles west of Wood Mountain, was all but run over by an enormous herd being driven by Sioux. The commissary's *métis* scouts fired into the onrushing herd and split it, and they watched the terrified bison gallop past on both sides, and like apparitions the stripped brown Sioux on strong buffalo horses emerged from the dust and were gone.

In Fort Benton men during those years were confidently saying that the buffalo were getting more numerous because of the killing off of the wolves, but a herd like that was already a thing of the past in all the five hundred miles of plains eastward, and after another seven years the buffalo would be gone from this last desolate prairie too—gone as if the earth had opened. The surveyors witnessed one of the reasons: encountering hunting camps of *métis*, they noted that every day each hunter would kill six or eight buffalo, from which his women would take the tongues and hump ribs and leave the rest, even the hides. Across this "arid cactus plain" between the Frenchman and the Milk the boundary line was pushed through the carrion stink of a way of life recklessly destroying itself.

In seventeen days they surveyed 108 miles across the cactus flats where we would later homestead. They held their noses against the smell of carrion, they gagged when they drank the brackish water full of wigglers or nauseous with buffalo urine. With undiminished speed they moved on toward the Three Buttes, or Sweetgrass Hills, a natural divide like the Cypress Hills and Wood Mountain, but on the south side of the 49th parallel. A few miles from their depot camp they came upon the bodies of twenty Crow Indians, scalped, half mummified in the dry heat— one more manifestation, belated like the spendthrift camp of *métis* buffalo hunters, of an ecology still furiously vital on the very eve of its extinction. As a power, the Blackfoot in 1874 were almost as dead as this Crow war party they had killed, but they did not yet know it, and neither did their enemies. Neither did the surveyors. The escort in these dangerous longitudes included not only the customary two companies of cavalry but five companies of the 6th Infantry based upon Fort Buford, and Major Reno had issued orders that not even that substantial command was to be divided too much—a precaution that his superior would ignore, to the sorrow of many widows and orphans, on the Little Big Horn.

Perhaps because of the big escort, perhaps because of their own lack of belligerence, the survey parties of both sides moved on without trouble from the Blackfoot. In the last week of August, 1874, they jointly located the last monument of the 1861 survey that had carried the boundary from the Pacific to the Rockies, and on a remote ridge above Waterton Lake they completed the line that now ran from sea to sea. Behind them, evidence of their personal contribution to international polity, stretched 388 cairns and pillars and forty astronomical stations. They could all go back to civilian jobs or to their normal army duties, leaving behind them that very open and penetrable fence; yet their work had drawn a line not merely between two countries, but between two periods of history. The final signatures of representatives of the two governments would be affixed to the official documents in London on May 29 of the next year. By that time Crow and Gros Ventre and Sioux and Blackfoot and Assiniboin would already know that the "Medicine Line," as they called it, was something potent in their lives.

Frontiers are lines where one body of law stops and another body of law begins. Partly by reason of that difference of basic law, and from the moment the boundary is drawn, they also become lines of cultural division as real for many kinds of human activity as the ecological boundaries between woods and plains, plains and mountains, or mountains and deserts. Likewise they have their inevitable corollaries. They create their own varieties of lawbreakers, smugglers particularly, and they provide for the guilty and the hunted the institution of sanctuary.

The coming of the precise international boundary in the neighborhood of such good hunting and trading ground as the Sweet-grass Hills, Cypress Hills, and Wood Mountain, made lawbreakers out of the whiskey traders who until that time had only been lawless. Along the western reaches of that lonely border, whose entire 800 miles were patrolled in the 1870's and 1880's by no more than two or three hundred men (some newspapers spoke of their being "massed" along the boundary), it remained easy to slip in and out. For whiskey or guns there was always a seller's market, and the excitement of successful rum- or gun-running was comparable, probably, to the Indian excitement in horse-stealing. And so there began in the Cypress Hills area a tradition of border-jumping that was still very much alive during my years there. The unmarked trails past our homestead, mere wagon tracks across a sea of grass, witnessed during 1918 and 1919 a remarkable lot of traffic in Marmons and Hudson Super Sixes, tightly side-curtained and so heavily loaded that their rear springs rode clear down on the axles. They drove mainly at night or in foul weather. We could see their lights far out across the plain groping toward Montana over the wracking burnouts, and we met them sometimes in the rain, traveling when no one else would risk the gumbo. Their tracks were often eight inches deep in the sod, ground down by the small hard tires, the heavy loads, and the constant low gear, with periodic wallows patched with sagebrush where they had bogged down and dug out again. It is astonishing how some unrecognized professions can last. The history of that country practically began with whiskey runners, and whiskey runners were using the same trails nearly half a century later, only this time they were running whiskey from wet Canada into dry Montana, and their customers were not Indian and *métis* hunters but Montana businessmen, mechanics, politicians, and housewives. Any real inequality or disparity between the laws of Canada and those of the United States starts a flow of contraband in one direction or the other.

But the most immediate effect of the completion of the boundary in 1874 was upon the Indians. It turned out that the Line which *should* not be crossed by raiding Indians literally *could* not be crossed by uniformed pursuers, and generally wasn't crossed even by the un-uniformed ones. The medicine of the line of cairns was very strong. Once it had been necessary to outrun your pursuing enemy until you were well within your own country where he did not dare follow. Now all you had to do was outrun him to the Line, and from across that magical invisible barrier you could watch him pull to a halt, balked, helpless, and furious. Sometimes raiders calmly camped, in plain sight but just out of gunshot, and jeered the cavalry foaming on the other side. The red coats of the Mounties, too, came only to the Medicine Line, like stars that rise only a certain distance into the sky. Altogether, a new and delightful rule was added to the game of raiding: there was a King's-X place.

It became clear very soon that the Canadian side was safer than the American, that the Mounted Police had more authority and were generally more to be trusted and easier to get on with than the blue-coated American cavalry, and much more to be trusted than Montana sheriffs or marshals or posses. The seethe of excitement on the American side—miners and cattlemen and army detachments and all the commercial complex of steamboats and stores and wagon trains that supported these—had as yet no counterpart on the Canadian side, where in the 1870's only a few Hudson's Bay Company posts, the random *métis* villages, a mission or two, and a handful of whiskey forts like Whoop-Up and Stand-Off and Slide-Out foretold white civilization. It was inevitable that, being emptier and having a more responsible law force and no irresponsible free settlers, western Canada should become a refuge for hostiles from the States. Well before the surveying of the Line or the formation of the Mounted Police, the Sisseton and Yankton Sioux set the precedent when they took refuge in Manitoba after the 1862 Minnesota Massacres. Farther west, as similar crises came upon them, Teton and Hunkpapa and Brulé Sioux, as well as Cheyenne and Nez Percé, would all take the same road, and request the protection of the Great Mother. The establishment of the Medicine Line let them know precisely, as they already knew approximately, where they could step across and be safe, and they took pains to avoid trouble north of the border because they did not want to jeopardize their sanctuary. That combination of facts helps to explain why the Boundary Commission surveyors who encountered Sissetons on Turtle Mountain in 1873, and the Mounted Police who ran into some Tetons east of the Cypress Hills in 1874, found them extremely friendly and apparently willing to believe that both the survey and the police were meant for the protection of the Great Mother's red children against their enemies. Four years before Black Hills gold hunters crowded the Sioux nation to desperate war, there were eight hundred lodges of Tetons camped in the Cypress Hills looking the place over as a possible new home.

This is all to say that with the coming of the first line of law on the prairie's face, responsibilities and problems that were not new, and not created by the line, were sharply clarified and brought within the possibility of control. The international boundary was the first indispensable legal basis of that control. The instrument, the Mounted Police, was being created at the same time as the survey, and arrived at the foot of the Rockies almost simultaneously with the completion of the border.

The police did not at once establish themselves in the Cypress Hills, having some preliminary pressing business among the whiskey traders along the Belly River. But the Cypress Hills Massacre had been the crucial incident that created them, and they very soon found that the Hills were the place where they were most needed. The base from which they operated during the most critical years of the northwest frontier was Fort Walsh, not far from the spot where Farwell's post had stood two years before their coming, and where Little Soldier's burned encampment was still whitened with human bones and skulls, and where Ed Grace, bravely dead in a doubtful cause, lay lost under the ashes of Solomon's fort. From Fort Walsh, which was headquarters for the Mounted Police from 1878 to 1882, the men in red coats watched over the death struggles of the Plains frontier.

8

Law in a Red Coat

The waiting room of the customhouse in Weyburn, Saskatchewan, had a yellow varnished wainscoting of tongue-and-groove boards, from above which framed portraits of men in red coats stared out across the smoky room. It was 1914 and I was five years old and we were going through the Canadian Plains equivalent of Ellis Island, preliminary to joining my father on the Whitemud River. This was my first look at Canada. I believe that for the half hour or so of our wait there I did not say a word, but was hushed as if in church and under orders to be quiet. The resolute, disciplined faces and the red coats glimmering in the shabby room filled me with awe. I can see those portraits yet; they were burned into me as if I had been photographic film.

No other memory of that trip from Iowa to Saskatchewan sticks to me in quite this way, not even Buck Murphy, who is at least half reconstruction from family reminiscences. But these portraits I never discussed with anyone, and the memory has to be from my own direct perception. They hang in my head unaltered and undimmed after nearly half a century, static, austere, symbolic. And if I had known all the history of Canada and the United States I could not have picked out a more fitting symbol of what made the Canadian West a different West from the American.

A long dirty train ride and a dusty jolting stage ride later, when we stumbled out of the stage at the edge of a rutted road in the construction camp of Whitemud, among overturned Fresno scrapers, lumber piles, and yellow mud puddles, the first thing I saw was another man in a red coat. He was stooping out the doorway of a shack across the road, a shack whose door bore the initials R.N.W.M.P., and he wore not only the scarlet tunic of the men in the portraits, but yellow-striped blue breeches, glistening boots, and a wide campaign hat. Holstered at his belt he had a revolver with a white lanyard, and he was altogether so gorgeous that I don't even remember meeting my father, who must have been there to welcome us and whom I had not seen for six months. This Mounted Policeman, like the portraits in Weyburn, was instantly part of me, as ineradicable as a scar. I can see him yet in the brilliant uniform, stooping to close the shack door behind him, as if moving out, as if in symbolic relinquishment of the West he had made tame and now left to us.

I have played with the notion, which is not out of the question, that this Mountie I saw on the moment of our arrival was the one who later shot Buck Murphy off a buckboard in the Shaunavon street, and I have contrived idle little comic scenes reminiscent of "The Bride Comes to Yellow Sky," in which the policeman and his troublemaking opponent confront each other, the armed roughneck dismounting from the stage encumbered by two small children and a lady to whom he pays a deferential and crippling attention. But these are only curlicues that the fancy makes, doodling around something more important. The important thing is the instant, compelling impressiveness of this man in the scarlet tunic. I believe I know, having felt it, the truest reason why the slim force of Mounted Police was so spectacularly successful, why its *esprit de corps* was so high and its prestige so great. I think I know how Law must have looked to Sioux and Blackfoot when the column of red coats rode westward in the summer of 1874.

Never was the dignity of the uniform more carefully cultivated, and rarely has the ceremonial quality of impartial law and order been more dramatically exploited. Since the middle of the 18th century the red coat of the British dragoons had meant, to Indian minds, a force that was non- and sometimes anti-American. The contrast was triply effective now that the blue of the American cavalry had become an abomination to the Plains hostiles. One of the most visible aspects of the international boundary was that it was a color line: blue below, red above, blue for treachery and unkept promises, red for protection and the straight tongue. That is not quite the way a scrupulous historian would report it, for if Canada had been settled first, and the American West had remained empty, the situation might well have been reversed. Certainly Canada had its own difficulties with the tribes when the buffalo disappeared and the crisis came on; and though its treaty system was better considered and its treaties better kept than the American, still Canada in red coats hunted down its hostiles in 1885 just as the blue-coated Long Knives had used to do. But given the historical context, red meant to an Indian in the 1870's friendship and protection, and it is to the honor of an almost over-publicized force that having dramatized in scarlet the righteousness of the law it represented, it lived up to the dramatization.

Lt. W. F. Butler, F.R.G.S., was an Irish officer who came west to Red River on a secret mission while Wolseley's expedition to suppress the *métis* was cutting its way through swamps and forests along the Dawson Route in the spring of 1870. Butler had his adventures, escaped a *métis* trap by jumping off the steamer *International* at the mouth of the Assiniboine, eluded pursuit until Riel called off the hunt and requested him to come in for a conference, made his investigation of the situation at Fort Garry, and finally delivered his report, along with two water-soaked bags of Her Majesty's mail, to Col. Wolseley at the mouth of the Winnipeg River on August 18. Six days later Wolseley marched into Fort Garry to find the *métis* leaders flown, and Lt. Butler was temporarily out of a job. By October he had another: on the 24th of that month, carrying a commission as the first Justice of the Peace for Rupert's Land and the North-West, and with two similar commissions to be conferred upon men out along the Saskatchewan, he set out with a *métis* guide to look into the state of the Indian tribes and the condition of law and order in the West.

Butler's journey, though by no means the first, was as rugged as any, for he made most of it in the dead of winter. It took him clear to British Columbia and back again, and the book he made of his wanderings is one of the best. Being a sort of magistrate-in-transit, he was concerned primarily with the trading posts and the beginning settlements, and so he followed the route of the fur trade along the Saskatchewan instead of cutting across through new territory, and he never came within two hundred miles of the

Cypress Hills, which at the time of his journey had been visited only by Father Lestanc, Captain Palliser, and the *métis* winterers. He witnessed plenty of lawlessness, but he never got into the border region where it was most uncontrolled, the Blackfoot country recently invaded by the whiskey traders from Fort Benton—a town which the historian John Peter Turner characterizes in somewhat Canadian terms as being inhabited mainly by "frontier heroes, fortune-hunting outcasts of both sexes, expungers of the law, side-armed sheriffs, desperadoes, murderers, and degenerates." Granting that the Fort Benton population was not quite that bad, there was plenty of justification for the recommendations Butler made for the establishment of civil law to replace the by now officially abdicated power of the Hudson's Bay Company.

Butler's report, dated from Red River in March, 1871, shortly after his return, closely follows suggestions that Sir John Mac-Donald had made in April of the year before, and anticipates suggestions that another investigator, Col. P. Robertson-Ross of the Canadian Militia, would make a year later. It contained three specific recommendations: 1) The appointment of a Civil Magistrate or Commissioner, after the model established in Ireland and India, who would reside on the upper Saskatchewan and make semi-annual tours of his territory; 2) the establishment of two government stations, one near Edmonton and one below Fort Carlton, and the extinction of the Indian title so that both banks of the river from Edmonton to Victoria, a distance of 80 miles, would be opened for settlement; and 3) the organization of "a well-equipped force of from 100 to 150 men, one-third to be mounted, specially recruited and engaged for service in the Saskatchewan; enlisting for two or three years' service, and at the expiration of that period to become military settlers, receiving grants of land, but still remaining a reserve force should their services be required."

This modest proposal—fantastically modest considering that the border from Lake of the Woods to the Rockies was 900 miles long, and that the region to be pacified was 300,000 square miles in extent and contained perhaps 30,000 of the most warlike Indians on the continent in addition to some of the toughest white border men—still seemed extravagant to many Canadians unused to the problems of an expanding continental hegemony. The implementing of Butler's suggestions took a little time, but not an excessive amount, for events in the West moved too fast for politicians to delay action. British Columbia entered the Canadian federation two months after Butler wrote his report, and the terms of its coming in made immediate and pressing the need for a transcontinental rail link. It was not alone Upper and Lower Canada, Quebec and Ontario, with their fatal hereditary schism, that confronted Ottawa lawmakers now, but two thirds of a tremendous continent in all stages of occupation: the settled East, then hundreds of miles of forest wilderness threaded only by canoe tracks and the Dawson Road, then the Red River settlements, then the vast emptiness of the Plains, then the Rockies, and then the remote Pacific province.

While Butler's report was being digested, Col. Robertson-Ross was on a reconnaissance that confirmed it. Robertson-Ross recommended troops—at least a regiment of 550 mounted riflemen, a customhouse on the Belly River to control the whiskey traders, and a chain of seven army posts for the protection of those who would be building the Pacific Railway. He was strong in his insistence that their coats be scarlet, for Indians who had seen Wolseley's militia at Fort Garry had asked him suspiciously who were the soldiers in the dark clothes. In their experience, the friendly ones wore red.

For the pacification of Rupert's Land and the North-West, added to Canada by Imperial proclamation on July 15, 1870, and the source of multiplying troubles from the moment the transfer began to be discussed, Sir John Macdonald in April, 1873, gave notice to Commons of a police bill based on the recommendations of Butler and Robertson-Ross, but with the numbers compromised at 300. The bill was in debate when word came eastward, roundabout through the United States, of the bloody skirmish in the Cypress Hills. Popular sentiment and anti-American hysteria swept the bill through Parliament, though in deference to American anxieties about a Canadian armed force along the border, Sir John scratched out the words "Mounted Rifles" and substituted "Mounted Police." That was on May 23, 1873, when the smell of human carrion still poisoned the air on Battle Creek, and when the Joint Boundary Commission, having closed the link between Lake of the Woods and the Red River, was assembling at Fort

Dufferin, on the west bank of the Red, to start its 800-mile traverse across the Plains.

There are several histories of the Royal North-West Mounted Police; this is not the place for another. Their beginnings may be put in briefest summary. Macdonald's order in council organizing the first three troops of fifty men each came at the end of August (the three troops were later doubled). The first three were sworn in at Fort Garry on November 3, and all six troops had gathered at Fort Dufferin, the Boundary Commission's base, by June 19, 1874. On July 8 they started, a spectacular cavalcade two miles long led by A Troop on dark bay horses, followed by B Troop on dark browns, C Troop on chestnuts, D Troop on grays and buckskins, E Troop on blacks, and F Troop on bright bays. They went, in spite of Sir John Macdonald's desire to have a force with as little "gold lace, fuss and feathers, as possible," with the pomp and circumstance at which the British have few equals: a stream of scarlet tunics, white helmets, white dragoon gauntlets, gleaming metal, polished leather, 275 picked officers and men on picked horses, the most brilliant procession that ever crossed those yellowing plains. Behind them lumbered the great freight wagons, 73 of them, and behind those 114 squealing Red River carts with *métis* drivers, and two 9-pounder field guns, and two brass mortars, and field kitchens, and portable forges, and mowing machines for making hay en route, and nearly a hundred cattle destined for slaughter before they reached the buffalo herds.

Out across the sun-beaten plains past the dying sloughs, through the clouds of mosquitoes and horseflies, into hailstorms of locusts, they rode like the Six Hundred at Balaklava. Much of the prairie had already been swept by fires, and forage was scarce. They had their trials from the first. On the second day out, the commander of F Troop, Inspector Theodore Richer, was sent back to Dufferin under arrest for gross insubordination. On Pembina Mountain they had word of white men murdered by Sioux five miles south. Their gallant procession sagged and drooped and strung out, the oxen were slow, the eastern horses refused the prairie water and grew weak on prairie grass. Some died, some were left behind, the heat was stifling though the wind blew hard, the air was thick with dust. Many of the men were sick with diarrhea. Before they had been out two weeks their track began to be marked every day by broken-down carts and wagons and by dead or abandoned animals. The sky was hot brass, the alkali dust burned in every sweaty crevice of the skin.

At Les Roches Percées part of A Troop, scheduled for permanent duty at Edmonton, broke off northward toward the Saskatchewan. The others, after a rest on good water in the valley of the Souris, slogged on. The rest was not enough; the eastern horses continued to fade under the hard riding and thin provender, and they stampeded at lightning and at hailstorms and at the rockets that the command sent up after dark to guide hunters back to camp. By now the riders were dismounting every hour to lead their horses, and even so they wore them out. They had swung north of the Boundary Commission road after crossing the west fork of the Souris, and were passing through country little known even to Pierre Léveillé and the other *métis* guides. The weather turned cooler, then turned rainy and cold, they were out of wood. Just after they crossed the Coteau of the Missouri a violent night storm blew all their tents down and soaked them to the shivering hide. They sent a party after supplies and oats down toward the Boundary Commission depot at Willow Bunch, and groaned on. On the night of August 6, after 26 exhausting miles uphill, they camped on top of the Dirt Hills and saw along the south the flames of a great prairie fire—set, the *métis* said, by Indians wanting to impede the march.

Their first tapping of Boundary Commission supplies brought them 4700 pounds of pemmican and dried meat. Their second, sent down from Old Wives Lake, got them 15,000 pounds of immediate oats, and a promise of more. They met and powwowed with a camp of Sisseton Sioux on a branch of Old Wives Creek, and a little further on encountered Père Lestanc, the missionary to the *métis* villages and the coadjutor of Bishop Taché during the Red River troubles of 1869-70. They also strengthened themselves, immediately and for the future, by persuading Louis Léveillé, the brother of their guide, to join them with his two sons. He would be one of the most valuable men in their service all during the pacifying of the border. He said now that in the Cypress Hills, which he had just left, there were plenty of grizzly bears and some Indians, but that the outlaws and ruffians and whiskey traders, hearing of the approach of the police, had pulled out. Commissioner George Arthur French, in command of the force, ordered his men to sleep in their clothes anyway, for now along the south they saw the rolling shoulders of the Hills that were claimed by all and owned by none, and the possibility of encountering Blackfoot was enough to make them anxious when their horses were so gaunt and exhausted. In the last two or three days, nine of them had died.

By the time they reached Swift Current Creek they could plainly see the timber in the folds of the Hills. They had plenty of ducks, they met the antelope in numbers, and for the first time they saw buffalo. The day after they ate their first hump ribs, Assistant Commissioner Macleod came in with another supply of oats, picked up this time from the Boundary Commission depot on the Frenchman below the 49th parallel. But oats could hardly bring back the lagging and ribby stock. A detachment of cripples had already been set up, following more slowly in the rear; to protect it, and impress any Indians with notions of horse-stealing, they also created a troop of twenty lancers. The only guide who knew the country, a Benton *métis* named Morriseau, led them on westward until they grew suspicious that he was a spy for the whiskey traders. But their confusion was only a matter of a few days long, and they were never more than a day's journey too far north. They made their immediate destination, the junction of the Belly and Bow Rivers, on September 11. Robertson-Ross's report had said that at the junction of the Bow and the Belly (South Saskatchewan) they would find the wicked Fort Whoop-Up. All they found, sitting their bonerack mounts and looking around with the eyes of men awakening from a laborious dream, was a little cluster of abandoned *hivernant* shanties. There was not a soul, Indian, white, or in between, in sight.

Bewildered, lost, suffering in the equinoctial blizzards, and in serious danger of losing the pitiful remnant of their stock, they retreated southward to the Three Buttes, or Sweetgrass Hills, and on September 19 they fell thankfully into bivouac in good grass on a louse-infested but otherwise deserted Indian campground 849 miles and 74 days out from Dufferin.

But they had not come out this far simply to rest, and their rest now was of the shortest. Within a few days, D and E Troops, which were scheduled to winter far back at the headquarters post that had been building at Swan River, near Fort Pelly on the Assiniboine, had started eastward again along the Boundary Commission trail. They had little enough time for traveling before winter set in, and it did not appear that they were needed here to suppress any borderers. Commissioner French, on a quick trip to Fort Benton, arranged for emergency supplies and found out where Fort Whoop-Up actually was. It was at the forks of the Bow and St. Mary's Rivers, south of the modern town of Lethbridge. He also picked up some information on the participants in the Cypress Hills Massacre, a matter that he was bound to investigate.

Within another few days, Assistant Commissioner Macleod had started for Whoop-Up with B, C, and F Troops and the remainder of A, and Commissioner French had started back east in a buckboard. He caught up with D and E Troops at Wild Horse Lake, seventy miles east of the Sweetgrass Hills, and they picked up the party of cripples, which had been detached at Old Wives Lake, just west of the Frenchman. And at the crossing of the Frenchman they found their first real evidence that their presence in the West was required: first a camp of twenty-nine lodges of Sioux, apparently friendly but unquestionably American Indians who presented a problem; and then in the river bottom a dead and naked *métis* tied to a tree. He had been tied there to die of exposure, the tree branches cut a good way up to let the sun have full play on him, and the river in plain sight, dimpling between its willows, to aggravate his thirst.

By the first week of November, when Indian Summer had faded and chilled and the wind from the northwest began to sing through the stiff prairie grass, the Mounted Police had taken possession of most of their oceanic range. Commissioner French was back at Dufferin with two troops and part of a third, keeping an eye on the Red River area. There was part of a troop at Swan River, the badly located, badly built, badly supplied, and short-lived headquarters post which had been intended as winter quarters for half the command. Hundreds of miles to the northwest, the bulk of A Troop was snugging into winter quarters at Edmonton, and three hundred miles south of Edmonton Macleod and his two and a half troops had a good start on the building of Fort Macleod in a horseshoe bend of the Old Man River. On his way in, he had paid calls on Forts Whoop-Up and Slide-Out, which the police had come west expecting to have to squash. They were both sleeping nearly deserted under the mild October sun. From his new post, Macleod proposed to see that they stayed that way. He was completely out of communication with the outside; his nearest sources of supplies or assistance were 200 miles away at Fort Benton or Fort Shaw, both in Montana; he was in the midst of a semi-outlaw element of unknown strength, and among thousands of demoralized and suspicious Indians.

What he did was characteristically prompt and decisive. He threw out patrols which very soon caught a whiskey trading party coming up the Whoop-Up Trail; Macleod confiscated the whiskey and threw the traders in his new log jail. Within weeks he held a conference with the Blackfoot for fear of whom the Mounties had slept in their clothes, coming past the Cypress Hills, and the conference resulted in a lasting pact of friendship with Crowfoot, greatest of the Blackfoot chiefs. Before the winter was over Macleod had not only stopped the drunken and murderous orgies that the liquor traffic had been promoting among the Blackfoot, but he had converted some of the traders, who turned out to be not so villainous as painted, to more legal pursuits. A village with three trading posts, a log billiard room, a blacksmith shop, and some other of the appurtenances of civilization grew up around Macleod's police barracks. The whiskey traders who were not amenable to reform were fined or jailed or run out.

Uncontrolled from 1868 to 1874, the whiskey traffic on the Whoop-Up Trail had gone a long way toward demoralizing Blood, Piegan, and Blackfoot, had brought on riots and murders, had pauperized families and made drunks out of hunters and squalid drabs out of hunters' wives. Left to run its course, it could hardly have avoided stirring up in the Alberta country a racial war as vengeful as the Minnesota Massacres of 1861-62, and it would as certainly have brought defeat and tribal collapse to the Blackfoot. The pattern had been repeated many times south of the Line. It was by no means out of the question that the Blackfoot might choose at any time to take the risk and wipe the little force of a hundred and fifty Mounties out. If the police had worn blue coats instead of red, the Blackfoot might well have tried.

Instead of that, and within a month of his coming, Macleod made a firm peace with the confederation which had never submitted and never did submit to the United States. As combined magistrate and peace officer, he would have his patrol duties, and occasional incidents of violence or illegality to handle, but to all intents and purposes he took care of the critical Whoop-Up problem the first winter. He took care of it, one might say, simply by being there. Altogether, his was a remarkable demonstration that law, when strictly and equitably enforced, is incomparably stronger than the random or violent powers ranged against it. *Rechtssicherheit* proved a quicker and surer way to peace with the Blackfoot than carbines and promises.

Thus the Whoop-Up danger dissolved when confronted. But in the other area which the police had their eye on there had been as yet no confrontation. That came when Superintendent J. M. Walsh with thirty men of B Troop rode the 160 miles eastward from Fort Macleod to the Cypress Hills, and almost precisely two years after the Cypress Hills Massacre, and within two miles of the spot where it had occurred, began to build Fort Walsh.

9

Capital of an
Unremembered Past

The Cypress Hills discovered that they had a history when the Old Timers' Association of Maple Creek planted some historical markers in 1942. In coming first to Fort Walsh they acknowledged that this was the true capital of the first stage of that frontier. In the old post cemetery, where the police graves were identifiable but the civilian ones a scramble of unmarked mounds, they erected crosses, and where they knew, they placed the appropriate names: Clark, Dumont, LaBarge, Quesnelle, McKay, Chief Little Bird—white, *métis*, Scotch halfbreed, Indian. From the graveyard they moved on to plant a cement monument where Abe Farwell's post had stood, and another where the wolfers and the Assiniboin had fought across Battle Creek. The foundations of Farwell's post were still faintly discernible after nearly seventy years, but the battlefield they could locate only through the memory of an old *métis* who as a boy of eighteen, in 1880, had kicked up human bones while herding the police beef herd on that ground.

Once discovered, history is not likely to be lost. But the first generation of children to grow up in a newly settled country do not ordinarily discover their history, and so they are the prime sufferers from discontinuity. If I, for instance, wanted a past to which I could be tribally and emotionally committed, I had to fall back on the American Civil War (my grandfather, whom I had never seen, had fought in it), or upon Norway (my maternal grandfather and grandmother had emigrated from it). Being a mama's boy, I chose Norway, which made a real hash of my affiliations. All through my childhood I signed my most personal and private books and documents with the Norwegian name that my grandfather had given up on coming to America. It seems to me now an absurdity that I should have felt it necessary to go as far as the Hardanger Fjord for a sense of belonging. I might have had —and any child who grows up in the Cypress Hills now can have —Fort Walsh, and all that story of buffalo hunter, Indian and halfbreed, Mounted Policeman and wolfer, which came to its climax just here.

The very richness of that past as I discover it now makes me irritable to have been cheated of it then. I wish I could have known it early, that it could have come to me with the smell of life about it instead of the smell of books, for there was the stuff of an epic there, and still is for anyone who knows it right—perhaps for some *métis* or Cree, a descendant of Gabriel Dumont or Big Bear or Wandering Spirit, who can see the last years of the Plains frontier with the distance of history and with the passion of personal loss and defeat. Often as it has been summarized, no one has properly told the story of the defeat of the Plains people, a people of many tribes but one culture. Fort Walsh saw its last years. This was where some of the last hopes flickered out and the irreconcilables gathered in hope of a last stand: Canadian Indians and American Indians, Cree and Assiniboin and Blackfoot who belonged, and Sioux and Nez Percé and Gros Ventre who fled here because of the Medicine Line and because here were the last of the buffalo. A way of life extremely rich in human satisfactions both physical and spiritual came to an end here. From their headquarters at Fort Walsh, a little over a hundred red-coated men patrolled its final agonies. A few years after it was essentially over for the Indians, the *métis* who lived by the same skills and were shaped to a similar habit of life broke out in their own final desperation, drawing with them some of their Indian relatives, and that could be another epic.

All of it was legitimately mine, I walked that earth, but none of it was known to me. I wish our homes or schools had given us stereopticon slides of Fort Walsh's old log stockade with its inward-facing buildings, its officers' and non-coms' quarters, its powder magazine, its blacksmith and carpenter shop, its thirty-horse stable, its kitchen, bakery, guardroom, quartermaster's store —all of it whitewashed clean and shining in the valley under the jackpine hills. I wish I had seen the Union Jack obeying the prairie wind from its tall pole, and heard the commands of drill and parade in that compound, and seen how competition among the troops brought out the spit and polish. They made full-dress parades in red coats, white helmets, pipe-clayed buckskin breeches, glittering boots. Sometimes, when a man was immaculately prepared for competition, his comrades carried him across the parade ground for fear he would get a wrinkle or a fleck of dust on him.

We were not informed in school that the graces of imported civilization first appeared here at Fort Walsh: amateur theatricals, pets, music, sports. Saskatchewan's first play, *Dick Turpin,* was acted by constables who had been out on patrol to pick up an offender called Four Jack Bob, and who barely had time to throw Bob in the guardhouse and get into their costumes before the curtain. The pets were young antelope, baby buffalo, a Canada goose who sat on a rock and alerted the guard when men sneaked in late from a pass, and who finally made the mistake of chasing an Indian dog, which killed him. The music was provided by men from F Troop, transferred from Calgary after Fort Walsh was made the headquarters of the force in 1878. The band died a riotous death, and one oddly incongruous with the traditional discipline of the Mounties, when its members, celebrating a British victory in Afghanistan, were betrayed by Commissioner Macleod's special issue of grog, and began beaning one another with the instruments.

The games, like the parades, often had the ceremonial full-dress quality that is reputed to keep men British in a far land. It must have been a rather remarkable sight to see cricketers and tennis players in white flannels walking across the compound, or bare-kneed constables and sub-constables lining up for a scrum at rugger. Sometimes they enlisted *métis* and Indians in their games, and educated them in how to take a rough body block or a kick in the shins without going for a knife. Sometimes they went out to meet the inhabitants, and raced horses against them outside the stockade. They kept an eye on sun dances where youths who had made a vow tore themselves from boyhood into manhood by hurling themselves against rawhide thongs threaded under their breast muscles. At Christmas or New Year there might be a banquet, even a dance. Outside the walls a village of three hundred families, mainly *métis,* had assembled by the late 1870's. It boasted a hotel, a restaurant, a log pool hall, a barber shop, and even a photographer's shop, for whose presence any historian has reason to give thanks. In the valley ringed by its timbered hills there might be at any time several hundred Indians. As the buffalo grew scarcer and hunger came as an unwelcome guest in the lodges, the hundreds grew into thousands, for whatever the Indians had coming to them by treaty was distributed here, and if new treaties were contemplated, this was where they would be discussed, and if non-treaty Indians wanted to beg a share of the dole, this was the place one begged in.

They were of many tribes, and their simultaneous presence might mean trouble either because of hereditary hostilities, or because of competition for the remaining game, or even because of the never quite quiet threat that they might ally in hostility against the whites. From Fort Walsh the Mounties patrolled south as far as Kennedy's Crossing on the Milk River, near the present hamlet of Wild Horse; and east through a chain of detachment posts to Wood Mountain. Disregarding Isaac Cowie's burned Hudson's Bay Company post, my home town dates from 1879, when Sitting Bull and his Teton Sioux made their winter camp on its site among the bends of the Whitemud. They were the first recorded inhabitants. That same winter, Walsh established a detachment post on the site of Cowie's cabins. Later we saw the chimneys of the police cabins sticking up through the grass and chokecherry bushes near the other line of chimneys from the old *métis* village when we went berrying in Chimney Coulee. It would have offended our Fenimore-Cooper-trained sensibilities to know that they were the relics not of savagery but of law.

Still, I wish we had known it. I wish we had heard of the coming of the Sioux, when they rode northward after annihilating Custer's five troops on the Little Big Horn, a whole nation moving north, driving the buffalo before them, and with the soldiers from every army post between Canada and Texas on their track. In

December, 1876, there were three thousand Ogalalas, Minneconjous, Hunkpapas, Sans Arcs, and Two Kettles camped near White Eagle's hundred and fifty lodges of Canadian Sissetons on Wood Mountain, and these were not all. Sitting Bull was reported to be on the Red Water, south of the Line, with a large band of Tetons, and there was a big band of agency Sioux, Yanktons under Medicine Bear and Black Horn, at a place called Burnt Timber, below where the Frenchman crossed the 49th parallel. These agency Indians too, though technically responsible to the authorities at Fort Peck, on the Missouri, had made sounds of wanting to cross the Line.

I wish somebody had told us how the tough Irishman Walsh, friendly to Indians but a realist, a good policeman and absolutely without nerves, rode in upon the camp of the first 3000 hostiles on Wood Mountain. With twelve men he rode through a fringe of warriors some of whom carried carbines wrenched from the hands of Custer's dying cavalrymen, past a horse herd many of whose horses and mules wore the United States Army brand, among lodges where American scalps still hung drying in the smoke, and in a meeting with White Eagle, Black Moon, Spotted Eagle, Little Knife, Long Dog, and their surly warriors, he told them how they would behave if they wanted to stay in the Great Mother's country. They said they were tired of war and wanted peace. Fine. They would do no injury to man, woman, or child; they would steal nothing, not so much as a horse; they would not fight, either among themselves or with the Canadian Indians; they would not hide behind the Medicine Line for the winter and then go raiding down south as soon as the prairies dried; they would not ever hunt beyond the Medicine Line, and they would smuggle no ammunition over it to their friends.

How bold a speech, how sublime a faith in the rightness of the Canadian occupation and the strength of Canadian law, considering that these Indians had hardly cooled from a bloodletting of white soldiers unmatched since Braddock's defeat, and that the police, outnumbered thirty or forty to one, had no chance of help nearer than several hundred miles. He told them the rules and they said they would obey: White Eagle, the Sisseton, had told them that the White Forehead Chief was a man of his word. They asked, almost humbly, for ammunition to hunt the buffalo, which they were forced now to lasso or to kill with lances made of knives bound to poles. Almost as if he possessed the power he assumed, Walsh granted to Jean Louis Legaré, the Wood Mountain trader destined to escort Sitting Bull back to captivity five years later, the right to sell the Sioux ammunition they could have taken by force any time they chose.

Later in the spring of 1877 Walsh repeated his lecture to fifty-seven lodges of Tetons under Four Horns, whom he intercepted just as they moved into Canada along the Frenchman. The Tetons were not as amenable as the first camp. One of their number persuaded them that Walsh could not be trusted, and they held him and his scouts in camp until messengers could be sent to confer with the Yanktons down at Burnt Timber. Next morning Medicine Bear and Black Horn and two hundred warriors painted for war poured across the Line and up to the Mud House Ford ready to revenge upon their own people any harm that might have come to Walsh. The nameless Teton who had called Walsh a Long Knife spy slid away in the excitement of the speech-making, and so saved his scalp.

Not too many days after that, Walsh repeated his lecture for the third time, this time to Sitting Bull himself, who had encamped with his band of Tetons near Pinto Horse Butte, between Wood Mountain and the Cypress Hills. He got from Sitting Bull the same answer he had had from Spotted Eagle and Four Horns and Long Dog. They were tired of war, they wanted to make their homes in the Great Mother's country, they would keep the peace.

Having clamped the lid on the kettle before it had a chance to boil, Walsh and later his replacement, Inspector L. N. F. Crozier, had to keep it on. The Sioux were not the only American Indians wandering north of the Line in 1877. Two months after Sitting Bull crossed over, there came a big encampment of South Assiniboin under Crow's Dance. They announced their arrival by roughing up a small camp of Canadian Saulteaux and demanding that the Saulteaux join them and submit to their hunting rules. Instead, the Saulteaux chief Little Child went to Walsh, and Walsh with seventeen men went directly to the camp of Crow's Dance. Arriving early in the morning, he left the surgeon and three men to build a barricade on which the others could fall back if a fight started. Then he and the other thirteen went into camp, entered the lodges, came out with twenty-two chiefs as prisoners, and bluffed their way out to the barricade, from which they stood off the Assiniboin frenzy without firing a shot. Crow's Dance and Crooked Arm, the head men, spent some months in a Mounted Police jail. The rest learned what the Sioux had had the wit to accept early: the law applied to everybody.

It kept the Mounties busy applying it. Time after time a handful of constables and scouts had to pluck horse thieves or stolen horses out of the midst of threatening clots of warriors. The daughter of the trader at Wood Mountain had the experience of being held with a knife at her throat while her Sioux captors demanded flour from her father, and her father stood with a pistol at the head of a powder keg threatening to blow them all up if the Sioux moved. Who made the move, finally, was a group of Mounties and ex-Mounties who burst in and threw the Sioux out—a procedure for which Walsh himself had set a precedent when he once threw Sitting Bull out the door, seizing the great man of the Sioux nation by the scruff and the seat and pitching him out in the dirt and then defying the furious stir of rage and threats until it subsided.

Through the almost five years of the Sioux visitation, from the end of 1876 to the summer of 1881, the Mounted Police kept the lid on, throttled the whiskey traffic, rode thousands of miles on patrol, noted in their patrol books the passage of every stray Indian or white or *métis*, every stray horse, every unfamiliar brand. When, in August, 1877, word came that the Nez Percé were headed for the Line pursued by General Howard and General Gibbon, Walsh had warning speeches to make to the aroused councils of the Sioux with all the war chiefs present. They were hot to start south to help the Nez Percé and have another go at the American cavalry. Walsh reminded them that if they went they would not be back; under those circumstances they would find the red coats hunting them as the blue coats hunted them now. The Sioux stayed. But when the refugees from Chief Joseph's long-running battle limped in, wounded, exhausted, stripped of everything but horse and gun, there was more need for Walsh's iron hand. He again calmed the angry Sioux, and he gave the Nez Percé sanctuary and his lecture on Canadian law.

They were White Bird and ninety-eight men, fifty women, and about fifty children, the battered remnant of a tribe that their conqueror General Miles called "the boldest men and the best marksmen" he had ever known. They had been friends of the whites since Lewis and Clark first met them under their other name of Chopunnish. Half Americanized, some of them Christians, house-dwellers, farmers, they had been cheated and abused until they made one of the last, the most desperate, and certainly one of the most heroic of the Indian revolts against the system that was destroying their life.

The heartbreaking Nez Percé refugees were not likely in themselves to add to the police burden. They were simply, like the Sioux and Gros Ventre and Assiniboin that kept drifting in, part of the ethnic junk heap that was piling up between Wood Mountain and the Cypress Hills as the Plains frontier worked toward the end of its first phase. But their condition so infuriated the Sioux, who were still powerful and capable of war, that there was constant fighting talk, and when Walsh brought word that General Alfred Terry and an American commission wanted to confer with the Sioux at Fort Walsh, it took all the prestige Walsh had, and all his argumentative persistence, to persuade Sitting Bull to attend. He would come only on the assurance that he had the protection of the Mounted Police, and he would promise nothing.

With twenty chiefs, Walsh left the camp near Pinto Horse Butte, and midway between there and Fort Walsh, probably near the bends where the Frenchman eased out of the Hills and where my town would later stand, they met Commissioner Macleod coming from the west, and they camped and feasted together. I know how that October river bottom would have looked and smelled with the skin lodges and the willow fires and the roasting meat—the smells of autumn and the muddy banks, the Indian Summer pungency of drying leaves and rose hips, the special and secret smell of wolf willow, the glint of yellow and red leaves shaking down over the camp in a chilly night wind. It is an actual pleasure to think that their boots and moccasins printed the gray silt of those bottoms where my bare feet would kick up dust years later. I like the thought of them camping there, great men of their time and kind, bent upon an errand that would bring other great men from below the 49th parallel, including correspondents from the New York *Herald* and the Chicago *Times*. Except for Henri Julien, who had accompanied the Mounties on their march west in 1874 as artist and correspondent for the *Canadian Illustrated News*, those were almost the only newspapermen who were ever lured to our Hills by anything.

The conference for which Sioux, red coats, and American officers assembled at Fort Walsh on October 17, 1877, was one of the briefest and least productive in history. There was one meeting. General Terry offered the Sioux amnesty, reservations, cattle, and allotments, and suggested that they had better come on home. The Sioux rose one by one and said that the Americans were liars, that they had never kept a promise, and that the Sioux would be fools to believe them now after having been cheated and deceived so often. They ironically introduced the squaw of Bear That Scatters, a move that in itself was an insult, since women did not sit on Indian councils. The wife of Bear That Scatters had been coached in a short speech. The Long Knives, she complained, were not giving her time to breed. She would like to stay here and have some children. The chiefs, for their part, said many times that they would not go back, that they wanted to be Canadian Indians. They shook hands many times with Macleod and Walsh, and wrapped their robes around them when it might have been time to shake hands with General Terry or his commissioners. So the commissioners gave it up and went home, and the Sioux stayed around Fort Walsh and made themselves sick on plum pudding and other items that Macleod had brought over for the occasion.

But the Sioux were not, whatever their desire, Canadian Indians, and Walsh and Macleod had to tell them so. They were not entitled to payments under any of the seven treaties which Canada had made with the tribes, and when others came in for treaty money the Sioux were left out. In 1877 there were still plenty of buffalo along the Frenchman, but by 1879 they were almost gone, and when starvation began to look in the lodge flaps of all the Indians on that border, it looked longest and most hungrily in on Sioux and Nez Percé. By persistent tactics of never dealing with Sitting Bull as head chief, but undercutting his power by consulting others, Walsh and Crozier whittled the great magician of the Tetons down to smaller and smaller size, and by

1880 had whittled away more than twelve hundred of his followers and persuaded them to return to agencies south of the Line. On July 11, 1881, Sitting Bull and his last supporters, quarreling over a few bags of flour and bitter at what they had been brought to, started out from Willow Bunch with Louis Legaré, and made their scarecrow march southward through the whitened buffalo bones. A week later they met Captain Clifford at the place now called Plentywood, Montana. The day after that, the gates of Fort Buford closed behind them and their guns were stacked in the yard and the Plains Indians were done.

Fort Walsh was almost done, too. It had never been a healthful site. Unexplained fevers swept it and its satellite village; the water from Battle Creek, polluted by buffalo and horse carcasses in the swamps above, brought typhoid into their tin cups and canteens. And two great movements of history, one just closing and one about to begin, united in persuading the police that another headquarters would serve them better, and that even as a post Fort Walsh should not be maintained. After the starving winters it became clear that reservations farther north, in the fertile belt along the North Saskatchewan, would provide more chance for farming and Indian self-sufficiency. More than that, the Hills were too close to the border. However successfully the police might deal with Sitting Bull's exiles, they were never able to control the horse-stealing that went on in both directions across the Line, and it seemed sound policy to move the Canadian Indians far enough north so that they would neither be tempted to raid, nor be tempting objects of raids from the American side. Finally, the Canadian Pacific was building very rapidly west, and one of the major police jobs of the new era would be protecting the men who were doing the building. By the winter of 1882, headquarters had been moved to Wascana or Pile o' Bones Creek, on the CPR main line, and the city that was being built there and called Regina after the queen. In May, 1883, Fort Walsh was dismantled and as much of its building material as could be salvaged was hauled to Maple Creek, on the railroad, to be used in building detachment posts there and in Medicine Hat, farther west on the South Saskatchewan. From the Maple Creek post, patrols could still ride the trail south to Kennedy's Crossing, or east to Eastend. Pinto Horse Butte, and Wood Mountain.

The wild and dangerous frontier had gone out like a blown match. Instead of taming wild men in wild places, the Mounted Police would increasingly find themselves protecting civilized men in places rapidly becoming tame. As for the Cypress Hills, only a little more than a decade after Cowie moved cautiously into them they lay all but empty from Medicine Lodge Coulee to Eastend, cleared of their grizzlies and elk, their flanks swept clean of buffalo, their ravines and valleys emptied of Indians. Only a few transitional figures remained. Abe Farwell, now ranching on a tributary of the Frenchman near where it flows out of Cypress Lake, was one; several Mounted Policemen who had served their terms and taken their allotments of land, certain *métis* who had squatted along the creeks, certain hide hunters who had seen the handwriting on the wall, made a thin and scattered population. Little by little, in the next twenty-five years, cattle would replace the buffalo, some of them whiteface and "shorthorn"—meaning anything not a longhorn—and some of them ringy old longhorns driven all the way up from the Rio Grande to stock the northern ranges. There would be room in the history of the Hills for one cowboy generation, and like its earlier counterpart it would be made up of many kinds: drifters from the American Plains all the way from Texas to Montana, Irish immigrant boys, venturesome English youths with too little self-control or too many elder brothers, made-over Mounties, French aristocrats, *métis* squatters, reformed whiskey traders. They would have this kingly range to themselves until 1906, long after nesters, barbed wire, and weather had pinched off the open-range running of cattle in the States.

I wish I had known some of this. Then, sunk solitary as a bear in a spider-webby, sweaty, fruit-smelling saskatoon patch in Chimney Coulee on a hot afternoon, I might have felt as companionship and reassurance the presence of the traders, *métis*, Indians, and Mounties whose old cabins were rectangles of foundation stones under the long grass, and whose chimneys crumbled a little lower every year. Kicking up an arrowhead at the Lazy-S ford, I might have peopled my imagination with a camp among the bends of the Whitemud and had the company of Sitting Bull, Long Dog, Spotted Eagle, Walsh, Macleod, Léveillé—some Indian Summer evening when smoke lay in fragrant scarves along the willows and the swallows were twittering to their holes in the clay cutbanks and a muskrat came pushing a dark-silver wedge of water upstream. I knew the swallows and the muskrats, and was at ease with them; we were all members of the timeless natural world. But Time, which man invented, I did not know. I was an unpeopled and unhistoried wilderness, I possessed hardly any of the associations with which human tradition defines and enriches itself.

I have sat many times all alone just inside the edge of one of the aspen coulees that tongued down from the North Bench, and heard the soft puffs of summer wind rattle the leaves, and felt how sun and shadow scattered and returned like disturbed sage-hen chicks; and in some way of ignorance and innocence and pure perception I have bent my entire consciousness upon white anemones among the white aspen boles. They were rare and beautiful to me, and they grew only there in the dapple of the woods—flowers whose name I did not know and could not possibly have found out and would not have asked, because I thought that only I knew about them and I wanted no one else to know.

Those are most peaceful images in my mind. I don't know why, remembering them, I think of Marmaduke Graburn. Perhaps because his grave lies under the same sky, with the same big light and the same quiet over it; perhaps because he died in such a coulee as this, and died young.

In 1879 he was nineteen years old, a rookie sub-constable recently recruited in Ottawa, a boy with an itch for adventure and a name that might have come out of a Victorian novel. Graburn Coulee, back of Fort Walsh a few miles, is the name the maps now give to the draw where he rode alone after an axe he had left behind, and was followed and shot in the back of the head by Star Child, a Blood Indian with a grudge. He died alone and uselessly, the victim of brainless spite. *Métis* trackers led by Jerry Potts and Louis Léveillé found first the tracks of his shod horse where they were joined by two barefoot Indian ponies; then his pillbox forage cap beside the trail; then his body, dumped into a ravine. He was not the first Mountie to die on the job. Others had died of fever, or gone under in the quicksand of rivers, but he was the first to die by violence. In their first five years, from the beginning of the march from Fort Dufferin to the time when Star-

Child raised his sawed-off fusee behind the unsuspecting boy in an aspen-whispering coulee in 1879, the Mounted Police had neither killed nor been killed. Merely by the unusualness of his death, young Graburn demonstrated the quality of the force to which he belonged. They had come to the Cypress Hills in 1875 to smother a hornet's nest. In 1883 they left the Hills pacified and safe, almost as peaceful as when I wandered through the coulees with a .22 and found nothing more dangerous than cottontails and anemones, or a lynx that might have been the product of my yearning imagination.

III

THE WHITEMUD
RIVER RANGE

*To snatch in a moment of courage, from the remorseless
rush of time, a passing phase of life, is only the beginning
of the task. The task approached in tenderness and faith
is to hold up unquestioningly, without choice and without
fear, the rescued fragment before all eyes in the light of
a sincere mood. It is to show its vibration, its colour, its
form; and through its movement, its form, and its colour,
reveal the substance of its truth—disclose its inspiring
secret: the stress and passion within the core of each convincing moment. In a single-minded attempt of that kind,
if one be deserving and fortunate, one may perchance
attain to such clearness of sincerity that at last the presented
vision of regret or pity, of terror or mirth, shall awaken in
the hearts of the beholders that feeling of unavoidable solidarity; of the solidarity in mysterious origin, in toil, in joy,
in hope, in uncertain fate, which binds men to each other
and all mankind to the visible world.*

JOSEPH CONRAD, Preface to *The Nigger of
the "Narcissus"*

1

Specifications for a Hero

In our town, as in most towns, everybody had two names—the one his parents had given him and the one the community chose to call him by. Our nicknames were an expression of the folk culture, and they were more descriptive than honorific. If you were underweight, you were called Skinny or Slim or Sliver; if overweight, Fat or Chubby; if left-handed, Lefty; if spectacled, Four Eyes. If your father was the minister, your name was Preacher Kid, and according to the condition and color of your hair you were Whitey, Blacky, Red, Rusty, Baldy, Fuzzy, or Pinky. If you had a habit of walking girls in the brush after dusk, you were known as Town Bull or T.B. If you were small for your age, as I was, your name was Runt or Peewee. The revelation of your shape at the town swimming hole by the footbridge could tag you for life with the label Birdlegs. The man who for a while ran one of our two grocery stores was universally known as Jew Meyer.

Like the lingo we spoke, our nicknames were at odds with the traditional and educational formalisms; along with them went a set of standard frontier attitudes. What was appropriate for Jimmy Craig in his home or in church or in school would have been shameful to Preacher Kid Craig down at the bare-naked hole. When we were digging a cave in the cutbank back of my house, and someone for a joke climbed up on top and jumped up and down, and the roof caved in on P.K. and he had to be dug out and revived by artificial respiration, even P.K. thought the hullabaloo excessive. He did not blame us, and he did not tattle on anyone. His notions of fortitude and propriety—which were at the other end of the scale from those of his parents—would not have let him.

When we first arrived in Whitemud the Lazy-S was still a working ranch, with corrals, and calves, and a bunkhouse inhabited by heroes named Big Horn, Little Horn, Slivers, Rusty, and Slippers. There was a Chinese cook named Mah Li, who had been abused in imaginative ways ever since he had arrived back at the turn of the century. In the first district poll for a territorial election, in 1902, someone had taken Mah Li to the polls and enfranchised him on the ground that, having been born in Hong Kong, he could swear that he was a British subject and was not an Indian, and was hence eligible to vote. When I knew him, he was a jabbering, good-natured soul with a pigtail and a loose blue blouse, and I don't suppose a single day of his life went by that he was not victimized somehow. He couldn't pass anybody, indoors or out, without having his pigtail yanked or his shirt tails set on fire. Once I saw the cowboys talk him into licking a frosty doorknob when the temperature was fifteen or twenty below, and I saw the tears in his eyes, too, after he tore himself loose. Another time a couple of Scandinavians tried to get him onto a pair of skis on the North Bench hill. They demonstrated how easy it was, climbed up and came zipping by, and then offered to help his toes into the straps. But Mah Li was too many for them that time. "Sssssssssss!" he said in scorn. "Walkee half a mile back!" When I was ten or eleven Mah Li was a friend of mine. I gave him suckers I caught in the river, and once he made me a present of a magpie he had taught to talk. The only thing it could say was our laundry mark, the number O Five, but it was more than any other magpie in town could say, and I had a special feeling for Mah Li because of it. Nevertheless I would have been ashamed not to take part in the teasing, baiting, and candy-stealing that made his life miserable after the Lazy-S closed up and Mah Li opened a restaurant. I helped tip over his backhouse on Hallowe'en; I was part of a war party that sneaked to the crest of a knoll and with .22 rifles potted two of his white ducks as they rode a mud puddle near his shack in the east bend.

The folk culture sponsored every sort of crude practical joke, as it permitted the cruelest and ugliest prejudices and persecutions. Any visible difference was enough to get an individual picked on. Impartially and systematically we persecuted Mah Li and his brother Mah Jim, Jew Meyer and his family, any Indians who came down into the valley in their wobble-wheeled buckboards, anyone with a pronounced English accent or fancy clothes or affected manners, any crybaby, any woman who kept a poodle dog and put on airs, any child with glasses, anyone afflicted with crossed eyes, St. Vitus's dance, feeble-mindedness, or a game leg. Systematically the strong bullied the weak, and the weak did their best to persuade their persecutors, by feats of courage or endurance or by picking on someone still weaker, that they were tough and strong.

Immune, because they conformed to what the folk culture valued, were people with Texas or Montana or merely Canadian accents, people who wore overalls and worked with their hands, people who snickered at Englishmen or joined the bedevilment of Chinamen, women who let their children grow up wild and unwashed. Indignation swept the school one fall day when the Carpenter kids were sent home by the new teacher from Ontario. She sent a note along with them saying they had pediculosis and should not return to school until they were cured. Their mother in bewildered alarm brought them in to the doctor, and when she discovered that pediculosis meant only the condition of being lousy, she had to be restrained from going over and pulling the smart-alec teacher's hair out. We sympathized completely. That teacher never did get our confidence, for she had convicted herself of being both over-cleanly and pompous.

Honored and imitated among us were those with special skills, so long as the skills were not too civilized. We admired good shots, good riders, tough fighters, dirty talkers, stoical endurers of pain. My mother won the whole town because once, riding our flighty mare Daisy up Main Street, she got piled hard in front of Christenson's pool hall with half a dozen men watching, and before they could recover from laughing and go to help her, had caught the mare and remounted and ridden off, tightly smiling. The fact that her hair was red did not hurt: among us, red hair was the sign of a sassy temper.

She was one of the immune, and so was my father, for both

had been brought up on midwestern farms, had lived on the Dakota frontier, and accepted without question—though my mother would have supplemented it—the code of the stiff upper lip. She had sympathy for anyone's weakness except her own; he went strictly by the code.

I remember one Victoria Day when there was a baseball game between our town and Shaunavon. Alfie Carpenter, from a river-bottom ranch just west of town, was catching for the Whitemud team. He was a boy who had abused me and my kind for years, shoving us off the footbridge, tripping us unexpectedly, giving us the hip, breaking up our hideouts in the brush, stampeding the town herd that was in our charge, and generally making himself lovable. This day I looked up from something just in time to see the batter swing and a foul tip catch Alfie full in the face. For a second he stayed bent over with a hand over his mouth; I saw the blood start in a quick stream through his fingers. My feelings were very badly mixed, for I had dreamed often enough of doing just that to Alfie Carpenter's face, but I was somewhat squeamish about human pain and I couldn't enjoy seeing the dream come true. Moreover I knew with a cold certainty that the ball had hit Alfie at least four times as hard as I had ever imagined hitting him, and there he stood, still on his feet and obviously conscious. A couple of players came up and took his arms and he shook them off, straightened up, spat out a splatter of blood and teeth and picked up his mitt as if to go on with the game. Of course they would not let him—but what a gesture! said my envious and appalled soul. There was a two-tooth hole when Alfie said something; he freed his elbows and swaggered to the side of the field. Watching him, my father broke out in a short, incredulous laugh. "Tough kid!" he said to the man next, and the tone of his voice goose-pimpled me like a breeze on a sweaty skin, for in all my life he had never spoken either to or of me in that voice of approval. Alfie Carpenter, with his broken nose and bloody mouth, was a boy I hated and feared, but most of all I envied his competence to be what his masculine and semi-barbarous world said a man should be.

As for me, I was a crybaby. My circulation was poor and my hands always got blue and white in the cold. I always had a runny nose. I was skinny and small, so that my mother anxiously doctored me with Scott's Emulsion, sulphur and molasses, calomel, and other doses. To compound my frail health, I was always getting hurt. Once I lost both big-toe nails in the same week, and from characteristically incompatible causes. The first one turned black and came off because I had accidentally shot myself through the big toe with a .22 short; the second because, sickly thing that I was, I had dropped a ten-pound bottle of Scott's Emulsion on it.

I grew up hating my weakness and despising my cowardice and trying to pretend that neither existed. The usual result of that kind of condition is bragging. I bragged, and sometimes I got called. Once in Sunday School I said that I was not afraid to jump off the high diving board that the editor of the *Leader* had projected out over the highest cutbank. The editor, who had been a soldier and a hero, was the only person in town who dared use it. It did not matter that the boys who called my bluff would not have dared to jump off it themselves. *I* was the one who had bragged, and so after Sunday School I found myself out on that thing, a mile above the water, with the wind very cold around my knees. The tea-brown whirlpools went spinning slowly around the deep water of the bend, looking as impossible to jump into as if they had been whorls in cement. A half dozen times I sucked in my breath and grabbed my courage with both hands and inched out to the burlap pad on the end of the board. Every time, the vibrations of the board started such sympathetic vibrations in my knees that I had to creep back for fear of falling off. The crowd on the bank got scornful, and then ribald, and then insulting; I could not rouse even the courage to answer back, but went on creeping out, quaking back, creeping out again, until they finally all got tired and left for their Sunday dinners. Then at once I walked out to the end and jumped.

I think I must have come down through thirty or forty feet of air, bent over toward the water, with my eyes out on stems like a lobster's, and I hit the water just so, with my face and chest, a tremendous belly-flopper that drove my eyes out through the back of my head and flattened me out on the water to the thickness of an oil film. The air was full of colored lights; I came to enough to realize I was strangling on weed-tasting river water, and moved my arms and legs feebly toward shore. About four hours and twenty deaths later, I grounded on the mud and lay there gasping and retching, sick for the hero I was not, for the humiliation I had endured, for the mess I had made of the jump when I finally made it—even for the fact that no one had been around to see me, and that I would never be able to convince any of them that I really had, at the risk of drowning, done what I had bragged I would do.

Contempt is a hard thing to bear, especially one's own. Because I was what I was, and because the town went by the code it went by, I was never quite out of sight of self-contempt or the contempt of my father or Alfie Carpenter or some other whose right to contempt I had to grant. School, and success therein, never fully compensated for the lacks I felt in myself. I found early that I could shine in class, and I always had a piece to speak in school entertainments, and teachers found me reliable at cleaning blackboards, but teachers were women, and school was a woman's world, the booby prize for those not capable of being men. The worst of it was that I liked school, and liked a good many things about the womanish world, but I wouldn't have dared admit it, and I could not respect the praise of my teachers any more than I could that of my music teacher or my mother.

"He has the arteestic tempera*ment*," said Madame Dujardin while collecting her pay for my piano lessons. "He's *sensitive*," my mother would tell her friends, afternoons when they sat around drinking coffee and eating Norwegian coffee cake, and I hung around inside, partly for the sake of coffee cake and partly to hear them talk about me. The moment they did talk about me, I was enraged. *Women* speaking up for me, noticing my "sensitivity," observing me with that appraising female stare and remarking that I seemed to like songs such as "Sweet and Low" better than "Men of Harlech," which was *their* sons' favorite—my mother interpolating half with pride and half with worry that sometimes she had to drive me out to play, I'd rather stay in and read Ridpath's *History of the World*. Women giving me the praise I would have liked to get from my father or Slivers or the Assiniboin halfbreed down at the Lazy-S. I wanted to be made of whang leather.

Little as I want to acknowledge them, the effects of those years remain in me like the beach terraces of a dead lake. Having been weak, and having hated my weakness, I am as impatient with the weakness of others as my father ever was. Pity embarrasses me for the person I am pitying, for I know how it feels to be pitied. Incompetence exasperates me, a big show of pain or grief or any other feeling makes me uneasy, affectations still inspire in me a mirth I have grown too mannerly to show. I cannot sympathize with the self-pitiers, for I have been there, or with the braggarts, for I have been there too. I even at times find myself reacting against conversation, that highest test of the civilized man, because where I came from it was unfashionable to be "mouthy."

An inhumane and limited code, the value system of a life more limited and cruder than in fact ours was. We got most of it by inheritance from the harsher frontiers that had preceded ours— got it, I suppose, mainly from our contacts with what was left of the cattle industry.

So far as the Cypress Hills were concerned, that industry began with the Mounted Police beef herd at Fort Walsh, and was later amplified by herds brought in to feed treaty Indians during the starving winters after 1879. In practice, the Indians ate a good deal of beef that hadn't been intended for them; it took a while to teach them that the white man's spotted buffalo were not fair game when a man was hungry. The raiding of cattle and horse herds was never controlled until the Canadian Indians were moved to reservations far north of the Line after 1882. Nevertheless it was the Indians who first stimulated the raising of cattle on that range, and the departure of the Indians which left the Whitemud River country open to become the last great cattle country.

In some ways, the overlapping of the cattle and homesteading phases of the Plains frontier was similar to the overlapping of the horse and gun cultures earlier, and in each case the overlapping occurred latest around the Cypress Hills. Cattle came in from the south, homesteaders from the east and southeast. Among the homesteaders—Ontario men, Scandinavians and Americans working up from the Dakotas, and Englishmen, Scots, and Ukrainians straight off the immigrant boats—there was a heavy percentage of greenhorns and city men. Even the experienced dryland farmers from the States were a prosaic and law-abiding lot by comparison with the cowboys they displaced. As it turned out, the homesteaders, by appropriating and fencing and plowing the range, squeezed out a way of life that was better adapted to the country than their own, and came close to ruining both the cattlemen and themselves in the process, but that is a later story. What succeeded the meeting and overlapping of the two cultures was a long and difficult period of adaptation in which each would modify the other until a sort of amalgamation could result. But while the adaptations were taking place, during the years of uneasy meeting and mixture, it was the cowboy tradition, the horseback culture, that impressed itself as image, as romance, and as ethical system upon boys like me. There were both good and bad reasons why that should have been true.

Read the history of the northern cattle ranges in such an anti-American historian as John Peter Turner and you hear that the "Texas men" who brought the cattle industry to Canada were all bravos, rustlers, murderers, gamblers, thugs, and highwaymen; that their life was divided among monte, poker, six-guns, and dancehall girls; and that their law was the gun-law that they made for themselves and enforced by hand. Allow sixty or seventy per cent of error for patriotic fervor, and Mr. Turner's generalizations may be accepted. But it is likewise true that American cow outfits left their gun-law cheerfully behind them when they found the country north of the Line well policed, that they cheerfully cooperated with the Mounted Police, took out Canadian brands, paid for grazing leases, and generally conformed to the customs of the country. They were indistinguishable from Canadian ranchers, to whom they taught the whole business. Many Canadian ranches, among them the 76, the Matador, the Turkey Track, and the T-Down-Bar, were simply Canadian extensions of cattle empires below the border.

So was the culture, in the anthropological sense, that accompanied the cattle. It was an adaptation to the arid Plains that had begun along the Rio Grande and had spread north, like gas expanding to fill a vacuum, as the buffalo and Indians were destroyed or driven out in the years following the Civil War. Like the patterns of hunting and war that had been adopted by every Plains tribe as soon as it acquired the horse, the cowboy culture made itself at home all the way from the Rio Grande to the North Saskatchewan. The outfit, the costume, the practices, the terminology, the state of mind, came into Canada ready-made, and nothing they encountered on the northern Plains enforced any real modifications. The Texas men made it certain that nobody would ever be thrown from a horse in Saskatchewan; he would be piled. They made it sure that no Canadian steer would ever be angry or stubborn; he would be o'nery or ringy or on the prod. Bull Durham was as native to the Whitemud range as to the Pecos, and it was used for the same purposes: smoking, eating, and spitting in the eye of a ringy steer. The Stetson was as useful north as south, could be used to fan the fire or dip up a drink from a stream, could shade a man's eyes or be clapped over the eyes of a bronc to gentle him down. Boots, bandanna, stock saddle, rope, the ways of busting broncs, the institution of the spring and fall roundup, the bowlegs in batwing or goatskin chaps—they all came north intact. About the only thing that changed was the name for the cowboy's favorite diversion, which down south they would have called a rodeo but which we called a stampede.

It was a nearly womanless culture, nomadic, harsh, dangerous, essentially romantic. It had the same contempt for the dirt-grubbers that Scythian and Cossack had, and Canadian tillers of the soil tended to look upon it with the same suspicion and fear and envy that tillers of the soil have always expressed toward the herdsmen. As we knew it, it had a lot of Confederate prejudices left in it, and it had the callousness and recklessness that a masculine life full of activity and adventure is sure to produce. I got it in my eyes like stardust almost as soon as we arrived in Whitemud, when the town staged its first stampede down in the western bend. Reno Dodds, known as Slivers, won the saddle bronc competition and set me up a model for my life. I would grow up to be about five feet six and weigh about a hundred and thirty pounds. I would be bowlegged and taciturn, with deep creases in my cheeks and a hide like stained saddle leather. I would be the quietest and most dangerous man around, best rider, best shot, the one who couldn't be buffaloed. Men twice my size, beginning some brag or other, would catch my cold eye and begin to wilt, and when I had stared them into impotence

I would turn my back contemptuous, hook onto my pony in one bowlegged arc, and ride off. I thought it tremendous that anyone as small and skinny as Slivers could be a top hand and a champion rider. I don't think I could have survived without his example, and he was still on my mind years later when, sixteen years old and six feet tall and weighing a hundred and twenty-five pounds, I went every afternoon to the university gym and worked out on the weights for an hour and ran wind sprints around the track. If I couldn't be big I could be *hard*.

We hung around the Lazy-S corrals a good deal that first year or two, and the cowpunchers, when they had no one else to pester, would egg us into what they called shit-fights, with green cow manure for snowballs; or they would put a surcingle around a calf and set us aboard. After my try I concluded that I would not do any more of it just at that time, and I limped to the fence and sat on the top rail nursing my sprains and bruises and smiling to keep from bawling out loud. From there I watched Spot Orullian, a Syrian boy a couple of years older than I, ride a wildly pitching whiteface calf clear around the corral and halfway around again, and get piled hard, and come up wiping the cow dung off himself, swearing like a pirate. They cheered him, he was a favorite at once, perhaps all the more because he had a big brown birthmark on his nose and so could be kidded. And I sat on the corral rail hunching my winglike shoulder-blades, smiling and smiling and smiling to conceal the black envy that I knew was just under the skin of my face. It was always boys like Spot Orullian who managed to be and do what I wanted to do and be.

Many things that those cowboys represented I would have done well to get over quickly, or never catch: the prejudice, the callousness, the destructive practical joking, the tendency to judge everyone by the same raw standard. Nevertheless, what they themselves most respected, and what as a boy I most yearned to grow up to, was as noble as it was limited. They honored courage, competence, self-reliance, and they honored them tacitly. They took them for granted. It was their absence, not their presence, that was cause for remark. Practicing comradeship in a rough and dangerous job, they lived a life calculated to make a man careless of everything except the few things he really valued.

In the fall of 1906 it must have seemed that the cowboy life was certain to last a good while, for the Canadian range still lay wide open, and stockmen from the western states had prospected it and laid large plans for moving bigger herds across the Line to escape the nesters and sheepmen who had already broken up the Montana ranges. Probably the entire country from Wood Mountain to the Alberta line would have been leased for grazing, at the favorable Canadian rate of a few cents an acre, if the winter of 1906-07 had not happened.

That winter has remained ever since, in the minds of all who went through it, as the true measure of catastrophe. Some might cite the winter of 1886-87, the year of the Big Die-Up on the American range, but that winter did not affect the Whitemud country, where cattle came in numbers only after 1887. Some who had punched cows in Alberta in the early days might cast a vote for the fatal Cochran drive of 1881, when 8000 out of 12,000 cattle died over by Lethbridge; and some would certainly, just as weather, mention the April blizzard of 1892, or the winter that followed it, or the big May blizzard of 1903. But after 1907 no one would seriously value those earlier disasters. The winter of 1906-07 was the real one, the year of the blue snow. After it, the leases that might have been taken up were allowed to lapse, the herds that might have been augmented were sold for what they would bring—fifteen to twenty dollars a head with suckling calves thrown in. Old cattlemen who had ridden every range from Texas north took a good long look around in the spring and decided to retire.

The ranches that survived were primarily the hill ranches with shelter plus an access to bench or prairie hay land where winter feed could be cut. The net effect of the winter of 1906-07 was to make stock farmers out of ranchers. Almost as suddenly as the disappearance of the buffalo, it changed the way of life of the region. A great event, it had the force in the history of the Cypress Hills country that a defeat in war has upon a nation. When it was over, the protected Hills might harbor a few cowboys, and one or two of the big ranches such as the 76 might go on, but most of the prairie would be laid open to homesteading and another sort of frontier.

That new frontier, of which my family was a part, very soon

squeezed out the Lazy-S. The hay lands in the bottoms were broken up into town lots, my father was growing potatoes where whitefaces had used to graze, the punchers were drifting off to Alberta. But while we had them around, we made the most of them, imitating their talk and their walk and their songs and their rough-handed jokes; admiring them for the way they tormented Mah Li; hanging around in the shade of the bunkhouse listening to Rusty, who was supposed to be the second son of an earl, play the mouth organ; watching the halfbreed Assiniboin braid leather or horsehair into halter ropes and hackamores. I heard some stories about the winter of 1906-07, but I never heard enough. Long afterward, digging in the middens where historians customarily dig, I found and read some more, some of them the reminiscences of men I knew. What they record is an ordeal by weather. The manner of recording is laconic, deceptively matter of fact. It does not give much idea of how it feels to ride sixty or eighty miles on a freezing and exhausted pony, or how cold thirty below is when a fifty-mile wind is driving it into your face, or how demoralizing it is to be lost in a freezing fog where north, south, east, west, even up and down, swim and shift before the slitted and frost-stuck eyes.

They do not tell their stories in Technicolor; they would not want to seem to adorn a tale or brag themselves up. The calluses of a life of hardship blunt their sensibilities to their own experience. If we want to know what it was like on the Whitemud River range during that winter when the hopes of a cattle empire died, we had better see it through the eyes of some tenderfoot, perhaps someone fresh from the old country, a boy without the wonder rubbed off him and with something to prove about himself. If in inventing this individual I put into him a little of Corky Jones, and some of the boy Rusty whose mouth organ used to sweeten the dusty summer shade of the Lazy-S bunkhouse, let it be admitted that I have also put into him something of myself, the me who sat on a corral bar wetting with spit my smarting skinned places, and wishing I was as tough as Spot Orullian.

2

Genesis

The summer of 1906 was very wet. It seemed to rain for weeks and the coulees ran knee deep and the Frenchman River was as high as a spring flood. The dirt roofs of the log houses of that day became so sodden that water dripped from them whether it rained or not. It stayed so wet that we had difficulty getting the hay in. The winter started early with a light snow on the 5th of November, followed by a terrific three-day blizzard that started on the 11th. From then till Christmas was a succession of bad storms. The range cattle were dying in December.

CORKY JONES AS AN OLD MAN

It seemed to the young Englishman that if anyone had been watching from the bench he would have seen them like a print of Life on the Western Plains, or like a medieval procession. The sun was just rising, its dazzle not yet quite clear of the horizon, and flooding down the river valley whitened with the dust of snow, it gilded the yellow leaves that still clung to the willows, stretched the shadow of every bush and post, glazed the eastern faces of the log ranch buildings whose other side was braced with long blue shadows. And moving now, starting to roll, the outfit was strung out along the Mounted Police patrol trail. He was enclosed in it, moving with it, but in his excitement he saw it as it would look from outside and above, and it made him want to stand up in his stirrups and yell.

Leading the lithograph procession went the five hounds—the four Russian wolfhounds and the thing its owner called a staghound, a dog as big as a calf and with a head like a lioness. Across the bottoms in the morning cold they cut loose and ran for the love of running; within seconds they were out of sight among the willows by the ford. Behind them rode Schulz, the wolfer, as new to the outfit as the Englishman himself; and after him his fifteen-year-old son driving a packhorse; and after them old Jesse in the wagon pulled by a team of hairy-footed Clydesdale stallions. Then the horse herd, seventy or eighty saddle horses in a flow of dark tossing motion across the flat, and then the riders, two and two.

They carried no lances or pennons, the sun found no armor from which to strike light, but in the incandescence of being nineteen, and full of health, and assaulted in all his senses by the realization of everything splendid he had ever imagined, the English boy knew that no more romantic procession had ever set forth. The Crusades could not have thrilled him more. Though they went, and he with them, like an illumination in an old manuscript, they had their own authentic color. Among the bays and blacks and browns and buckskins and roans of the horse herd was one bright piebald; in substitution for slashed doublets and shining silks they offered two pairs of woolly goatskin chaps and Ed Spurlock's red mackinaw.

Only a week in that country, the Englishman with practically no urging would have started running with the dogs. It rattled the brains in his head like seeds in a pod to think where he was—here, in Saskatchewan, not merely on the way to the great lone land, or on its edge, but in it, and going deeper. He had lived a dream in which everything went right. Within an hour of the time he stepped off the train in Maple Creek, hesitant and a little scared, he had learned that all the big cattle outfits using the open range east of the Cypress Hills were shorthanded. Within two hours, he had found a ride with Joe Renaud, the mail driver. Within twelve, he was sleeping in the T-Down bunkhouse, an authentic cowboy. Within a week here he went, part of a company bound for adventure, on the late fall roundup to gather and bring in to feeding stations the calves that could not be expected to winter on the range.

He was face to shining face with everything new. Names he had heard here knocked and clanged in his mind—places where anything could happen, and from the sound of them, *had* happened—Jumbo's Butte, Fifty-Mile, Pinto Horse Butte, Horse Camp Coulee, the War Holes. He blew his exultant breath out between his pony's ears, and when he breathed in again he felt the cold at the root of every bared tooth. He noticed that the horses felt as he did: though they had been on the roundup and then on the long drive to Montana and then on the long drive back, and had been worked steadily since May, they were full of run; they joined him in snorting smoke.

The column turned down toward the river, and looking back the Englishman saw Molly Henry, the foreman's wife, hugging her elbows by the ranch-house door. He waved; her hand lifted. He and Ed Spurlock were the last in the line, and he saw how they would look to her, his new sheepskin and Spurlock's red mackinaw just disappearing into the willows. He thought it a lonesome piece of luck for a girl married only three weeks to be left now, with no help except a crippled handy man and no company except the Mountie on his weekly patrol from Eastend, and no woman nearer than twenty-five miles. To Spurlock, jogging beside him with his mittened hands stacked on the horn, he said with feeling, "I'm certainly glad it's not *me* being left behind!"

Spurlock glanced sideward with restless brown eyes; he said nothing; his expression did not change.

The Englishman grew aware, under Spurlock's glance, that he was posting to his pony's jogtrot. As if stretching muscles he pushed down hard into the unfamiliarly long stirrups, shoved back against the cantle, leaned a little and stacked his hands casually on the horn in imitation of Spurlock's. As soon as he had them there he felt that he seemed to be hanging on to ease the jolt of sitting the trot, and he took his hands away again. With a complex sense of being green, young, red-headed, and British—all potentially shameful—but at the same time strong, bold, high-spirited, and ready for anything, he appraised Spurlock's taciturnity and adjusted his seat in the big strange saddle and threw at random into the air a look that was cocky, self-conscious, and ingratiating all at once.

The wagon had crushed through the thin ice at the ford, and

the horses waded into the broken wake and stood knee deep, bobbing away ice-pans with their noses, plunging their muzzles to suck strongly. Here and there one pulled its nose out and stood with a thoughtful, puckered, tasting expression at the corners of its dripping lips; they looked as if the water had made their teeth ache.

Then Slippers and Little Horn and Ray Henry rode in and hazed them across, and Buck and Panguingue and Spurlock and the Englishman picked up the stragglers. The cold sound of splashing became a drumming and thudding on the bank. Above and ahead, the wagon was just tilting out of sight over the dugway edge. They took the herd up after it in a rush, and burst out onto the great glittering plain.

It was tremendous, it was like a plunge over a cliff. The sun looked them straight in the eyes, the earth dazzled them. Over and under and around, above, below, behind, before, the Englishman felt the unfamiliar element, a cleanness like the blade of a knife, a distance without limits, a horizon that did not bound the world but only suggested endless space beyond. Shading his eyes with his hand while his pony rocked into a lope, he saw all ahead of him the disk of the white and yellow world, the bowl of the colorless sky unbearable with light. Squatting on the horizon right under the searchlight sun were a pair of low mounds, one far off, one nearer. The closer one must be Jumbo's Butte, the far one Stonepile. They were the only breaks he saw in the plains except when, twisting backward, he found the Cypress Hills arched across the west, showing in coulees and ravines the faded white and gold of aspen, the black of jackpines. By the time they had ridden five minutes the river valley out of which they had risen was almost invisible, sunk below the level of sight.

The wolfer and his son were already far ahead, the dogs only running specks out on the shining plain. Jesse and the pilot wagon were leading the rest of them on a beeline toward Jumbo's Butte, and as the Englishman settled down and breathed out his excitement and relaxed to the shuffle of his pony he watched the broad wheels drop and jolt into holes and burnouts and old Jesse lurch and sway on the high seat, and he let his back ache with sympathy. Then he saw Jesse's teeth flash in his face as he turned to shout something at Ray Henry riding beside the wagon, and he decided that sympathy was wasted. Jesse had been a bullwhacker with supply trains between Fort Benton and the Montana mining camps in the early days, he had known these plains when the buffalo were still shaking them, he had been jolting his kidneys loose across country like this for thirty years. If he had wanted another kind of job he could have had it. The Englishman admired him as a man who did well what he was hired to do. He believed old Jesse to be skilled, resourceful, humorous, close-mouthed, a character. Briefly he contemplated growing a mustache and trying to train it like Jesse's into a silky oxbow.

The saddle horses followed along smartly after the pilot wagon, and there was hardly any need to herd them, but the boys were fanned out in a wide semicircle, riding, as if by preference, each by himself. And among them—this was the wonder, this was what made him want to raise his face and ki-yi in pure happiness —rode Lionel Cullen, by now known as Rusty, the least of eight (as he admitted without real humility) but willing, and never more pleased with himself. That morning in early November, 1906, he would not have traded places with Sir Wilfrid Laurier.

He wanted to see everything, miss nothing, forget nothing. To make sure that he would not forget what happened to him and what he saw, he had begun a journal on the train coming west from Montreal, and every evening since then he had written in it seriously with posterity looking over his shoulder. He watched every minute of every day for the vivid and the wonderful, and he kept an alert eye on himself for the changes that were certain to occur. He had the feeling that there would be a test of some sort, that he would enter manhood—or cowboyhood, manhood in Saskatchewan terms—as one would enter a house. For the moment he was a tenderfoot, a greenhorn, on probation, under scrutiny. But at some moment there would be a door to open, or to force, and inside would be the self-assurance that he respected and envied in Jesse, Slippers, or Little Horn, the calm confidence of a top hand.

As they moved like the scattered shadow of a cloud across the face of the plain he knew practically nothing except how to sit a horse, and even that he knew in a fashion to get him laughed at.

But he was prepared to serve an apprenticeship, he would prove himself as and when he must. And in the pocket of his flannel shirt he had a notebook and two pencils, ready for anything.

At noon, a little to the east of Jumbo's Butte, they stopped to boil coffee and heat a kettle of beans. The thin snow did not cover the grass; the crust that had blazed in their eyes all morning was thawing in drops that clung to the curly prairie wool. On a tarpaulin spread by the wagon they sprawled and ate the beans that Jesse might just as well not have heated, for the cold tin plates congealed them again within seconds. But the coffee burned their mouths, and the tin cups were so hot to hold that they drank with their mittens on. The steam of their coffee-heated breath was a satisfaction; Rusty tried to blow rings with it.

When he finished he lay on the tarp next to Panguingue. There was always, it seemed, room next to Panguingue: it was said of him that he took a bath every spring whether he needed it or not. In the cold, and so long as Panguingue wore a sheepskin and overshoes, Rusty did not mind. And anyway, since arriving he had seen no one take a bath, not even Buck, who was fastidious; certainly he had taken none himself. So he relaxed by Panguingue and felt the ground satisfyingly hard under the tarp, and let Panguingue thump him monotonously between the shoulder blades and dust cigarette ashes through his hair. With half-closed eyes he heard the horses working on the curly grass all around, he saw a snowbird come boldly to pick at a scrap of salt pork by the edge of the tarp; his ears heard the sounds of ease, the scratchings, the crackle of a match; his nose smelled sour pipe, smelled Bull Durham, smelled Ray Henry's sybaritic cigar. He loved every minute, every sensation, and when, just as they were rising to tighten cinches and move on, they heard the hysterical yapping of hounds, and saw Schulz's pack, two miles away, pursue and run down a coyote, he climbed on the wagon and watched as eager as a spectator at a horse race. He thought of Schulz as belonging somehow with Jesse, the two of them survivors of an earlier stage of Plains life; he rather envied Schulz's boy, brought up to lonely cabins, skimpy cowchip campfires on the prairies, familiarity with wild animals, the knack and habit of casual killing. From high on the wagon seat, bracing himself on Jesse's shoulder, he watched Schulz ride in and scatter the hounds and dismount, while the boy gathered up the loose packhorse. He expected that the wolfers would come in and get something to eat, but he saw Schulz mount again and the three horses and the five dogs move out eastward. Even more than the cowboys, these were the wild ones; they had gone as far as it was possible to go back toward savagery. He regretted not seeing them ride in with the scalp of the coyote, the hounds bloody-muzzled from the kill. He hoped to get a chance to course a coyote or a wolf across such a marvelous plain as this on such a glorious day, when you could see for twenty miles. It was tremendous, every bit of it.

During the afternoon the country roughened, broke into coulees that opened down toward the river. They rode, it seemed, endlessly, without a break and with little talk. Rusty stiffened in the saddle, he rode lounging, stood in the stirrups, hung his feet free while under him the shaggy little horse shuffled on. The sun went down the sky toward the Cypress Hills, now no more than a faint clean lifting of the horizon. They felt the thin warmth on their necks if their collars were down; their faces felt the cold.

When they arrived at Stonepile the sun was already down. The sky back over the hills was red, the snow ahead of them lay rosy across the flats. Until they reached the coulee's rim they would not have known it was there; as for the river, it was sunk among indistinguishable rough coulees to the north, but no more than a mile away. As they dipped downward toward the Stonepile buildings, once a Mounted Police patrol post, the valley was already full of violet shadow. Rusty creaked and eased himself, letting the horse pick his way. He was stiff and chilled, his face felt like sheet metal, his eyes watered and smarted from the day's glare.

They were not talkative as they unsaddled and turned the horses loose, or during the time while they lugged bedrolls and food into the old barracks. Two or three men would be stationed here later to feed to the calves the three hundred and fifty tons of wild hay stacked in the coulee; they had brought flour, rice, oatmeal, sugar, matches and prunes, tinned corn and syrup and jam and peas, dried apples and peaches, to stock the place. There was a good deal of tracking in and out from the cold blue dusk. Jesse had stuck two tallow dips in china holders that said *Peerless Hotel*. They were all in each other's way in the narrow bunkhouse, and all in the way of Jesse, trying to get supper going. They bumped shoulders, growled. Rusty, who had thrown his bedroll forehandedly into one of the upper bunks, came in with a load later and found that Ed Spurlock had thrown it out and put his own in its place. There were only six bunks for the ten of them. In the end, Rusty spread his bed beside Panguingue's on the floor, and the wolfers, coming in a half hour after them, looked in the door briefly and decided to sleep in the stable with the Clydes, the night horses, and the dogs.

"Be careful them studs," Jesse told Schulz. "It wouldn't do if them and your lion got to mixing it."

The wolfer was a man, Rusty thought, to be noticed, perhaps to be watchful of. He still wore, in the warming barracks, a muskrat cap with earlaps. Under it his eyes were gray as agates, as sudden as an elbow in the solar plexus. His face was red, his mustache sandy. Between his eyes, even when he smiled, which was not often, he wore a deep vertical wrinkle. He had what Rusty thought of as a passionate taciturnity. He looked watchful and besieged, he would be quick to strike back, he was not a man you could make a joke with. In a low growling voice he said that he valued his hound too highly to let any forty-dollar horse kick him in the head.

Jesse looked at him, holding a stove lid half off the smoking fire, and his silky mustaches moved as if a small animal had crawled under the thatch. He said, "If one of the Clydes hit him, that wouldn't be no forty-dollar kick. That would be a genuine gold-plated eight-hundred-dollar kick guaranteed to last."

Schulz grunted and went out: Rusty told himself that he had been right in guessing him as a man with whom you did not joke. The boy, sullen-looking, with a drooping lip and eyes that looked always out their corners, went silently after him. They came back in for supper, cleaned their plates, and went out again for good.

"What's the matter with him?" Spurlock asked. "Don't he like our company?"

"Likes his dogs better," Buck said. He reared his red turkey neck up and glared out into the jammed corridor between the bunks. From the end, where he sat braced against the wall fooling with the harmonica, Rusty saw the disgust on his skinned-looking face. "What about somebody that would sleep with a God damn dog?" Buck said.

From the lower, talking around the dead cigar that poked upward from his face, Little Horn said gently, "We ain't got any right to criticize. We all been sleepin' with Panguingue for a year."

"B.S.," Panguingue said. "My feet don't smell no worse'n yours."

"Well for the love of God," Jesse said, hanging the dishpan on the wall, "let's not have any contests. There ain't a man here would survive it."

Rusty took the slick metal of the harmonica from his mouth and ventured: his feelers, tentative always to estimate his own position as one of them, told him that now, while they were criticizing the unsociable wolfer, his own position was more solid; and yet he admired the wildness and the obvious competence of the wolfer, too. The very fact that he rode in moccasins and thick German socks gave him a distinction over the rest of them in their overshoes. Rusty said, "Do you suppose it's only that he's used to living out alone, don't you know . . . that he's almost like a wild animal himself? He seems that way to me . . . or is that only fancy?"

They hooted at him, and he felt his ears grow red. "Aow, it's only fawncy, p'raps," they told each other for the next minute or two. "Deah!" they said. "Rilly?" Rusty blew into the mouth organ. He heard Little Horn saying, "It's natural enough. Yell at a dog, he minds. Yell at one of you sonsofbitches, what does he do? I don't blame the guy. There's no satisfaction in a cowpuncher's company like there is in a dog's."

Spurlock said, "Can his kid talk? I never heard him say a word yet."

"Probably all he knows is 'bow-wow,'" Buck said.

Jesse pawed his yellow-white silky mustache and said with the look of foolery in his faded blue eyes, "Schulz don't look to me like he's got a steady conscience. I'd say mebbe he was a windigo."

Rusty waited, hoping someone else would take the bait, but

resigning himself when no one spoke. And anyway, he was interested. "What's a windigo?"

"What the Crees used to call an Injun that had made use of man-meat," Jesse said. "Most generally seemed to sort of drive a man wild, he wasn't right afterwards. I recall hearing Bert Willoughby tell about one the Mounties had to go get up on the Swift Current, back in the early days. His tribe got suspicious, he come out of a starvin' winter lookin' so fat and slick. Also his fambly was missin'. So they collared this buck and he took 'em up to his winter camp on Bigstick Lake, and here was all these bones and skulls around, and he'd kick 'em and laugh, and say, 'This one my wife, hee hee hee,' and 'That one my mother-in-law, ho ho,' and 'This one here my father, ha ha.' He'd et the whole damn bunch, one after the other."

"Well," Little Horn said. "I wonder if somebody is settin' oncomfortable on old Schulzie's stomach?"

"Maybe we could get him to eat Panguingue before he gets too God damn high," Spurlock said.

Little Horn said regretfully, "I doubt if even a windigo would take a chance on Panguingue."

"B.S.," Panguingue said.

From the white cloud of cigar smoke that filled the enclosed space above his bunk, Ray Henry whispered, "You can all take it easy. Schulz and his boy will be stayin' here or at Bates Camp all winter, while you boys is up to your ass in dried apple pies back at the ranch."

"Good," Buck said.

"Sure, Ray," said Jesse, "I know that was the arrangement. But is it safe?"

"Safe, how?"

Jesse kicked the stove leg. "This-here my boy," he said. "Hee hee hee."

They left Schulz and his silent boy behind them at the Stonepile camp and made a hard drive eastward to the Fifty-Mile Crossing of the Whitemud, on the eastern boundary of the range that, by mutual consent among all the outfits, was called the T-Down's. Already, within a day, Rusty felt how circumstances had hardened, how what had been an adventure revealed itself as a job. He rose from his bed on the floor so stiff he hobbled like a rheumatic dog, and when he stumbled out of the foul barracks and took a breath of the morning air it was as if he had had an icicle rammed clear to his wishbone. Another cold day—colder than the one before by a good deal—and an even harder ride ahead. And leaving the Schulzes affected him unpleasantly: these two were being separated off to carry on a specific and essential duty, but no one was sorry to see them go. The outfit that he had thought of as ten was really only eight. If the others chose to find him as disagreeable as they found Schulz, it was only seven. He hung at their fringes, hoping to earn a place among them. He was painfully alert, trying to anticipate what was expected of him. What was expected was that he should climb in the saddle, on a new pony this morning—one with a trot like a springless wagon over cobblestones—and ride, and ride, and ride, straight into the blinding glare of the sun.

The night before, he had entered in his journal information on how the open range from Wood Mountain on the east to Medicine Lodge Coulee on the west was run. From the Whitemud north to the Canadian Pacific tracks the Circle Diamond and the 76, both very large outfits, divided it. South of the river there were several. Between Wood Mountain and Fifty-Mile was the Turkey Track, running about 25,000 head. Then their own outfit, the T-Down Bar, running 10,000. Between the T-Down ranch house and the Cypress Hills the Z-X ran about 2000 purebred shorthorns and whitefaces, and through the Cypress Hills to Medicine Lodge Coulee an association of small ranchers called the Whitemud Pool ran their herds together. It seemed reasonable; it even seemed neat; but it seemed terribly large when you had to ride across it at the wagon's pace.

By noon the sky had hazed over. They blessed it because of their eyes and cursed it because the wind developed a sting. Then away out on the flats in the middle of a bleak afternoon they met the wagon and four riders from the Turkey Track, bound for a camp they had on the big coulee called the War Holes. They were on the same errand as the T-Down boys: combing parts of the range missed in the spring roundup, and separating out the calves and bulls to be wintered on hay in the sheltered bottoms. Their greeting was taciturn and numb. The

T-Down boys looked to them exactly as they looked to the T-Down, probably: frostbitten, with swollen watery eyes, their backs humped to the cold wind, their ponies' tails blowing between their legs as they waited out the fifteen minutes of meeting.

It had not been made clear to Rusty Cullen, until then, that they were on a belated and half-desperate job. A green hand did not inquire too closely for fear of asking foolish questions; an experienced hand volunteered nothing. And so he was surprised by the gloominess of the Turkey Track boys and their predictions of heavy losses on the range. They quoted signs and omens. They ran mittened hands against the grain of their ponies' winter hair, to show how much heavier it was than normal. They had seen muskrat houses built six feet high in the sloughs—and when the rats built high you could depend on a hard winter. Mounted Police freighters reported a steady drift of antelope from the north across the CPR tracks.

The chinook winds, he gathered, should keep the range clear enough for the stronger animals to get feed, but calves didn't winter well. Fortunately all the stock was fat: the summer range had been good. If they could get the calves in where there was feed, maybe there wouldn't be too much loss. Having exchanged omens, predictions, reassurances, and invitations to Christmas blowouts, they raised their mitts to each other and ducked each his own way into or away from the wind, and the tracks that had briefly met crawled apart again across the snow.

Somehow the brief, chilled, laconic encounter in the emptiness and cold of the flats left Rusty depressed. By the time they dragged in to camp in the willows of the river bottom at Fifty-Mile his eyes were swollen almost shut, and burned and smarted as if every little capillary and nerve in them had been twisted and tied in knots; he knew how streaked and bloodshot they were by looking at the eyes of the others. He was tired, stiff, cold; there was no immediate comfort in camp, but only more cold hard work, and the snow that was only a thin scum on the prairie was three inches deep down here. They shoveled off a space and got the tent set up in the blue dusk, and he looked it over and felt that their situation was gloomily naked and exposed. When he chopped through the river's inch of ice and watched the water well up and overflow the hole it seemed like some dark force from the ancient heart of the earth that could at any time rise around them silently and obliterate their little human noises and tracks and restore the plain to its emptiness again.

The wind dropped after sundown, the night came on clear and cold. Before turning in Rusty stepped outside and looked around. The other boys were all in their bedrolls, and the light in the tent had been blown out so that even that pale human efflorescence was gone; the tent was a misty pyramid, the wagon a shadow. Tied to the wheels, the blanketed night horses and the Clydes moved their feet uncomfortably and rustled for a last grain of oats in the seams of their nosebags.

The earth showed him nothing; it lay pallid, the willows bare sticks, the snow touched with bluish luminescence. A horn of moon was declining toward the western horizon. But in the north the lights were beginning, casting out a pale band that trembled and stretched and fell back and stretched out again until it went from horizon to horizon. Out of it streaks and flares and streamers began to reach up toward the zenith and pale the stars there as if smoke were being blown across them.

He had never felt so small, so lost, so inconsequential; his impulse was to sneak away. If anyone had asked his name and his business, inquiring what he was doing in the middle of that empty plain, he would have mumbled some foolish and embarrassed answer. In his mind's eye he saw the Turkey Track camp ten or fifteen or twenty miles out in the emptiness, the only other thing like themselves, a little lonesome spark that would soon go out and leave only the smudge of the wagon, the blur of the tent, under the cold flare of the Northern Lights. It was easy to doubt their very existence; it was easy to doubt his own.

A night horse moved again, a halter ring clinked, a sound tiny and lost. He shuddered his shoulders, worked his stiffened face, stirred up his numbed brains and shook the swimming from his eyes. When the tent flap dropped behind him and he stooped to fumble the ties shut the shiver that went through him was exultant, as if he had just been brushed by a great danger and had escaped. The warmth and the rank human odors of the tent were mystically rich with life. He made such a loud, happy, unnecessary row about the smell of Panguingue's feet when he crawled into his bedroll in their cramped head-to-foot sleeping space that three or four sleepy voices cursed him viciously and Panguingue kicked him a few good hard ones through his blankets and kicked the vapors out of him.

Sometime during that roundup they may have had a day of decent weather, but it seemed to Rusty it was a procession of trials: icy nights, days when a bitter wind lashed and stung the face with a dry sand of snow, mornings when the crust flashed up a glare so blinding that they rode with eyes closed to slits and looked at the world through their eyelashes. There was one afternoon when the whole world was overwhelmed under a white freezing fog, when horses, cattle, clothes, wagon, grew a fur of hoar frost and the herd they had gathered had to be held together in spooky white darkness mainly by ear.

On bright days they were all nearly blind, in spite of painting their cheekbones with charcoal and riding with hats pulled clear down; if they could see to work at all, they worked with tears leaking through swollen and smarting lids. Their faces grew black with sun and glare, their skin and lips cracked as crisp as the skin of a fried fish, and yet they froze. Every night the thermometer dropped near zero, and there was an almost continuous snake-tongue of wind licking out of the north or west.

The river bottom and the big rough coulees entering from the south held many cattle, and they soon collected a large herd. They were hard to move; if he had had a gun Rusty would have been tempted more than once to make immediate beef of them. The Canadian cattle, whiteface or whiteface-and-shorthorn cross, were impenetrably stupid and slow; their whole unswerving intention was to break past a rider and get back into the bottoms. The longhorns, most of which carried the Turkey Track or Circle Diamond brand and which had to be cut away from their own, were exactly the opposite: fast, agile, wicked, and smart. They could lead a man a wild chase, always in a direction he didn't want to go; they hid among other cattle and couldn't be cut out; they milled and stampeded the T-Down herd at every chance; all the boys had spills, chasing longhorns through rough country and across the icy flats; and they wore the horses, already weak and thin, to the bone.

On the third day out from Fifty-Mile, Slip, Panguingue, and Rusty were cutting out a bunch of ten or fifteen Circle Diamond longhorns from a dozen T-Down whitefaces. They wanted the whitefaces up on the bench where they could turn them into the herd; the longhorns were welcome to the coulee. Of course the whitefaces hung onto the coulee and the longhorns stampeded up onto the flats. It was astonishing how fast those cattle could move and how much noise they made. Their horns cracked; their hoofs cracked; their joints cracked; it seemed as if even their tails snapped like bullwhips. In a wild clamor they went up the coulee bank, agile as goats, with Rusty after them.

He came out onto the rim in a sting of snow and wind. The longhorns were well ahead of him, racing with their bag-of-bones clatter toward the wagon and the herd that Jesse and Spurlock were holding there. Rusty ducked his head and squinted back at Slip; he was waving and shouting: Rusty understood that he was to head the longhorns before they got too close to the herd.

The cattle, very fast for a short distance, began to slack off. His dogged little horse came up on a roan haunch, then on a brindle, then past a set of wild horns, and finally up on the leader, so close the boy could have kicked his laboring shoulder or reached out and grabbed his thirty-inch horn. He lashed him with the rope across the face; still going hard, the steer ducked and began to turn.

The next he knew, Rusty was over the pony's head like a rock shot from a slingshot. It happened so fast he knew nothing about it until he was flying through the air frantically clawing at nothing, and lit sliding, and rolled. His wind and wits went out of him together; he sat up groggily, spitting blood and snow.

And oh, how beautiful a thing it is to work with men who know their job! He sat up into a drama of danger and rescue. The steer had turned and was coming for him; Slip was riding in hard from the side to head him off. But he was too far back; Rusty saw it with the hardest sort of clarity, and he was up on hands and knees, into a crouch, his eyes estimating distances, watching the wide horns and the red eyes of the steer, noting even how the stiff ice-encased hairs sprayed back from his nostrils. While he crouched there laboring to get wind back into his lungs, Rusty saw Slip's bay in the air with all four legs stiff, coming down to a braced landing. The wide loop came snaking in the air, Slip's left hand was making a lightning dally around the horn. The timing was so close that the rope did not even sag before the steer's rush took up the slack. It simply whistled out straight and was snapped tight and humming as the pony came down stiff-legged in the snow. The steer was yanked off his feet, the horse slipped, went nearly down, recovered, the air was full of hoofs and horns, and the longhorn crashed as if he had fallen from the sky. Liquid dung rolled from under his tail; Rusty thought he had broken his neck.

Shakily he went toward the steer to unhook Slip's rope for him, but Slip warned him sharply away. His horse stepped nervously, keeping the rope tight when the steer tried to rise. A little way off, Panguingue was reaching from his saddle to catch the trailing reins of Rusty's pony. "Bust anythin'?" Slip said.

"No," Rusty said. He had sense enough to swallow his gratitude. With his cracked and blackened face, Slip looked like a dwarfish Negro jockey on that big strong horse. He was watching the herd, and Rusty turned to look too, just as Panguingue rode up and handed him his reins. All three stood a moment looking toward the wagon and listening to the uproar of shouts and curses that came from Spurlock and Jesse.

"God damn!" Panguingue said.

The longhorns, bursting into the compact herd of whitefaces, were stirring them like a great spoon. Even as they watched, the milling movement spread, the edges scattered, the whole herd was on the run back toward the coulee. Slip shook off his rope and he and Panguingue started off at a lope without a glance at Rusty. The steer rose and stood spraddling, watching him with red eyes. Limping, cursing the treacherous icy hole-pocked prairie, sorry for himself in his unregarded pain, Rusty reached his numb left arm up and took hold of the horn and mounted. Gritting his teeth, he spurred the pony into a trot, but that so agonized his arm and shoulder that in a moment he slowed to a walk. Then he swore and kicked him into a canter. He would show them. He would ride it out the whole mortal day, and they would never know until that night, after he had done without a complaint all the duty demanded of him, that he was really a stretcher case with a broken shoulder or collarbone or something. He knew he was going to be laid up, but he would stay in the saddle till he dropped. A grim campaigner, a man with the right stuff in him, he crippled along after Slip and Panguingue and the accursed cows.

He managed to get through the rest of the day, but when he was unsaddling that night at the wagon, his face skinned, his left hand helpless and his right fumbling and clumsy, no one came around with help or sympathy. One or two of them gave him bleary glances and went on past as he picked at the latigo with one freezing unmittened hand. Perhaps he dropped a tear or two of rage and weakness and pain into the snow. When he finally got the saddle off and turned the pony loose, he stumbled into the tent and lay down and turned his back to them. He heard Jesse's cooking noises, he smelled the smoke of frying meat, he felt the heat of the stove filling the canvas space. The boys talked a little, growling and monosyllabic. The wind puffed on the tent wall near his face; he cradled his aching arm the best he could and concentrated on stoicism.

Panguingue came in, crawled into his bed to warm up, and kicked Rusty companionably to get his attention. The jar shook such pain through the boy that he rose up with gritted teeth. Panguingue's astonished grin glimmered through his beard, and he said to the tent at large, "You should of seen old Rusty get piled today. How'd that feel, Rusty? You was up in the air long enough to grow feathers."

"It felt like hell, if you want to know. I think I broke my shoulder."

"Oh well," Panguingue said. "Long as it wasn't your neck."

His callousness absolutely enraged Rusty, but Spurlock enraged him more when he remarked from the other corner of the tent, "You sure chose a hell of a time to get piled, I'll say that. You fall off and we lose the whole God damn herd."

"Fall off?" Rusty said shrilly. "*Fall* off? What do *you* do when your pony steps in a hole?"

"Not what you did," Spurlock said. In the light of the two candles Jesse had stuck onto his grub box, his bloodshot eyes moved restlessly, here, there, first on Rusty, then on one of the others, never still. There was a drooping, provocative smile on his face. Rusty pulled his anger in and stayed silent.

Slippers said into the air from where he lay on his back next to Panguingue, "Rusty was doin' all right. He was headin' 'em."

"When he see his horse was too slow, he took off and flew," Panguingue said.

In imbecile good nature his rough hand jarred out, half blow and half push, and Rusty fell awkwardly on the bad shoulder. "Look out, you silly bastard!" he screamed, so much like a hysterical schoolboy that he turned again, ashamed, and gave his back to them. He knew they were watching, speculatively and with expressions of calculated neutrality. Judgment was going on in their minds, and he hated what they were thinking.

In a few minutes Ray Henry came in, the last but one into camp.

"Somebody'll have to spell Buck in an hour," he said. "After that we can take it in two-hour shifts. Little Horn, you take it first, then Panguingue, then Slip." His inflamed eyes came around to Rusty, blinked at him across the stove and candles. "Rusty, you healthy? Was that you took a spill today?"

"That was me."

"Hurt yourself?"

"I don't know. I can't move my left arm."

The foreman picked his way between the bedrolls and squatted. "Roll over and let's see." Obediently, justified and finally vindicated, Rusty helped unbutton sheepskin and both flannel shirts he wore, and the thick hands probed and squeezed and punched around his shoulder and collarbone and down the arm. Rusty flattered himself that he did not wince.

For a second or two Ray stayed squatting there, dark-faced, burly as a boulder, expressionless. "I don't think she's bust," he said. "It don't wiggle anywhere. I'll take your shift tonight, and you better lay up with the wagon tomorrow and see how it goes."

"No," Rusty said. "I can work."

"Excelsior," said Spurlock from his corner.

"What?" Ray said.

Nobody said anything.

That was always a bad time, that few minutes before supper, when they came in and lay around the tent waiting for food with their bones melting away with tiredness. But it didn't last. They were cheerful enough afterward, lying in bed, smoking, and Spurlock even went to the length of rolling Rusty a cigarette and passing it across in silence. "Oh, I say," Rusty said. "Thanks very much!" Spurlock threw his muzzle in the air and gave himself up to silent laughter, or to communion with his ironic gods, and shook his head in amused despair, but the edge was out of him, out of all of them.

Buck came in, cold and morose, and fussily hunted up a pan and heated water in it and washed himself before he ate the supper Jesse had kept warm. Little Horn, groaning, hunched into his sheepskin and went out. They could hear him asking the sympathy of the horse as he saddled up.

One by one the other boys made their way outside and in a few seconds came chattering in again. When it came Rusty's turn he ducked out with his arm hugged against his chest. The cold froze his teeth clear to the roots at the first breath; he shuddered and shook. It is awkward enough for a man to button and unbutton his pants with his right hand at any time, but in that freezing circumstance he might as well have tried to do it with tongs. The big pale earth was around him, the big mottled sky arched over with a slice of very white moon shining on icy-looking clouds. It was so quiet he heard his own heart thudding. For a moment he stood taking it in, and then he opened his mouth and let out a very loud yell, simply to announce himself and to crack the silence. When he went back in, hissing and shaking, he found them all staring at him.

"What in hell was that?" Buck said.

"That was me," Rusty said. "It was too quiet to suit me."

Jesse was paring a sliver of tobacco off a plug, working at it slowly and carefully as he might have peeled an apple. His faded eyes glinted up, his oxbow mustaches parted briefly. "You hadn't ought to do a thing like that, son," he said. "I reckon you don't know, though."

"Know what?"

"When it's this cold," Jesse said, "man has to be careful how loud he talks."

"What?" Rusty said. "Get too cold air into your lungs, you mean? Freeze your windpipe?"

"Tell you," Jesse said. "I used to know this feller name Dan Shields."

Rusty crept into his blankets, not willing to give any of them, even Jesse, a handle. "Anybody feel like a game of stud?" Spurlock said.

"Too damn cold," Panguinge said. "You'd freeze your hands."

"Down by where I used to work," Jesse said, in his soft insisting voice, "down there by Sheridan, there's this guy Dan Shields. He's tellin' me one time about some cold weather *he* seen. Said him and another guy was up on the mountain workin' a gold mine one winter, and it chilled off considerable. Man walk along outside, he'd steam like a laundry. Wood froze so hard it'd last all night in the stove—they never had a bit of fuel trouble. Go to spit, you'd have to break yourself free before you could walk away. They figured seventy-five, eighty below. Couldn't tell, the thermometer froze solid at sixty-five."

"I hope they had a steam-heated backhouse," Panguingue said. "I had to break myself free out there just now."

"Better look close, Pan," said Spurlock. "Man could make a serious mistake breakin' too careless."

"B. S.," Panguingue said. "Even broke off short I'll match you."

"Said they had them a nice warm cabin and they made out fine," Jesse said, "except the grub began to run low. One mornin' they're talkin' about what they should do, and they step outside to sort of look at the weather. They're standin' there talkin', and it seems to Dan this other guy's voice is sort of failin' him. He gets squeakier and squeakier, and finally he pinches out. The fella looks surprised and clears his throat, and spits, and breaks himself loose, and tries again. Not a whisper.

" 'Is your tonsils froze, or what?' Dan says to him—and you know, *he* don't break the silence any, either. He tries his lips, and they're workin', and he wags his tongue, and *it* ain't bogged down, and he takes a big breath and tries to rip off a cussword, and nothin' happens at all.

"His partner is lookin' at him very queer. He says somethin' that Dan don't get. 'By God,' says Dan at the top of his voice, 'there's somethin' almighty damn funny here!' and all he hears is nothin', just nothin'. They turn their heads and listen, and there ain't a sound.

"Dan cusses some more, thinkin' he may jar somethin' loose the way you'd kick a jammed endgate. He can't make a peep. Said he was beginnin' to get scared. Said he looks across at his partner and the sweat was up on the guy's forehead size of buckshot. The drops froze as fast as they popped out, and they roll off his face and hit the snow. You'd think they'd patter—sort of human hailstones. Not a speck, Dan says. They roll off his partner's brow and hit the ground and he can see them bounce and they don't make no more noise than feathers.

"The partner begins to get excited. His mouth is goin' like a stampmill, and yet it's just as quiet as three o'clock in the mornin'. His eyes bug out, and he makes these yellin' motions, and all of a sudden he busts inside the cabin and throws his stuff together and takes off down the mountain."

"And never was seen again," Spurlock said. "The end."

"Well, that relieves the grub situation, and after Dan has gone inside and warmed up he tries out his voice again and it works, so he stays on. The weather never lets up, though, not till way 'long in the spring. Then one mornin' the sun comes up bright and first thing Dan notices the thermometer has thawed out and begun to slide down, and she's only sixty below, and then a little later she's fifty. She's gettin' so mild he sits down on the doorstep after breakfast and smokes a pipe. While he's sitting there he hears his partner, somewhere a good ways away, but comin' closer, sayin' somethin' like, 'figger we could get down and back in three-four days if on'y it wasn't so God damn cold.'

"Said it cheered him like anythin' to hear a human voice again, and he raises up on the doorstep and looks down the trail, but ain't a sign of anybody. He's lookin' all around when his partner says, quite close, 'I don't mind bein' out of sugar, but I sure as hell don't aim to stay long where they ain't any Climax Plug.'

"'I see what you mean,' Dan says conversationally. 'I expect you get the bulk of your nourishment thataway,' and then he looks very fast behind him and all around that front yard, because it ain't him that's said it, he ain't moved his mouth or had any intention of sayin' anything. It ain't him but it's his voice.

" 'My notion is we ought to go on down,' the partner says, very clear and close, and then there is a good deal of hackin' and spittin' and clearin' of the throat and the partner says, 'What in the God damn hell is happenin' to me?' and Dan hears his own voice say, 'Is your tonsils froze, or what?' and then there is a very considerable duet of cussin' and yellin', and more throat clearin' and more yellin' and a sound like a hailstorm patterin' all around, and out of this big uproar the partner says, 'By God, I'm gettin' out of here!' Well that's just what Dan does. He ducks inside that cabin and leans against the door till all the fuss dies down outside, and when she's quiet he gathers together his plunder and he hightails her off the mountain too.

"He had it figured out by then, easy enough. It was so cold out there while they was talkin' that their words froze right there in the air, froze up plumb solid and silent. Then when that quick thaw comes on they broke up all at once and come down on old Dan's head like icicles off a roof. But Dan said he didn't want to stay up there even after he figured it out. Said it made him uncomfortable to think that any time somebody might yell right in his ear three months ago. Said he never did learn to care for cold-storage conversation as well as the fresh article."

"Now ain't it funny?" Buck said. "That ain't my taste at all. I'd just as soon have everything you just said all froze up nice and solid so the coyotes could listen to it next spring and I could just lay here now with no noise going on and get some sleep."

"That's the biggest pile of cold-storage bullshit I ever heard," Spurlock said. "Jesse, you could chop that up and use it for cowchips for a month."

"I guess," Jesse said mildly. "But I tell you, kid, don't you go yellin' so loud outside there no more. This is one of those winters when you might deefen somebody in 1907."

With his arm hanging in a sling made of a flour sack and a horse-blanket pin, and the loose sleeve of his sheepskin flapping, Rusty managed to go on riding. The weather was clear and bitter, full of signs that the boys said meant change—sundogs by day, Northern Lights by night. Even the noontime thermometer never climbed much above twenty. Flushing the stubborn cattle out of coulees and draws, they left behind them a good many cold-storage curses to startle the badgers and coyotes in the first thaw.

Day by day they worked their herd a few miles closer to Horse Camp Coulee; night by night they took turns riding around and around them, beating their arms to keep warm, and after interminable star-struck icy hours stumbled into the sighs and snores and faint warmth of the tent and shook the shoulder of the victim and benefactor who would relieve them. Some days one or another couldn't see to work, and when that happened they all suffered, for Jesse rode with the hands, instead of making camp, and in the icy evening they all had to fall to and shovel off a patch of prairie and set up the tent and fit the sooty lengths of stovepipe through the roof thimble, and anchor themselves to the earth with iron picket pins, the only thing they could drive into the frozen ground.

After an hour or two the stove would soften up the ground close around it, but near the edges and under their beds it never thawed more than just enough to moisten the tarps and freeze the beds fast, so that they pulled them up in the morning with great ripping sounds. The tent walls that they banked with snow to keep out the wind had to be chopped free every morning, and wore their clots and sheets of ice from one day to the next.

That cloth house stamped itself into Rusty's mind and memory. It spoke so plainly of the frailty and impermanence of their intrusion. And yet that frailty, and the implication of danger behind it, was what most nettled and dared and challenged him. Difficult as this job was, it was still only a job, and one done in collaboration with seven others. It called only for endurance; it had very little of the quality of the heroic that he had imagined Saskatchewan enforced upon the men who took its dare. Sometime, somehow, after he had gone through this apprenticeship in the skills of survival, he would challenge the country alone—some journey, some feat, some action that would demand of him every ounce of what he knew he had to give. There would be a real testing, and a real proof, and the certainty ever afterward of what one was. The expectation had no shape in his mind, but he thought of it in the same way he might have thought of sailing a small boat singlehanded across the Atlantic, or making a one-man expedition to climb Everest. It would be something big and it would crack every muscle and nerve and he would have to stand up to it alone, as Henry Kelsey had, wandering two years alone among unheard-of tribes in country not even rumored, or as young Alexander Mackenzie did when he took off from Fort Chippewyan to open the mysterious Northwest and track down the river that carried his name. There were even times when he thought of the wolfer Schulz with near envy. Like him or not, he didn't run in pack, he was of an older and tougher breed, he knew precisely what he was made of and what he could do, and he was the sort from whom one might learn something.

Meantime he was the greenhorn, the outcast tenderfoot of the outfit, and he would remain so until he personally turned a stampeding herd, or rode seventy-five miles and back in twenty-four hours to bring a doctor for someone critically hurt, or plucked somebody from under the horns of a crazy longhorn steer. He nursed his sore shoulder, evidence of his so-far failure to perform heroically, like a grudge that must sometime be settled, or a humiliation that must be wiped out.

The first night, when he had come out and confronted a sinking moon and a rising banner of Northern Lights, and the other one, after his fall, when he had been tempted into a yell of defiance, had several counterparts. Sometimes, riding around the dark mass of the herd, numbly aware of the click of hoofs, the sigh of a cow heaving to her feet, the flurry of movement from a scared or lost calf, the muted tramplings and mooings and lowings, it seemed he guarded all life inside his round, and heard its confusion and discomfort and dismay, and witnessed its unsleeping vigilance against the dangers that might come at it from outside the ritual circle his pony trod. The fact of living, more even than the fact of a job or a duty or the personal need to prove himself fit to call himself man in this country's own terms, bound him to the cattle. The steam that hung above them was relative to the breath that plumed before his own face. It seemed to him a fact of tremendous significance that a cow never closed its eyes in sleep in all its life. These calves were on watch against the world from the time their mothers licked away the membrane from their wet faces until the axe fell between their eyes in Kansas City or Chicago. He felt that nothing living could afford *not* to be on guard, and that the warm blood of men and cattle was in league against the forces of cold and death. Like theirs, his mortality mooed and bellowed, keeping up its courage with its voice or complaining of its discomfort. He sang to the herd, or to himself, and sometimes played them tunes on the harmonica.

They had to be content with a limited repertoire—the mouth organ had been his study for no more than ten days, on the boat coming over—so that he found himself running through a few songs many times. Sometimes, for variety, he rendered, talking aloud to himself, the pony, and the cattle, like a fool or a hermit, certain poems, especially one he had memorized in his first enthusiasm for Canada—a ballad of *coureurs de bois* and of a stranger that walked beside them and left no footprints in the snow. When he had succeeded in scaring himself with ghosts and shadows he might fall back upon a jigging Canuck tune,

> *Rouli roulant, ma boule roulant,*
> *Rouli roulant ma boule.*

But everything he said or played or sang during his hours on the night herd was meant seriously, even soberly, even ritually, for he felt in every deceptive snow-shadow and every pulse of the Northern Lights and every movement of the night wind the presence of something ancient and terrible, to which the brief stir and warmth of life were totally alien, and which must be met head on.

On those miraculously beautiful and murderously cold nights glittering with the green and blue darts from a sky like polished dark metal, when the moon had gone down, leaving the hollow heavens to the stars and the overflowing cold light of the Aurora, he thought he had moments of the clearest vision and saw himself plain in a universe simple, callous, and magnificent. In every direction from their pallid soapbubble of shelter the snow spread; here and there the implacable plain glinted back a spark—the beam of a cold star reflected in a crystal of ice.

He was young and susceptible, but he was probably not far wrong in his feeling that there never was a lonelier land, and one in which men lived more uneasily on sufferance. And he thought he knew the answer to the challenge Saskatchewan tossed him: to be invincibly strong, indefinitely enduring, uncompromisingly self-reliant, to depend on no one, to contain within himself every strength and every skill. There were evenings when he sorted through the outfit, examining models, trying on for fit Ray Henry's iron, Slip's whalebone, Little Horn's leather. Though he had ambitions beyond any of them, he admitted that there was not a man in the outfit who could not teach him something, unless it was Spurlock. And Spurlock, he perceived, was the one on whom he might have to prove himself. The others would tease him, Little Horn and Jesse would pull his leg, Panguingue would thump him in brainless good humor, but Spurlock would push his nasty little nagging persecution until he might have to be smashed. It even occurred to Rusty once or twice that that was exactly what Spurlock wanted: a test of strength. Well, so be it. Riding narrow-eyed, he compared their physical equipment. Spurlock probably had some weight on him, and Rusty had a picture in his mind of big hands, thick wrists. On the other hand, Spurlock must be at least thirty-five, and it was said that for five years he had dealt in a Butte gambling joint, an occupation to soften and weaken a man. Let him come; he might not be half as tough as he sounded or acted; and in any case, let him come.

And then, with singing stopped, and talking stopped, and harmonica stopped, riding slowly, thinking of challenges and anticipating crises and bracing himself against whatever might come, he might have word from his night companions of the prairie, and hear the *yap-yap-yap* and the shivering howl of coyotes, or the faint dark monotone of the wolves. Far more than the cattle or their protectors, they were the proper possessors of the wilderness, and their yelling was a sound more appropriate there than human curses or growls or songs, or the wheezy chords of the mouth organ, and certainly than the half-scared screech of defiance he had let off that one night. The wolves' hunting noises were always far off, back north in the river bottoms. In the eerie clarity of the white nights they seemed to cry from inexpressible distances, faint and musical and clear, and he might have been tempted to think of them as something not earthly at all, as creatures immune to cold and hunger and pain, hunting only for the wolfish joy of running and perhaps not even visible to human eyes, if he had not one afternoon ridden through a coulee where they had bloodied half an acre with a calf.

By day the labor and the cold and the stiffness of many hours in the saddle, the bawling of calves, the crackle and crunch of hoofs and wheels, the reluctant herded movement of two or three hundred cows and calves and six dozen horses, all of whom stopped at every patch of grass blown bare and had to be whacked into moving again. By night the patient circling ride around the herd, the exposure to stars and space and the eloquent speech of the wolves, and finally the crowded sleep.

Nothing between them and the stars, nothing between them and the North Pole, nothing between them and the wolves, except a twelve by sixteen house of cloth so thin that every wind moved it and light showed through it and the shadows of men hulked angling along its slope, its roof so peppered with spark holes that lying in their beds they caught squinting glimpses of the stars. The silence gulped their little disturbances, their little tinklings and snorings and sighs and the muffled noises of discomfort and weariness. The earth and the sky gaped for them like opened jaws; they lay there like lozenges on a tongue, ready to be swallowed.

In spite of his dream of a test hoped-for, met, and passed, the tenderfoot pitied himself, rather. The pain of his arm as he lay on the frozen ground kept him turning sleeplessly. Some nights his fingers throbbed as if he had smashed them with a maul, and his feet ached all night with chilblains. To be compelled to bear these discomforts and these crippling but unvaliant pains he considered privately an outrage.

They told each other that it couldn't last—and yet they half prayed it would, because cold as it was, it was working weather: they could collect and move their herd in it. Nevertheless the boys spoke of change, and said that this early in November, weather like this shouldn't last more than a few days, and that the sundogs meant something for sure. Not at all fond of what they had, they feared what might replace it.

At the end of the eighth day, with a herd of nearly four hundred cows and calves and two dozen bulls, they camped within ten miles of Horse Camp Coulee. The streaked sky of sunset hazed out in dusk. Before Jesse had supper hot the wind was whistling in the tent ropes and leaning on the roof in strange erratic patches, as if animals were jumping on the canvas. In an hour more they were outside trying to keep the tent from blowing away, half a dozen of them hauling the wagon by hand around on the windward side and anchoring the tent to it. The darkness was full of snow pebbles hard and stinging as shot, whether falling or only drifting they couldn't tell, that beat their eyes shut and melted in their beards and froze again. While they were fighting with the tent, Slip came in from the cattle herd and talked with Ray. He did not go back; it would have been risking a man's life to try to keep him riding. They did not discuss what was likely to happen to the cattle, though even Rusty could guess; they crawled into their beds to keep warm, let the fire go out to save fuel, gave at least modified thanks for the fact that they would not have to ride night herd, and because they could do nothing else, they slept.

They slept most of the time for the next two days. When the wind eased off and they dug their way out, the wagon and the tent were surrounded by a horned dune of snow. Snow lay out across the plains in the gray, overcast afternoon, long rippled drifts like an ocean petrified in mid-swell, a dull, expressionless, unlit and unshadowed sea. There was not a sign of the herd; the only horses in sight were the four they had kept miserably tied to the wagon—Jesse's Clydes and two night saddle ponies.

Slip and Little Horn hunted up the horses, far downwind, before dark. They reported bunches of cattle scattered through all the coulees in that direction for a dozen miles. They also found that range steers had drifted in among them during the storm, which meant that all of that separation of whiteface and longhorn and steer and cow and calf had to be gone through again.

The prospect appalled Rusty Cullen; he waited for them to say it couldn't be done, that they would give it up and head for the ranch. It apparently never even occurred to Ray that they might quit. They simply chased and swore and floundered through the drifts, and wore out horses and changed to others, and worked till they couldn't see, and fell into their beds after dark with about a hundred head reassembled. Next day they swung around in a big half circle to the south and east and brought together about a hundred and fifty more.

Sweeping up a few strays as they went, they moved on the third day toward the corrals at Horse Camp Coulee and made half of the ten miles they had to cover. The hard part was about over. They spoke at supper of Molly Henry's dried apple pies, disparaging Jesse's beefsteak and beans. That night, sometime between midnight and dawn, the wind reached down out of the iron north and brought them a new blizzard.

Into a night unfamiliarly black, whirling with snow, a chaos of dark and cold and the howl of a wind that sometimes all but lifted them from their feet, they struggled out stiff and clumsy with sleep, voiceless with outrage, and again anchored themselves to that unspeakable plain. While they fought and groped with ropes in their hands, ducking from the lash of wind and snow, apparitions appeared right among them, stumbled over a guy rope and almost tore the tent down, snorted and bolted blindly into the smother: range horses drifting before the storm. The cowboys cursed them and repaired their damage and got themselves as secure as they could and crawled back into their blankets, knowing sullenly what the drifting horses meant. When they dug out of this one they would have lost their herd again.

Jesse had started the fire as soon as it seemed clear that the tent would not go down. When Rusty had got back into his bed next to Buck, with Panguingue's feet jammed for a headboard against his skull, he could see the glow through the draft door and feel his stung face loosening in the warmth. The canvas roof bucked and strained, slacked off, stiffened in a blast. The wind came through in needles of cold. It was close to morning; he could make out the faint shapes inside the tent. He waited for Ray to say something—something to console them, perhaps, for their failure and their bad luck—but no one spoke at all. They lay appraising the turmoil half seen and half heard on the straining roof. Finally, after several minutes, Jesse said, "Anybody feel like a cup of coffee?"

Only then did Ray speak. His hoarse, ironic whisper croaked across the tent, "Looks like you boys could have the day off. Sleep in, if you want."

"Sleep!" Ed Spurlock said. "How could anybody sleep when he thinks where them God damn cows are going?"

"Just the same you better sleep," Ray whispered. "You'll need your rest, boy."

"You going to try rounding them up again?"

Ray said, "We're in this business to raise calves, not fertilize some prairie with their carcasses."

"*Jesus!*" Spurlock said. He rocked his head back and forth on his rolled mackinaw, glaring at the tent roof with eyes that shone oilily in the glimmer from the firebox. The wind took hold of the tent and shook it, testing every rope; they waited till the blast let go again. "You can't drive cows in this kind of weather, Ray," Spurlock said.

"I know it," Ray whispered. "That's why you get the day off."

"I bet you we end up by leaving the whole herd to scatter."

"We do, we'll lose ever' damn calf," Ray said. His face turned and craned toward Spurlock, above and across from him. His indomitable croak said, "I don't aim to lose any, if work'll save 'em."

"No, I can see," Spurlock said. "You might lose a few of us though."

Ray laughed through his nose. "Why, Ed," he said, "you sound like you thought you was more valuable than a calf."

"I'd kind of like some coffee, myself," old Jesse said. "Don't anybody else feel thataway?"

"Shut up!" said Buck's voice from under the blankets. He had a capacity for always sounding furious, even when he was talking through four layers of wool. "Shut up and let a guy get some sleep."

Panguingue produced a few exaggerated snores.

There was a brief silence. The wind gripped the tent, fell away, pounced once more; they could hear it whining and ricocheting off the guy ropes. "Good God," Ed Spurlock said restlessly, "listen to the God damn wind blow."

"I think I'll just put the pot on anyhow, long as we got that fire," Jesse's soft voice said. Rusty heard the stiff creak of his bedroll tarp and the fumbling sounds as he got on his boots. There was a grunt, and Spurlock said savagely, "God damn it to hell, Jesse, watch out where you put your feet!"

"Don't leave your face hanging out, then," Jesse said. "How can I see your face in this dark? I been huntin' for ten minutes with both hands, and I just now found my ass."

"Step on me once more and you'll find it in a sling," Spurlock said. "Why can't you stay in bed? There's nothing to get up for."

"Yes there is," Jesse said. "Coffee."

His shape reared up against the graying canvas; when he opened the lid the glow from the stove illuminated his intent face with the white bristles on cheeks and chin, and the mustache drooping in a smooth oxbow. This, Rusty thought, was all familiar to Jesse. He must have done this same thing, camped in the same brutal kind of weather, a hundred times, with Indians, with *métis hivernants*, with hide hunters, with wagon trains hauling supplies into the Montana camps, with cattle outfits like this one. His relation to the country was almost as simple as that of the wolves; no matter how fast the province changed, it remained to Jesse merely a few known forms of hardship, a known violence of weather, one or two simple but irreplaceable skills. He had the air, standing ruminatively above his stove, of a man who could conceive of no evil that a cup of hot coffee or a beefsteak fried in flour would not cure.

Daylight came as dusk and stayed that way. They dozed, and when the fire was up high for cooking they took advantage of the warmth to play poker or blackjack. When anyone had to go outside he took a look at the horses, which they had picketed to give them a little more chance to move around and keep warm, but which crowded close up against the wagon for the little shelter it gave them. Morning and evening someone hung on their noses a nosebag of their limited oat supply.

Their wood was running low too; they had been depending on getting fuel from the willows in Horse Camp Coulee. After meals they had to let the fire die, and then if they played cards they passed around a lighted candle to warm their hands by. When even that got too cold they dug down under their blankets to sleep or think. Talk flared up like matches and went out again; they cocked their ears to the howl of the wind, remoter as the tent snowed in. Once or twice one of them went out and carefully cleared the worst of the snow off the roof while the rest, inside, watched with concern the sausage-tight canvas which a careless shovel might easily slit, leaving them exposed to the storm like an out-turned nest of mice. Every hour or so Ray Henry, taciturn and expressionless, took a look outside.

When he had got his hands well warmed under the blankets, Rusty played the harmonica. There were more requests than he could gratify, with a heavy favoritism for old Red River tunes which they tried to teach him by whistling or humming. If he quit, with his hands too numb to feel the fingers and his chapped lips sore from the sliding of the little honeycomb back and forth across them, they urged him for a while, and then cursed him languidly and gave up. The afternoon waned; they yawned; they lay resting.

Once the notebook in his shirt pocket crunched as Rusty turned over, and he took it out and amused himself for a while reading the journal entries he had made. There was nothing since his catalog of information about the Stonepile Camp, but before that there was a very windy and prize-essay series of notations. He had put them down in the first place as colorful items to be incorporated into letters home: they expected him not to write very often, and he would oblige them; but they expected him, when he did write, to fill pages with cowboys and Indians and wild game and the adventures and observations of a well-educated young gentleman in the North American wilderness. In this too he had set out to oblige them. He read what he had had to say about the ranch, and the thumbnail sketches he had made of some of the cowboys, and the lyrical flights he had gone into during the days of perfect Indian Summer hay-making weather that preceded the first storm—only the night before they had set out on this belated roundup. He could imagine the family all around his mother as she read, and he cocked an inner ear to the sound of his own prose describing the apelike Panguingue with his good nature and his total disregard for cleanliness, and wry little birdy Slippers with his sore feet, as if he had walked all the way from Texas; even on roundup he wore no boots like the rest of them but elastic-sided slippers under his overshoes. Rusty told them Slip was the best bronc rider in Saskatchewan, which may have been going it a bit strong, and about how Buck kept a row of tobacco tins on the two-by-four above his bunk, with all his smaller private effects filed away in them in neat and labeled order. He described, with the proper tone of sober appraisal and respect, Ray Henry and his new wife, whom he had brought from Malta, Montana, in a buckboard, a hundred and twenty miles across country, for a wedding trip. Rusty had loaded that part of the journal with data on the country, much of it, as he saw now, in error. It was the sort of stuff which, written as a letter, would surely set his younger brother to itching, and produce another emigration from the family, but it seemed false and shrilly enthusiastic and very, very young when he read it over in the tent, while a frozen guy rope outside, within three feet of his ear, hummed like a great struck cable.

"What you got there, Rusty?" Little Horn said. "Something to read?"

"No," he said. "Oh no, just an old notebook."

"Notebook?" Spurlock said.

"Just . . . notes, don't you know," Rusty said. He was frantic with the notion that they would sit on him and take it away from him and read in it what he had said about them. If they tried it he would die fighting. He put it in his shirt pocket and buttoned it down. "Things I wanted to remember to put in letters home," he said.

"All about the cow country and the cattle business, uh?" Little Horn said.

"More or less."

"She's a real good business," Little Horn said. "You ought to think about her, Rusty." Staring at the roof, his red nose one of a half dozen projecting toward the lashed and laboring canvas, he plucked a thread from the frayed edge of his blanket and drew it dreamily between his front teeth. "Young fella from the old country could do a lot worse," he said. "There's this Englishman over on Medicine Lodge Coulee, kind of a remittance-man colony they got over there, he was tellin' me about cattle ranchin' one time. He said there was millions in it. All you do, you just get some cows and a few bulls, and you turn 'em out on the range. Say you start with a hundred cows. You get a hundred calves the first year, and fifty of them are cows and fifty you make into steers. Next year you got a hundred and fifty cows and they give you a hundred and fifty calves, and you make seventy-five steers and keep the seventy-five cows, and that builds your breeding herd to two hundred and twenty-five. That year you get two hundred and twenty-five calves, and by now you're sellin' your two-year-old and three-year-old steers, and your herd keeps growin' and you keep sellin' the bull calves, and that's all they is to her. He had it all mapped out. You ought to talk to him, Rusty."

"I'll look into it the first chance I get," Rusty said. "I've been inquiring around for a good opportunity."

"You do that," Little Horn said. "If I didn't have me this job here with Ray, I'd do somethin' about it myself. There ain't a thing to her. Once you get your herd and start them cows to calfin', all you do is set back and count the dollars rollin' in.

"They'll tell you: mange. Hell, they ain't nothin' to mange. All you got to do about that, you dip 'em twice a year. You get yourself one of them steam boilers and a tank, and you lay in some sulphur and so on. And you dig yourself a big hole in the ground, maybe a hundred feet long, say, and thirty wide, and at one end you build a couple corrals, one big one to hold maybe a couple hundred head and the other a little one to take a dozen or so. From this little one you build a chute that leads down into the hole. At the other end of the hole you make a slatted slope out of planks for the cows to climb out on, and a couple drippin' pens where the ones that has been dipped can stand, and under those pens you dig a ditch so the dip that runs off them can run back into the vat. It ain't anything, hardly. If you got ten or fifteen hands around it'll only take you a couple-three weeks' hard work altogether to build this rig.

"Then you bring your stock into the big corral, see, and feed 'em out a few at a time into the little corral and on into the chute, and on both sides of the vat you put guys with long poles with a yoke onto them, and they get the yoke over these cattle as they come down the chute and duck 'em clear under. Then you prod 'em on through the vat and up the slope and into the drippin' pens and you're done with that bunch.

"They'll tell you it's lots of work. Shucks. You got, say, ten thousand head to dip, like we would on the T-Down, and you got maybe twelve men in the outfit. You can do a dozen ever' twenty minutes, thirty-six an hour, three hundred and sixty in a ten-hour day, thirty-six hundred in ten days. You can get the whole herd through in three or four weeks, if you can get the inspector there when you want him. They'll tell you it's hell to catch the inspector, and hard to keep the herd together that long, and hard to keep the sulphur mixture strong enough and the right temperature, and a lot like that, but it ain't nothing to bother a man. Some people would talk down anything.

"Or they'll tell you it's dangerous. Shoot! Suppose one of them steers does get on the peck when he's pushed under and gets his eyes full of sulphur, what can he do? He can thrash around in the vat, maybe, and drowned himself or some other steer, or maybe he climbs out and chases you up onto the barn, or he scrambles back into the corral and gets them to millin' there till they break something down, but that ain't only a little delay. Even if some old ringy longhorn catches you before you can climb out of the corral, what can he do to you? His horns is so wide he just rams you against the fence with his forehead and holds you there till somebody twists his tail or spits Bull Durham in his eye and pulls him off, and there you are good as ever, maybe bruised up some is all.

"No, sir," Little Horn said, pulling his thread back and forth, "it's a mistake to listen to these calamity howlers about what a tough business the cow business is. Mange, that's only a sample of how they exaggerate. They'll tell you: wolves. Wolves! They won't pick off more'n one calf in ten or twenty all winter long. Sure three or four of them will pull down a cow sometimes, get her by the hind leg and a flank and pull her over and pile on, but mostly it's just calves. Say you start with two thousand head in the fall, you still got eighteen hundred in the spring. And if you want to, you can hire somebody like this Schulz to wolf your range."

"Schulz!" Buck said from down under. "I wonder if he's et his boy yet?"

"Only cost you ten dollars a scalp," Little Horn said. "If he puts out poison baits, course you might lose a few dogs. Sure a wolf is hard to poison and he's too smart to step in a trap or come within gunshot very often, but that don't have to bother you. There's other ways of handlin' wolves. You just lay around and keep an eye open and when you catch one out on the flats you can run him down on a horse. I did it once myself. I had me a little old pony that could run, and I come right up on that old white wolf and run over him. I missed him that first time, somehow, and had to come over him again, and I missed him again, but I kep' tryin'. This wolf can't get away—he's down there under the pony's feet somewhere duckin' and snarlin'. I'd of had him sure if the pony hadn't of stepped in a hole. The wolf run off then and I couldn't chase him. I was out quite a few miles, and after I shot the horse I had me quite a walk carryin' the saddle, but that experience taught me quite a bit about runnin' down wolves, and I know how it's done. I'll show you sometime, if you want."

"Oh, I say, thanks," Rusty said.

"Old Rusty, I bet he figures just like your other Englishman," Spurlock said. "Ain't it the fact, Rusty? You come out here thinking you'd get yourself a few thousand acres and a herd of cows and be a lord of the manor like Dan Tenaille, uh?"

"That's right," Rusty said. "Just now, I'm out here learning the business first hand from the experts."

"Or did you *have* to come out?" Spurlock said. "You're a remittance man too, ain't you? Tell us the story of how you happened to leave England. I bet it'd be interesting. Help pass the time, don't you know."

"I'm afraid you'd find it a bit dull."

"A bit dull?" Spurlock said heartily. "Not at all, lad, not at all. Come on, give us your reasons for trailing out to the cow country."

They were not a talking bunch, and so far as he knew they had not discussed him. He was too common a phenomenon. Unless he took pains to prove himself otherwise, any young Englishman in that country was assumed to be the second son, third son, scapegrace son, of a baronet, a KCB, a shooting partner of Edward VII. Or he was a cashiered guardsman or disgraced country vicar. Rusty was none of those, but it seemed unnecessary to insist. He said only, "I'm afraid my reasons wouldn't be as colorful as yours."

He put into his voice just the quantity of sneer that would

make Spurlock rise up without realizing precisely where he was stung. Or perhaps the sneer did not do it at all, perhaps Spurlock was only bored, uncomfortable, irritable, ready to pluck any little thread that would ravel, quarrelsome out of no motive except tedium. If that was it, fine; let him come. And there he came, rearing up on one elbow and throwing across the tent a literary badman look as if he thought he was wearing black gloves and black guns like a villain in *The Virginian*. "What do you mean by that, exactly?"

From the side, Ray Henry's whisper said, "The kid's not crowding you any, Ed."

"I can tell when I'm crowded," Spurlock said.

"Pull in your elbows," Ray whispered, amused. "Then you'll have more room."

Spurlock lay down again. "Little English punks," he said. "Coming out pretending to be cowhands."

Rusty looked at Ray, but Ray only smiled. The boy said, fairly hotly, "The cows can't tell the difference."

"No," Spurlock said, "no, but a man sure can."

"I haven't heard any *men* discussing it."

Once more he reared up on his elbow. "Is its little arm sore?" he said. "Got piled, did it?"

"How are its little sore eyes?" Rusty said. Out of nothing, out of nowhere, as random and unprepared for as an August whirlwind kicking up a dust, Spurlock had produced the quarrel he evidently wanted. Rusty was angry enough to take him on, arm or no arm. He pretended to himself that he was annoyed with Ray when the foreman whispered equably, "In about a second I'm kickin' both you quarrelsome bastards out in the snow."

Rusty lay ready, smoldering, waiting for Spurlock to say something else that could not be borne, or to rise and stalk outside where it would be necessary to go out and fight him. But Spurlock did not move or speak; he only breathed through his nose in so eloquent and contemptuous a way that Rusty had to hold himself back from springing over and smashing him. The wind slammed against their canvas roof in a furious gust. Against some rope or edge or corner it howled like a wolf, and then trailed off to the steady whisper and rush again.

"They'll tell you," Little Horn said dreamily, "they'll say to you it's terrible hard work. Why, God damn, now, you just can't pay attention to that. How long we been on this-here roundup? Since first of May, more or less? And it's only November now. And they'll tell you it gets cold, but where would you find a nicer, more comfortable little tent than this one, if we only had some wood?"

Jesse crawled out and stood stretching in the narrow space among the mussed beds. Rusty noticed that he was careful to stay clear of Ed Spurlock's blankets. "Well," he said, "time for a little grub?"

Ray went past Jesse and pulled the flap aside and looked out. Beyond him the horizontal blast streaked with snow dipped and swirled; flakes settled and whirled away again; there was a curved drift building up at the tent corner. Ray's back looked bulky and solid; he was a powerful man, single-minded and devoted. A little hollow in the solar plexus from the nearness of a fight, Rusty had a wry feeling that if Spurlock and he had started something, and the foreman wanted to interfere, he could have thrashed them both. But what his hunched back and his bent head reminded Rusty of really was the burden he bore. He was foreman, he wore responsibility for both men and cattle, and he had left his bride of less than a month at the ranch house with only a crippled handy man for company. Rusty did not envy Ray, but he respected him a great deal. He wanted to do well for him; he was ashamed of having had to be reprimanded along with Spurlock. The foreman dropped the flap and came back and sat down.

"They'll tell you," Little Horn said, endless and ironic and contemplative, "they'll say, all that ridin' and brandin' and weanin' and nuttin' and chasin' cows up and down the hills and dales. How else would you want a cowpuncher to spend his time? He don't have any work to do, he just gets himself into trouble playin' cyards and fightin' and chasin' women. Lots better for him to be out in a nice tent like this, camped out comfortable in some blizzard."

Sometime before the gray afternoon howled itself out, Ray Henry shouldered into his sheepskin and went outside. The rest lay in their blankets, which they had inhabited too long for their blankets' good or their own, in their postures that were like the postures of men fallen in war. Panguingue sprawled with his drawn-up knees wide, his whiskered face glimmering a vacant grin straight upward. Little Horn and Buck were unexpected angles of arms and legs, Slip lay curled as if around a mortal body wound. Spurlock had locked his hands under the back of his head and crossed his knees under the covers. They listened to the undiminished wind. After what may have been ten minutes Jesse rose and said he guessed he'd take a look at the Clydes. He followed his jet of white breath outside, and they lay on.

Their cloth house shook, and gave way, and shuddered stiff and tight again. They heard the whistle and scream go flying through and away, and in a lull Buck said, "This one's the worst one yet." They lay considering this for quite a long time. At last Rusty heard the sound of feet, and with a relief that astonished him he cried, "Here they are!"

But no one entered. The wind pounded through and over and past. It had a curving sound; it dipped to the ear like telegraph wires to the eye. Everyone in the tent was listening for the steps Rusty had announced. At last Spurlock grumbled, "Just fawncy." Panguingue blurted a laugh.

"Christ a'mighty!" Slip said abruptly, and snapped nimble as a monkey out of his bed. He was stepping in his slippers across Ray Henry's tarp when the flap opened and Ray and Jesse stooped in on a flurry of snow. Slippers sat quietly down again on his blankets. His leathery, deeply lined, big-nosed face said nothing. Neither did any of the other smudged and whiskered faces around the tent. But they were all sitting up or half propped on their elbows; the concern that had moved Slip had been a fear in all of them. In silence they watched Ray throw down beside the cold stove three or four round cake-like chunks of ice. Rusty reached across and picked up a frozen cowchip.

"Are we burning ice now?"

With a wipe of a bare hand around on his wet, beef-red face, the foreman said, "We may be lucky to have that to burn, it's drifting pretty deep all over."

"Still from the northwest?" Buck asked.

"Oh dear," said Little Horn. "All those poor little calves and their mamas. They'll be clear the hell and gone down to Wood Mountain."

"Or else they'll be piled up in some draw," Ray said.

"You think it's pretty bad, then," Rusty said—a small, inconsequent, intrusive voice of ignorance and greenness that he himself heard with shame and dismay.

"Yes, kid," Ray said. "I think it's pretty bad."

They ebbed away into silence. With only a few sticks of wood left Jesse gave them no more for supper than warm gravy poured over frozen biscuits; not even coffee. Part of the stove, while the gravy was warming, held two of the cowchips that Ray had kicked up from under the snow, and the smell of wetted and baking manure flavored their supper. But at least the cakes dried out enough so that Jesse could use them for the breakfast fire.

The single candle gave a blotted light. When they were all still Rusty saw the humps of bedrolls fuming like a geyser basin with their eight breaths, until Little Horn said, "Well, nighty-night, kids," and blew out the candle. The wind seemed to come down on their sudden darkness with such violence that in the cold tent they lay tensely, afraid something would give. Both Slip and Little Horn had pulled their goatskin chaps over their beds for extra cover. Rusty's icy hands were folded into his armpits; he wore all his clothes except sheepskin and boots. He blew his breath into the air, moved his sore shoulder experimentally, smelled his own stale nest, thinking Holy Mother, if my people could see me now! There was a brief, vivid picture of rescuers in the spring reverently uncovering eight huddled figures, identifying each one, folding the tarp back over the frozen face. His head was full of vague heroisms related to Commodore Peary and the North Pole.

Once the thought popped whole and astonishing into his head: I might, except for one or two decisions made in excitement and stuck to through tears and argument, be sleeping in my old room right now, and if I opened my eyes I would see the model of the *Kraken* hanging from the ceiling like a ship of thanksgiving in a Danish church. Except for the excitement that his father thought wild whimsy and his mother thought heartlessness, he might be getting his exercise these days pushing a punt up and down the Cher, disturbing the swans (Swans! From here they sounded fabulous as gryphons), or drinking too much port with sporty undergraduates from his college, or sitting on some cricket pitch, or (assuming he *hadn't* chosen Oxford and the family's program) he might be guiding the tiller of the yawl with his backside while he shouted questions, jeers, comments, or other conversation at sailors leaning over the stern rails of old rustpots anchored in the stream off Spithead.

The fact that he was here in a tent on the freezing Saskatchewan plains, that one decision rashly made and stubbornly stuck to had taken him not only out of the university, out of home, out of England, but out of a whole life and culture that had been assumed for him, left him dazed. A good job he didn't have much chance to think, or he might funk it yet, and run straight home with his tail tucked. He was appalled at the effectiveness of his own will.

A numbness like freezing to death stole through him gradually, Panguingue restored him to wakefulness with a kick in the head, and he cursed Panguingue with a freedom he would not have adopted toward anyone else in the outfit. Sometime during or just after the flurry of profane protest he fell asleep.

Solitary flutes, songs from the Vienna woods, chirpings and twitterings so that he opened his eyes thinking *Birds?* and heard the awakening sounds of the outfit, and old Jesse whistling with loose lips while he stood over the stove. He lifted a can and tipped it in a quick gesture; the tent filled with the smell of kerosene. Jesse hobbled about in his boots like an old crone. His right knee crooked upward, there was a swoop and a snap, and a match popped into flame across his tight seat. The stove *whoofed* out a puff of smoke. The lids clanged on. Fire gleamed through the cracks in the ash door and Jesse shoved the coffee pot against the stovepipe. Looking, Rusty saw that Ray, Slip, and Buck were missing.

He sat up. "I say! The wind's died!"

"You say, hey?" Jesse said.

Rusty hustled to the door and looked out. Deep tracks went through the drift that curved all around them; the sky was palest blue, absolutely clear. Ray was trotting the Clydes up and down a fifty-foot trampled space, getting them warm. Their breasts and rumps and legs were completely coated in ice. Buck and Slip already had saddles on the night ponies. Whatever had been brown in the landscape had disappeared. There were no scraggly patches of bare grass in the snow waves, but packed, rippled white ran off into the southeast where the sun was just rising. He could almost see the plain move as if a current ran strongly toward where the sun squatted on the rim and sent its dazzle skipping across the million little wave crests into his eyes. Spurlock, looking over his shoulder, swore foully. "Here goes for some more God damn snowblindness." He stepped past Rusty and blew his nose with his fingers, first one nostril, then the other. Rusty shouted over to Ray, "Working weather!"

"Yeah." He laughed his dry laugh through his nose. "Come here and curry some of the ice out of these studs."

"Uh-huh!" Spurlock said behind Rusty, with I-told-you-so emphasis. The boy stared at him. "Working weather!" Spurlock said. "Jesus Christ! I guess."

His guess was right. Within minutes of the time Rusty woke he was working; they paused only long enough to bolt a steak and gulp scalding coffee and warm their hands over the fire; their last wood and all the cowchips had gone into it. Before they had more than spread their palms to the beautiful heat, Slip and Buck came in with the horse herd.

"Jesse," Ray said, "you better tear down here and get loaded and beat it on a beeline for Horse Camp. If we ain't there when you get there, which we won't be, you can improve your time and warm your blood gettin' in wood, and there ain't any such thing as too much. The rest of you is goin' to round up every cow within fifteen miles downwind, and we're going to put them all in the corrals at Horse Camp before we sleep any more. So pick you a pony with some bottom."

They looked at the shaggy, scrawny, long-maned and long-tailed herd picking at the wisps of a few forkfuls of hay that the boys had thrown out. There was not a pony among them whose ribs did not show plainly under the rough winter hair. Here and there one stood spraddled, head hanging, done in, ready to fall.

"Boneracks," Little Horn said. "Some of them ponies ain't goin' to make it, Boss."

"Then we got to leave them," Ray said. "They can maybe make out, poor as they are, but unless we get a chinook this is starvin' time for cattle."

They saddled and rode out, Ray, Slip, Panguingue, and Rusty to the southeast, straight into the sun, Spurlock and Buck and Little Horn to the northeast. They would pinch everything in to the middle and then swing and bring them back. The tent was already coming down as they rode off.

They rode a long way before they raised any cattle. When they did, down in a draw, they were humped in the deep snow, making no effort to get out. They stood and bellowed; they moved as if their blood had frozen thick, and they had among them range steers, including a few longhorns, which the boys did not want at all but had no time to cut out. They threw them all into a bunch, and attended by an intensely black and unlikely looking crow, rode on into the diamond glitter, gradually swinging eastward so that they could get some relief by ducking their heads and pulling their hats clear down on the sun side. Ray kept them pushing hard through the difficult going, knee high sometimes, hock high the next moment, crusted just enough to hold the horse's weight for a split second before he broke down through. It was hard enough in the saddle; it must have been a good deal worse under it.

"Got to hustle," Ray said. "For some reason I'm gettin' so I don't trust the damn weather." They fanned out, riding wide. Far north, across a spread of flats and one or two shallow coulees whose depressions could hardly be seen in the even glare, the black dots that were Spurlock and Little Horn and Buck were strung out across a mile or so of snow. They headed in toward the center of their loop every sad whiteface whose red hide showed. The cattle bellowed, blinking white eyelashes, and they moved reluctantly, but they moved. The crow flapped over, following companionably, flying off on some investigation of his own and returning after a few minutes to coast over and cock his wise eye down and caw with laughter to hear them talk.

About noon, far to the south and east of where they had camped, they came to the river, angling down from the northwest in its shallow valley. The willows along the banks looked thin as a Chinaman's whiskers, hardly more than weeds, but they held a surprising number of cattle, which the outfit flushed out by the dozens and scores and hazed, plunging and ducking and blindly swinging back until a horse blocked them or a rope cut across their noses, up onto the flats. They had everything in that herd: whiteface, shorthorn, longhorn, all sorts of crosses; steers, cows, bulls, calves; T-Down, Circle Diamond, Turkey Track. Ray pointed some out to Rusty when they rested their ponies for a minute on the flat and let Slip chase a half-dozen whiteface yearlings back into the bottoms. "The Seventy-Six," he said. "Their range is way up by Gull Lake, on the CPR. They've drifted twenty-five miles."

Whatever they were, whoever they belonged to, if they could not be easily cut out the riders swept them in and drove them westward, pushing them without a pause toward Horse Camp. The afternoon changed from blue-white to lavender. The crow had left them—disgusted, Rusty thought, that they never stopped to eat and threw away no scraps. The trampled waste of snow bloomed for a minute or two a pure untroubled rose, and the sun was gone as if it had stepped in a hole. Gray-blue dusk, grateful to their seared eyes, lay in every slightest hollow; the snowplain was broken with unexpected irregularities. The "drag" of cows and calves slowed, poked along, stopped and had to be cursed and flogged into starting. Their ponies, poor boneracks, plodded gamely, and if a cow tried to break away or swing back they had to gather themselves like a tired swimmer taking one last stroke. Their breath was frozen all over them, stirrups and overshoes were enameled in ice; Rusty could hear his pony wheezing in his pipes, and his skinny ewe neck was down. He stumbled in the trodden snow.

It grew dark, and they went on, following Jesse's track, or whatever track it was that Ray kept, or no track at all, but only his wild-animal's sense of direction. The faint eruption of color in the west was gone; and then as the sky darkened, the stars were there, big and frosty and glittering, bright as lamps, and Rusty found the Dipper and Cassiopeia and the Pole Star, his total astronomy. He moved in his saddle, lame and numb, his face stiff, his shoulder aching clear down across his collarbone into his chest. Ahead of him, a moving blur on the snow, the herd stumbled and clicked and mooed, the joints of their random longhorns

cracked, the traveling steam went up. Off to his right he heard
Buck trying to sing—a sound so strange, revelatory, and forlorn
that he had to laugh, and startled himself with the voiceless croak
he produced.

How much farther? Up above, the sky was pure; the Northern
Lights were beginning to flare and stretch. He heard his old
friend the wolf hunting down the river valleys and coulees of his
ordained home and speaking his wolfish mind to the indifferent
stars. Lord God, how much longer? They had been in the saddle
since six, had eaten nothing since then. Neither horse nor rider
could take much more of this. But nobody said, We can stop now.
Nobody said, We'll camp here. They couldn't, obviously. Jesse
had taken their bubble of shelter God knew how many more
empty miles to Horse Camp. He thought to himself, with a qualm
of panic, My God, this is *desperate*. What if we don't find him?
What if a horse should give clear out?

He gave his pony clumsy mittened pats; he enlisted its loyalty
with words; it plodded and stumbled on.

Eventually there was a soft orange bloom of light, and shouts
cut through the luminous murk, and as he stopped, confused,
Ray Henry came riding from his left and they crowded the
cattle into a tighter mass. Over their moving backs and the
sounds of their distress and irritation he heard poles rattle; someone ki-yi-ed. Ray pushed his horse against the rear cattle and in
his almost-gone whisper drove and urged them on. They moved,
they broke aside, they were turned back; the mass crawled ahead,
tedious, interminable, a toss and seethe of heads and horns,
until suddenly it had shrunk and dwindled and was gone, and
Panguingue was down in the snow, ramming gate poles home.
The whole world smelled of cow.

They sat there all together, stupid with cold and fatigue; they
dismounted like skeletons tied together with wire. Ray croaked,
"Let's see if Jesse ain't got a spare oat or two for these ponies," and
they walked toward the wagon and the bloom of the tent. The
air, which had been bright at sunset and in the first hour of dark,
was blurred as if a fog were rising from the snow; beyond the
tent the faint shadow of the coulee fell away, but the other side
was misted out. Rusty's eyes were so longingly on Jesse's shadow
as he hopped around the stove, obviously cooking, that he fell

over the pile of willows stacked by the wagon: Jesse had not wasted his time; there was cooking wood for a week.

"Dad," Ray called, "you got any oats? These ponies are about done." The white head appeared in the flap, a hand with a fork in it held the canvas back, the soft old voice said, "I got a couple-three bushel left, I guess. That has to hold the Clydes and the night horses till we get back to the ranch."

"They'll have to get along," Ray said. "I'm afraid we're going to lose some ponies anyway. They just don't have the flesh for this kind of a job."

Rusty stood with the reins in his hand, letting Jesse and Ray heave the oat bag out of the wagon. The tent with its bloom of light and its smell of frying was a paradise he yearned for as he had never yearned for anything, but he had to stand there and care for the horse first, and he hated the poor beast for its dependence. It was no tireder than he was. Nevertheless Ray's was an inescapable example. He unsaddled and threw the saddle into the wagon; he tramped a little hollow in the snow and poured out a quart or two of oats and pulled his pony's bridle and let him drop his head to them. One after the other the outfit did the same. After what seemed an hour Rusty found the tent flap and crept in. The little stove was red hot; the air was full of smoke. Jesse had unrolled their beds for them. Rusty stepped over Buck and fell full length and shut his eyes. What little strength he had left flowed out of him and was soaked up; his bones and veins and skin held nothing but tiredness and pain.

Jesse hopped around, juggling pans, going on cheerfully. He had thought by God they were never going to get in. Chopped wood till he like to bust his back. (Yeah, said somebody, *you* did a day's work!) Horse herd come all the way with him, right along behind the pilot. Those few scraps of hay the other day made tame ponies of the whole bunch. Looks like you guys got a pretty good herd of calves, considering. Anybody like a cup of coffee now?

"By God," he said after a short silence, "you fellers look *beat*."

And after another little silence in which nobody spoke, but somebody groaned or grunted, Jesse said, "Here, I don't reckon coffee has got enough nourishment for the occasion."

Beside Rusty, Buck rolled over. Rusty opened his eyes. Slip and

Little Horn had rolled over too. Ray was sitting on his bed, holding a quart of whisky, shaking his head. "Jesse," he said, "by God, remind me to raise your wages."

Their common emotion while Ray worked on the cork was reverence. They sat or lay around in a ring, as bleary a crew as ever ate with its fingers or blew its nose with the same all-purpose tool, and they watched each motion of his thick wrist and big dirty hand. None of them had shaved for more than two weeks; they had all, except possibly Buck, lost any right to browbeat Panguingue about his filthiness. They felt—or at least Rusty did—that they had endured much and labored incredibly. He wondered, as the greenest hand there, how well he had done, and hoped he had done at least passably, and knew with unaccustomed humility that he could not have done more. Considering everything, the three hundred odd cattle they had finally brought to the Horse Camp corrals were an achievement. The work still to be done, the separating and weaning, and the driving of calves and bulls to the home ranch, could only be trifling after what they had been through.

The stove's heat beat on their bearded red faces, the candles gleamed in their bloodshot eyes. They watched Ray Henry's thick hands, and when the cork slipped out of the neck with a soft *pok* some of them smiled involuntarily, and Panguingue giggled, a high, falsetto sound that set off another round of smiles and made Jesse say, "Listen at old Pan, he sounds like a jack after a mare."

Ray held the bottle to the light and looked through it; he shook it and watched the bead rise. He was like a priest before an altar. He would not hurry this. "Well," he said at last, "here's looking at you, boys," and tipped the bottle to his blackened mouth. They watched the contents gurgle around the spark of candle that lived inside the amber bottle. He let the bottle down. "Whah!" he said. "Kee-rist!" and wiped the neck politely with the heel of his palm and passed it to Slip, whose bed lay beside his next to the wall. The smell of whisky cut through the smoke of the tent; they sat like Indians in the medicine lodge and passed the ceremonial vessel around, and each, as he finished, wiped the neck carefully with his palm. Slip to Jesse, Jesse to Little Horn, Little Horn to Spurlock, Spurlock to Panguingue. Panguingue drank and shook his head and wiped the neck once and started to pass the bottle and then, as if not satisfied, wiped it again. Rusty loved him for it, he loved them all; he felt that he had never known so mannerly a group of men. Buck took the bottle from Panguingue, and from Buck it came to the greenhorn, its neck flavored with all their seven mouths and hands. He raised it to his mouth and let its fire wash down his throat and felt it sting in his cracked lips. His eyes watered. He lowered the bottle and choked down a cough, and as he passed the bottle back to Ray and talk broke out all at once, he took advantage of the noise and cleared his throat and so was not shamed.

"Well, Jesse," Ray said, "what do you think? Want to save that little-bitty dab?"

"Why, I can't see it'd be much good from now on," Jesse said.

They passed it around again, and their tongues were loosened. They told each other how cold it had been and how hard they had worked. Jesse had made up a raisin-and-rice pudding, practically a pailful. It was pure ambrosia; they ate it all and scraped the kettle, and for a few minutes after supper Rusty even roused up enough strength to get out the harmonica. There was not the slightest remnant left of the irritability they had felt with one another in the snowed-in time; the boy could feel how they had been welded and riveted into a society of friends and brothers. Little Horn sang some filthy verses of "The Old Chisholm Trail." Spurlock supplied some even filthier ones from "Johnny McGraw." The whole bunch joined in a couple of songs.

Then all at once they were done in again. The talk dropped away, Rusty put the harmonica in his pocket. They went outside and walked a few steps from the tent and stood in a row and made water, lifting their faces into the night air that was mistier than ever, and warmer than any night since they had left the ranch.

"I don't know," Ray said, sniffing for wind. "I don't quite like the looks of the sky."

"Oh but hell," they said. "Feel how warm it is."

He gave in doubtfully to their optimism. The mild air might mean snow, but it also might mean a chinook coming in, and that was the best luck they could hope for. There was not enough grass bare, even out on the flats, to give the cattle a chance to feed. Rusty had never seen or felt a chinook, but he was so positive this was the birth of one that he offered to bet Little Horn and Panguingue a dollar each that it was a chinook coming. They refused, saying they did not want to hoodoo the weather. Ray remarked that such weather as they had had couldn't be hoodooed any worse. They kicked the snow around, smelling the night air soft in their faces; it smelled like a thaw, though the snow underfoot was still as dry and granular as salt. Every minute or so a hungry calf bawled over in the corral.

"Well," Ray said, "maybe this is our break."

Rusty hardly heard him. His eyes were knotted, the nerves and veins snarled together, the lids heavy with sleep. Back inside the tent there was a brief flurry of movement as they crawled in. Somebody cursed somebody else feebly for throwing his chaps across him. He heard the fire settle in the stove; after a minute or two he was not sure whether it was the stove or the first whiffling of some sleeper. Then he was asleep too, one of the first.

But not even his dead tiredness could lift from him the habits of the last ten days. In his dreams he struggled against winds, he felt the bite of cold, he heard the clamor of men and animals and he knew that he had a duty to perform, he had somehow to shout "Here!" as one did at a roll call, but he was far down under something, struggling in the dark to come up and to break his voice free. His own nightmared sounds told him he was dreaming, and moaning in his sleep, and still he could not break free into wakefulness and shove the dream aside. Things were falling on him from above; he sheltered his head with his arms, rolled, and with a wrench broke loose from tormented sleep and sat up.

Panguingue was kicking him in the head through his blankets. He was freezing cold, with all his blankets wound around his neck and shoulders like shawls. By the light of a candle stuck on the cold stove lid he saw the rest all in the same state of confused, unbelieving awakening. There was a wild sound of wind; while he sat leaning away from Panguingue's feet, stupidly groping for his wits, a screeching blast hit the tent so hard that old Jesse, standing by the flap, grabbed the pole and held it until the shuddering strain gave way a little and the screech died to a howl.

Rusty saw the look of disbelief and outrage on every face; Panguingue's grin was a wolfish baring of teeth, his ordinary dull-witted good nature shocked clear out of him. "What is it?" Rusty asked idiotically. "Is it a chinook?"

"Chinook!" Buck said furiously.

He yanked his stiff chaps on over his pants and groped chattering for his boots. They were all dressing as fast as their dazed minds and numbed fingers would let them. Jesse let go the tent pole to break some willow twigs in his hands and shove them into the stove. At that moment the wind swooped on them again and the tent came down.

Half dressed, minus mittens, boots, mackinaws, hats, they struggled under the obliterating canvas. Somebody was swearing in an uninterrupted stream. Rusty stumbled over the fallen stovepipe and his nostrils were filled with soot. Then the smothering canvas lifted a couple of feet and somebody struck a match to expose them like bugs under a kicked log, dismayed and scuttling, glaring around for whatever article they needed. He saw Jesse and Ray bracing the front pole, and as the match died he jumped to the rear one; it was like holding a fishing rod with a thousand pound fish on: the whole sail-like mass of canvas flapped and caved and wanted to fly. One or two ropes on the windward side had broken loose and the wall plastered itself against his legs, and wind and snow poured like ice water across his stockinged feet. "Somebody get outside and tie us down," Ray's grating whisper said. Little Horn scrambled past, then Spurlock. Panguingue crawled toward the front flap on hands and knees, Slip and Buck followed him. Braced against the pole, old Jesse was laughing; he lit a match on his pants and got a candle going and stuck it in its own drip on the stove. The stovepipe lay in sooty sections across the beds.

Ropes outside jerked; the wall came away from Rusty's legs, the tent rose to nearly its proper position, the strain on the pole eased. Eventually it reached a wobbly equilibrium so that he could let go and locate his boots in the mess of his bed. The five outsiders came in gasping, beating their numbed hands. In the gray light of storm and morning, they all looked like old men; the blizzard had sown white age in their beards.

"*God* A'mighty!" Slip said, and wiped away an icicle from under his nose.

"Cold, uh?" Ray whispered.

"Must be thirty below."

"Will the tent hold?"

"I dunno," Slip said. "Corner ropes is onto the wheels, but one of the middle ones is pulled plumb out."

They stood a second or two, estimating the strain on the ropes, and as if to oblige their curiosity the wind lit on them and heeled them halfway over again. The whole middle of the windward wall bellied inward; the wind got under the side and for an instant they were a balloon; Rusty thought for certain they would go up in the air. He shut his eyes and hung on, and when he looked again three of the boys had grappled the uplifting skirt of the cloth and pinned it down.

"We got to get in off these flats," Jesse said.

"I guess," Ray said. "The question is how. It's three-four miles to the river."

"We could keep the wind on our left and drift a little with it. That'd bring us in somewhere below Bates Camp."

"Well," Ray said, and looked at the rest of them, holding the tent down, "we haven't got much choice. Slip, you reckon we could find any horses in this?"

"I reckon we could try."

"No," Ray said. "It'd be too risky. We couldn't drive them against this wind if we found them."

"What about the cattle?" Buck said.

"Yeah," said Little Horn. "What about them?"

"D'you suppose," Ray whispered, and a spasm like silent mirth moved his iron face, "after we get things ready to go, you boys could pull about three poles out of the corral gate?"

"You mean turn 'em loose?"

"I mean turn 'em loose."

Ed Spurlock said, "So after all this, we wind up without a single God damn calf?" and Ray said, "You rather have a corral full of dead ones?"

Rusty leaned against the swaying pole while the furious wind whined and howled down out of the Arctic, and he listened to them with a bitterness that was personal and aggrieved. It seemed to him atrocious, a wrong against every principle and every expectation, that the devoted and herculean labors of eight good men should be thwarted by a blind force of nature, a meteorological freak, a mere condition of wind and cold.

Now on with the boots over feet bruised and numb from walking stocking-footed on the frozen ground, and on with the overshoes, and stamp to get life going. Now button the sheepskin collar close and pull the fur cap down, earlaps and forehead piece, leaving exposed only the eyes, the chattering jaw, the agonized spuming of the breath, *huh-huh-huh, huh-huh-huh-huh.* Clumsy with clothing, beat mittened hands in armpits, stoop with the others to get the stovepipe together, the grub box packed, the beds rolled. "Keep out a blanket apiece," Ray Henry says.

The tent tugs and strains, wanting to be off. In the gray light, snow sifts dry as sand down through the open stovepipe thimble and onto the stove—a stove so useless that if anyone touched it with a bare hand he would freeze fast.

As in a nightmare where everything is full of shock and terror and nothing is ever explained, Rusty looks around their numb huddle and sees only a glare of living eyes, and among them Panguingue's eyes that roll whitely toward the tent roof to ask a question.

"We'll leave it up till we get set," Ray says. "It ain't a hell of a lot, but it's something."

They duck outside, and shielding faces behind shoulders and collars, drive into the wind. The paralyzing wind hammers drift against eyelids, nose, and lips, and their breath comes in gasps and sobs as they throw things into the wagon. Jesse and Ray are harnessing the Clydes over their yellow blankets, Slip pounds ice off the blanket of the night pony getting ready to throw the saddle on. From their feet plumes of drift streak away southward. Beyond the figures in the squirming dusk the whole visible world moves—no sky, no horizon, no earth, no air, only this gray-white streaming, with a sound like a rush of water, across and through it other sounds like howling and shouting far off, high for a moment and lost again in the whistle and rush.

The cheek Rusty has exposed feels scorched as if by flame. Back in the icy, half-cleared tent, the hollow of quiet amid the wind seems a most extravagant sanctuary, and he heaves a great breath as if he has been running. He does not need to be told that what moves them now is not caution, not good judgment, not anything over which they have any control, but desperation. The tent will not stand much more, and no tent means no fire. With no horses left but the Clydes and one night pony, they will have to walk, and to reach either of the possible shelters, either Stonepile or Bates Camp, they will have to go north and west, bucking the wind that just now, in the space of a dozen breaths, has seared his face like a blowtorch. He has a feeling outraged and self-pitying and yet remotely contemplating a deserved punishment, a predicted retribution, the sort of feeling that he used to have in childhood when something tempted him beyond all caution and all warnings and he brought himself to a caning in the iodine- and carbolic-smelling office where his father, the doctor, used to look him down into shame before laying the yardstick around his legs. They have got what they deserved for daring Authority; the country has warned them three separate times. Now the punishment.

Into the wagon, jumbled any old way, goes everything the tent holds—grub box, saddles, stove, stovepipe, kerosene can, and again they gather in the still, icy hollow, strangely empty without the stove. Ray Henry has two lariats in his hands, Buck an axe, and Jesse a lighted lantern. The foreman wipes his nose on the back of his mitt and squints at old Jesse. "Dad, you sure you want to drive? It'll be colder up there than walkin'."

The old-timer shakes the lantern, and his eyes gleam and his square teeth gleam. "Lantern between m'feet, buffler robe over the top," he says, "I don't care how cold I get upstairs if I'm warm from the tail down."

"Long as you don't set yourself afire," Ray says. "How about somebody ridin' up there with you?"

"Dee-lighted!" Jesse says, flashing his teeth like Teddy Roosevelt, and they laugh as if they were all short of wind. The foreman's gray thinking eyes go over them. When his look pauses on Rusty Cullen, the boy's breath is held for a moment in sneaking hope, for he has never been so miserable or so cold; the thought of going out there and fighting across six miles of snowflats in the terrible wind has paralyzed his nerve. Also, he tells himself, he is the injured one; his arm still hurts him. The possibility pictures itself seductively before him: to ride, bundled under the buffalo robe and with the lantern's warmth. Like a child pretending sleep when a night emergency arises and the rain beats in an open window or the wind has blown something loose, to sit snug beside old Jesse, relieved of responsibility, while the grownups take care of it . . . He cannot read the foreman's gray eyes; he feels his own wavering down. A crawl of shame moves in his guts, and he thinks, if he picks me it will be because I'm the weakest as well as the greenest.

The thinking eye moves on. "Slip," Ray says, "you ain't got the feet for walkin'. You can spell Dad with the lines. It'll be bad on the hands."

To cover his relief Rusty is beating his hands rhythmically in his armpits and jiggling on nerveless feet. He watches Ray pass the lariats to Little Horn. "If you're tied together, we won't lose nobody."

"Where'll you be?"

"I'll be ridin' pilot."

They are all moving constantly, clumsily. Spurlock has wrapped a woolen muffler around his mouth so that only his restless eyes show. Buck and Panguingue already have hung blankets over their heads and shoulders. Little Horn pulls off a mitt to pat the chimney of Jesse's lantern with a bare hand. "Well," Ray says, "I guess it's time she came down."

They lurch outside. Rusty, unsure of what to do, astonished at their instant obedience, finds himself standing stupidly while Buck with the butt of the axe knocks out one picket pin, then another, and chops off the ropes that tie the tent to the wheels. Jesse and Panguingue, at the ends, reach inside the flaps and lift and yank at the poles, and down it comes in a puddle of frozen canvas that they fall upon and grapple together and heave into the wagon. They curse and fight the wind, pushing and folding the tent down, throwing the poles and two saddles on it to hold it, hauling and lashing the wagon cover tight. Rusty looks back at where their shelter has been and his insides are pinched by cold panic. Drift is already streaking across the patch of thawed and refrozen grass; the little space their living warmth has thawed there in the midst of the waste looks as passionately and finally abandoned as the fresh earth of a grave.

Little Horn is tying them together, using the rope to snug and hold the blankets they have wrapped around themselves, when out of the tattered edge of storm cattle appear, longhorns that swerve away at a stumbling half-trot. After them and among them, a streaming miserable horde, come the whiteface and shorthorns, cows and calves, some steers, a few bulls, with no noise except an occasional desperate blat from a calf, and the clicking of longhorn hoofs and joints carried headlong southward by the wind. Well fleshed and round-bellied no more than a week ago, they stream and flinch past, gaunt ghosts of themselves, and Rusty thinks sullenly, while Little Horn ties the rope tight around him and their four hands tuck the blanket under, that it has been human foolishness that has brought the cattle to this condition. Driven all day by cowboys, and every other night by blizzards, they have eaten hardly anything for days. Left alone, yarding up in the coulees and river bottoms, they could at least have gnawed willows.

He is furious at their violent futile effort, and at Ray Henry for insisting upon it. Inhuman labor, desperate chances, the risk of death itself, for what? For a bunch of cattle who would be better off where their instinct told them to go, drifting with the storm until they found shelter. For owners off in Aberdeen or Toronto or Calgary or Butte who would never come out themselves and risk what they demanded of any cowboy for twenty dollars a month and found.

The tip of his mitt is caught under the rope; he tears it loose, and for a moment Little Horn's barely exposed eyes glint sideways, surprised. Out of the storm behind the last straggling cattle rides Ray Henry, already plastered white. He waves, somebody shouts, the wind tears the sound away and flings it across the prairie, the Clydes jerk sideways, the frozen wheels of the wagon crackle loose and crush through a crested foot-deep drift. The five walkers bunch up to get the protection of the wagon for their faces and upper bodies; the wind under the box and through the spokes tears at their legs as they swing half around and jolt off angling across the storm—northeast, Rusty judges, if the wind is northwest—following the stooped figure of the foreman on the horse. As they pass the corrals, Rusty sees the stained ground humped with carcasses already whitening under the blast of snow and wind.

He huddles his blanket across his chest, clenching and un-
clenching his numb hands; he crowds close to the others, eager to
conform; he plants his feet carefully, clumsily, in the exact footprints of Ed Spurlock, and he tries to keep the rope between
them just slack enough so that it does not drag and trip him.
His face, unless he carelessly falls behind, is out of the worst
lash of the wind; with walking, he has begun to feel his feet again.
It seems possible after all—they can walk under these conditions
the necessary five or six miles to shelter. He is given confidence
by the feel of the rope around his waist, and the occasional tug
when Spurlock or someone else up ahead stumbles or lurches, or
when he feels Little Horn coming behind. Beside his cheek the
wheel pours dry snow, and every turning spoke is a few inches
gained toward safety.

Once, as they bounced across the flats, Slippers leaned out and
shouted something down to Buck, leading the single-file walkers.
An unintelligible word came down the line, the wheels beside
them rolled faster, and they were forced into a trot to keep up.
Rusty staggered sideways in the broken snow, kept himself from
falling under the wheel by a wild shove against the wagon box,
lurched and was yanked forward into step so roughly that it
kinked his neck. The line of them jogged, grunting in cadence,
trotting awkwardly armless, wrapped in their blankets, beside
the ponderous wagon. Eventually Buck shouted up at the seat,
and they slowed to a walk, but the run had done them good. The
blood was out at their edges and extremities again. Rusty felt
it sharp and stinging in his cheeks.

Up ahead, revealed and half covered, and revealed and nearly
obscured, moving steadily through the lateral whip and crawl of
the storm, went the whitened horse, the humped white figure of
Ray Henry. Once when Rusty looked he was down, walking and
leading the pony. A few minutes later he was up again. The
plain stretched on, interminable. Rusty dropped his head turtle-
fashion, wiped an edge of the blanket across his leaking and
freezing nose, concentrated on putting his feet precisely into the
tracks of Ed Spurlock. Dreamlike and hypnotic, body moved,
brain moved, but both sluggishly, barely awake. Life was no more
than movement, than dull rhythm. Eyes were aware only of the

drooping rope, the alternating feet ahead, and once in a while the glimpse of Ray Henry moving through the blizzard out at the edge of visibility. Walking or riding, he went with the inevitability of a cloud driving across the sky; to look up and find him not there would have been a shock and a dismay. And yet he went ambiguously too, something recognized or remembered from an old charade or pantomime or tableau, Leader or Betrayer, urgent, compulsive, vaguely ominous, so that one hurried to keep him in sight and cursed him for the way he led on, and on.

In the thudding hollows of the skull, deep under the layered blanket, the breath-skimmed sheepskin, inside the stinging whiskered face and the bony globe that rode jolting on the end of the spine, deep in there as secret as the organs at the heart of a flower or a nut inside shell and husk, the brain plodded remotely at a heart's pace or a walking pace, saying words that had been found salutary for men or cattle on a brittle and lonesome night, words that not so much expressed as engendered what the mind felt: sullenness, fear, doubt.

Up ahead the foreman moved steadily, dusky stranger, silent companion, and if he did not "bend upon the snowshoe with a long and limber stride," he had a look as tireless and unstoppable as if he had in fact been that Spirit Hunter, that Walker of the Snow, one of the shapes with which the country deluded frightened men.

The wind had changed, and instead of driving at their legs under the box between the spokes was coming much more from behind them. Rusty felt Little Horn's hand on his back, but when he turned to see what was wanted, Little Horn shook his head at him from under the blanket hood: only a stumble, or the wind hustling him along too fast. The pour of dry snow from the wheel blew on forward instead of sideward into their faces. Except for his hands and his impossible leaky nose, he was not cold. They must have come more than half of the three miles that would bring them to the river, where there would be protection among the willows and under the cutbanks, and where they might even choose to make some sort of shelter of the wagon and the tent—build a big wood fire and thaw out and wait for the storm to blow by. He hoped they would; he did not relish the thought of turning into the wind, even in the more sheltered river valley.

He saw The Walker coming back, bent double, his face turned aside. When he reached them his pony turned tail to wind and Jesse cramped the Clydes around and they stood for a brief conference. It seemed that the wind had not changed. The horses simply wouldn't head across it, and kept swinging. That meant they would hit the river lower down, and have a longer upwind pull to Bates.

Only Ray's eyes showed through the mask-like slot of a felt cap that came clear down around his throat. To Jesse and Slip he whisper-shouted something that Rusty could not hear, and mounted and rode off again. The wagon crunched after him, the segmented ten-footed worm beside it took up its lockstep. Deafened by fur and wool, anesthetized by cold and the monotony of walking, the next-to-last segment, joined to the segments before and behind by a waist of half-inch hard-twist rope, plodded on, thinking its own dim thoughts, which were concerned with cosmic injustice and the ways of God to man.

Why couldn't there be, just at this moment, the lucky loom of an unknown or unexpected cowcamp, the whiff of lignite smoke on the wind? Why, just once, could not rescue come from Heaven, instead of having to be earned foot by foot? He dreamed of how warmth would feel in the face, the lovely stink of four or five shut-in cowboys in a hot shack, and he sucked and sniffed at the drooling of his mouth and nose, a hateful, inescapable oozing that turned to ice in his beard and on his lips.

Head down, he plodded on, one step and then another. Once as he put his foot in the print that Spurlock's foot had just left, he caught the heel of Spurlock's overshoe with his toe, and saw Spurlock fling an irritable snarl over the shoulder. Oh, the hell, he thought. Can't you be decent even when we're like this? The rope tugged tight around him, he hopped to get in step again, walking carefully, left, right, left, right, wiping his leaking nose against the blanket's edge and feeling slick ice there.

> Sancta Maria, speed us!
> The sun is falling low;
> Before us lies the valley
> Of the Walker of the Snow!

Later—hours or days, for time whipped and snaked past in unceasing movement like the wind and the trails of drift, and all its proportions were lost—Rusty bumped into Spurlock and an instant later felt Little Horn bump into him in turn. The wagon had stopped, and Ray was back, leading his pony by the bridle. His visor of felt was iron-stiff with ice, so that he pulled it down and craned his neck and lifted his chin to shout over it to Jesse, perched on the high seat beside Slip with the buffalo robe folded up around him under the armpits. Rusty, squinting to see what they were looking at, felt the sticky drag of ice on his lashes as if his eyes were fringed with crickets' legs, and saw that ahead of them the land fell away beyond an edge where the grass was blown bare. Ahead or below, the ground-hugging trails of drift were gone, leaving only air murky as dusk, with fitful swirls and streaks of dark at its bottom which he realized were brush. He dragged at his wet nose. The river.

But the brief, gratified expectation he had that this would be an easier stage lasted no more than two minutes. The hills dipping down to the floodplain were gullied and washed, and drifted deep. Even with Ray riding ahead to try the going, the wheels dropped into holes and hollows, rose over knobs; the wagon canted at perilous angles, groaning and jolting its way slanting, with the wind almost dead behind it. Pulling out wide from the rocking wagon, the men were caught in the open wind and blown along. Rusty saw the Clydes braced back in the breeching, their hairy fetlocks coming up out of the snow rattling with balls of ice, and their muscular haunches bunching under the blankets, and then here came Slip digging out from under the buffalo robe to throw his weight on the brake. Ice against ice, shoe slid on tire and held nothing; the wagon rolled heavily down upon the Clydes, who braced lower, slipping. The walkers jumped aside and then, as the wagon lumbered past them, jumped to the endgate to try to hold it back. Its ponderous weight yanked them along, their dug heels plowed up snow. They could feel it under their hands getting away, they knew it without Jesse's yell that snapped off on the wind above their heads. Jesse rose half to his feet, braced between seat and box. The wagon jackknifed sharply as he swung the Clydes along the sidehill to slow them. The left side dropped down, the right

heaved up, and with a neat final motion like the end of a crack-
the-whip the wagon tipped over and cast off Slip in a spidery
leap down the hillside. Jesse, hanging to the tilted seat to the
end, slid off it to land on his feet with the reins in one hand and
the lantern in the other. By the time Ray discovered what had
happened and rode back, he had unhooked the Clydes and got
them quiet. The wagon lay with its load bulging out of the
lashed cover, the busy wind already starting to cover it with snow.

Rusty would not have believed that in that wind and cold it
was possible to work up a sweat, but he did. It was a blind and
furious attack they launched on the tipped wagon, unloading almost everything and carrying it down to more level ground
where the abrupt hill aproned off, stacking it there while they
floundered back to dig and pry at the jackknifed wheels. Ray
hitched on with his saddle horse, they heaved while their held
breath burst out of them in grunts and straining curses, until
they righted it, and straightened the wheels, and a spoke at a
time got them turning; three of them carrying the tongue and
the others ready to push or hold back, they angled it down onto
leveler and smoother ground.

There they wasted not a second, but hitched up and loaded
as if they raced against time. When the muffled-up figure of
Spurlock started to heave a saddle up, and slipped and fell flat
on its back with the saddle on its chest, Rusty coughed out one
abrupt bark of laughter, but no one else laughed. Panguingue
and Buck picked the saddle off Spurlock's chest and tossed it
aboard, and before Spurlock was back on his feet Little Horn
and Buck were starting to tie together the worm of walkers. Up
where Jesse and Slip were fussily folding the buffalo robe around
and under them it looked bitterly cold, but down where Rusty
stood it was better. He could feel his hands all the way, his feet
all but the tips of the toes. Where the fur cap covered it, his forehead was damp, and under the ponderous layers of clothing and
blanket his body itched a little with warmth. He was winded,
and dead tired, and his shoulder ached as if the fierce haul and
heave of the unloading and loading had pulled it from its
socket, but the dismay of the accident was worked off. They
were all right, they would make it yet.

He twisted to help Little Horn tuck the blanket-ends under the rope, and at that moment Spurlock, moving awkwardly in front, put his foot down crooked, reeled against him, landed on his foot and anchored him there, and bore him helplessly over in the drift. If it had been anyone else, Rusty might have laughed, reassured and warmed by work as he was; but since it was Spurlock he rose to one knee anticipating trouble. He was not wrong; the hand he put on Spurlock's arm was knocked off angrily, and through the layers of the muffler the words were savage: ". . . the Christ you're doing!"

The boy's anger blew up instant and hot, and he bounded to his feet freeing his elbows from the blanket. They faced each other, tied together by four feet of rope like gladiators coupled to fight to the death, and then the shadow above them made itself felt and Rusty looked up to see Ray Henry sitting hands-on-horn and looking down on them.

"What's trouble?" the foreman said.

The unintelligible growl that came out of Spurlock's muffled mouth could have told him nothing, but Rusty pulled the collar away from his chin and said passionately, "Look, put me somewhere else in this line! I'm not going to stand for . . ."

"What's trouble?" Ray said again.

"He keeps stumbling around and falling down and then blaming me . . ."

"If he falls down, help him up," Ray croaked, and kneed his frosted pony around and rode off in front. The wheels jerked, the icy axles shrieked, their feet automatically hopped to get in step, and they were walking again. Rusty pulled his chin back inside the collar and went sullenly, furious at the injustice of the rebuke, and alert to make the most of any slightest slip or stumble ahead of him.

Down in the bottoms among the willows the wind was less, and they could bring the horses to turn halfway into it, feeling for the river. But if the wind was less, the snow was deeper; the Clydes floundered belly deep and the wagon box scraped up a great drift that piled up over the doubletree and against the stallions' rumps and finally stopped them dead. They shoveled it away and cleared the Clydes' feet, never quite sure whether or not they would have their brains kicked out. Then they fell into two lines out in front and tramped a way for the horses and the wagon wheels down through smothered rosebushes and between clumps of willow whose bark gleamed red under the hood of snow. Ten feet of it was enough to wind a man; they panted their way ahead, turned to tramp backward and deepen the track, stopped every twenty yards to dig away the snow that the wagon box scooped up. They worked like people fighting a fire, exhausted themselves and stood panting a minute and fell to it again, frenzied for the easy going on the river ice.

The wagon eased over the edge of a bushy bank, the Clydes plunged as Jesse took them over straight on. The front wheels went down, pushing the stallions out onto the ice. Just as Rusty saw them lunging to pull the wagon through, a jerk from behind dragged him over in the drift and the whole line of walkers came down. When they got to their feet there was the wagon on the river.

Getting up watchfully, Rusty thought he felt Spurlock yanking at the rope, and he yanked back harshly. Sunk between the muskrat cap and the muffler, and blindered on both sides by the wings of the mackinaw collar, Spurlock's eyes peered out like the eyes of a fierce animal peering from a crack in the rock, but he turned away without a word, giving Rusty at least the smoldering satisfaction of having yanked last, of having finished something that the other had started.

The cutbank partially shielded them from the wind. Upriver was a straight reach with an irregular streak of clear, blown ice down its center, grading up to shelving drifts against both banks. Drift skated and blew down it like dust down an alley. The last lap of the road to shelter lay before them as smooth as a paved highway.

Ray Henry, leading his pony down the broken bank, stopped by them a moment where they hung panting on the wagon. "Everybody all right?"

They looked at him from among their wrappings.

"Ed?" Ray said.

It seemed to Rusty terribly unjust that particular attention should have been paid to Spurlock rather than to himself. It meant that the foreman still looked upon Spurlock as in the right, himself in the wrong. It meant that he had no concern for the one of his men who was hurt, and might be in trouble. He saw Ray's eyes within the visor that was like the helmet of a hero, and his unhappiness that he had lost prestige and respect drove words to his lips, impulsive and too eager, anything to be recognized and accepted again. He did not care about Spurlock, actually; he was already ashamed of that quarrel. But he wanted Ray Henry to notice him, and so he said, "What do we do now, Ray? Camp here till it's over?"

"Not hardly," Ray said. "The Clydes have had all the fresh air they need."

"How much farther?"

"Three miles, maybe four."

"Do we ride from here?"

The gray, thinking eye examined him from within the helmet of ice-hardened felt. The foreman said, "You reckon you're any more petered than them studs?"

He went stooping and slipping out in front to confer with Jesse and Slip, and Rusty, avoiding Little Horn's eyes and with his back to Spurlock and the others, watched the smothered rosebushes on the bank quiver in a gust. The slow warmth under all his wrappings might have come from the heavy work of getting the wagon through the brush and the drifts, but it might just as well have been shame, and he hated them all for never giving a man a chance, for taking things wrong, for assuming what should not be assumed. He hadn't been wanting to quit, he had asked only for information. Sullenly he waited, resolved to keep his mouth shut and plod it out. Once they got back to the ranch, he could simply leave the job; he was under no obligation to stay at it any longer than he pleased to. Neither Ray nor anyone else could compel a man to stick it through months of this kind of thing, no matter how short-handed the T-Down was. There was sure to be a great change as soon as he announced he was leaving. He could see Ray Henry's face—all their faces. Every man who left, left more for the remaining ones to do. Too late, chaps. Sorry. Ta-ta, gentlemen. Enjoy the winter.

In the river bottom the wind was louder, though he felt it less. The bare willows and the rosebushes, bent like croquet wickets into the drifts, whistled with it, the cutbank boomed it back in hollow eddies, every corner and edge and groove of the valley gave it another tongue. More than out on the flats, even, it echoed with hallucinatory voices, shouts, screams, whistles, moans, jeers. Rusty concentrated on it. He had only been asking a perfectly reasonable question, considering that they were running for their lives and still had an unknown distance to go. Would it be so terrible to climb up and let those big strong horses pull them for a little while along the level ice? Would it, for that matter, be entirely unheard of to sacrifice the Clydes, if necessary, to save eight lives? He asked himself what about a leader who thought more of his horses than of his men.

The blood in his veins was sluggish with cold, his mind was clogged with sullen hatred. Ray, shouting up to Jesse and Slip, and Spurlock, weaving bearlike from one foot to the other, were both part of a nightmare which he loathed and wanted to escape, but the numbness held him and he stood spraddling, squinting from behind the wagon box, hearing the shouts of those ahead torn from their lips and flung streaming down the ice to become part of the headlong illusory wailing that blew and moaned around the river's bends. His mind, groping among images, was as clumsy as his mittened unfeeling hands would have been, trying to pick up a coin from the snow. He thought of old Jesse's friend down by Sheridan, with his frozen conversation, and of how others had explained, not so humorously, the voices that haunted the wind in this country.

> For I saw by the sickly moonlight
> As I followed, bending low,
> That the walking of the stranger
> Left no footmarks on the snow.

The voices of all the lost, all the Indians, *métis*, hunters, Mounted Police, wolfers, cowboys, all the bundled bodies that the spring uncovered and the warming sun released into the stink of final decay; all the starving, freezing, gaunt, and haunted men who had challenged this country and failed; all the ghosts from smallpox-stilled Indian camps, the wandering spirits of warriors killed in their sleep on the borders of the deadly hills, all the skeleton women and children of the starving winters, all the cackling, maddened cannibals, every terrified, lonely, crazed, and pitiful outcry that these plains had ever wrung from human lips, went wailing and moaning over him, mingled with the living shouts of the foreman and the old-timer, and he said, perhaps aloud, remembering the legend of the Crying River, and the voices that rode the wind there as here, *Qu'appelle? Qu'appelle?*

Heartless and inhuman, older than earth and totally alien, as savage and outcast as the windigo, the cannibal spirit, the wind dipped and swept upon them down the river channel, tightening the lightly sweating inner skin with cold and the heart with fear. Rusty watched Ray hump his back and shake off the worst of the blast, saw the arm wave. The wagon rolled again. Ed Spurlock, unready, was pulled sideways a stumbling step or two by the tightening of the rope, and Rusty got one clear look into the brown, puckered eyes. Out of his fear and misery and anger he sneered, "Learn to walk!" But if Spurlock heard he made no sign. In a moment he was only the hooded, blanketed, moving stoop, not human, not anything, that Rusty imitated movement for movement, step for step, plodding up the river after the wagon.

Exhaustion and cold are a kind of idiocy, the mind moves as numbly as the body, the momentary alertness that a breathing spell brings is like the sweat that can be raised under many clothes even in the bitterest weather; when the breathing spell is over and the hard work past, mind and body are all the worse for the brief awakening. The sweaty skin chills, the images that temporary alertness has caught scrape and rasp in the mind like edged ice and cannot be dislodged or thought away or emptied out, but slowly coagulate there.

For Rusty they were the images of fear. No matter how much he tried to tie his mind to the plod-plod-plod of foot after foot, he heard the spirit of that bitter country crying for cold and pain. Under his moving feet the ice passed, now clear, with coin-like bubbles in it, now coated with a pelt of dry smooth snow, now thinly drifted. The world swung slowly, the dry snow under their feet blew straight sideward, then quartered backward; his quickly lifted eyes saw that the right bank had dropped to a bar and the left curved up in a cutbank. The wind lashed his face so that he hunched and huddled the blanket closer, leaving only the slightest hole, and still the wind got in, filled the blanket, threatened to blow it off his back. His eyes were full of water and he wiped them free, terrified that they would freeze shut. With his head bowed clear over, almost to the rope, he stumbled on. Through the slits of sight remaining to him he saw that the drift now was blowing straight backward from Spurlock's feet. The river had swung them directly into the wind. The line of walkers huddled to the left until they were walking bunched behind the feeble protection of the wagon.

The wagon stopped, the line of walkers bumped raggedly to a halt. Rusty had forgotten them: he was surprised to find them there, glaring from the frozen crevices of their clothes. From out in front Ray Henry came looming, a huge indomitable bulk, leading the pony whose bony face was covered with a shell of ice, the hairy ears pounded full of snow, the breast of the blanket sheathed. He unlooped the halter rope and tied it to the endgate, pulled the bridle and hung it on the saddle horn. For a minute he rubbed and worked at the pony's face, turned grunting, and said from inside his visor, "They just can't buck it. We're gonna have to lead 'em." He helped Little Horn pull open the loose, frozen knot in the rope and free himself from the others. "Rusty," he said, "see if you can find a blanket up in the load somewhere."

Rusty found the blanket, the foreman and Little Horn flapped off with it, the walkers huddled back to the wagon, eying the miserable pony which now took half their shelter. After a minute or two the yell came back, they turned, they stirred their stiffened legs and moved their wooden feet. The wind shrieked around the wagon, between the spokes, along the axles and the snow-clogged reach, and Rusty, colder now than at any time since he had awakened half frozen in his blankets, heard the blizzardy bottoms wild with voices. *Qu'appelle? . . . Qu'appelle? . . . Qu'appelle?*

In an hour, or four hours, or ten minutes, the river blessedly bent rightward, and the wind went screaming and flying above them but touched them only in swoops and gusts. There was a stretch where the inshore drifts let them go close up under the bank, and for a brief time the air was almost still, the snow settling almost gently as on any winter's day, a day to put roses in the cheeks.

Sancta Maria, speed us!

During that brief, numbed lull Spurlock tangled his feet and fell again, pulling over Panguingue ahead of him. Rusty, hopping awkwardly to keep from getting entangled with the sliding, swiveling figures, saw Buck squat and grab the rope to maintain his balance against the drag of the fallen ones. There went the three of them, helplessly dragged along on back or feet, and here came Rusty, a lead-footed dancer, prancing and shouting in their wake until those up ahead heard and they stopped.

Ray was back again. Panguingue and Buck stood up and cleared the rope, but Spurlock sat on the ice with his head down, pawing at his face and heaving his shoulders under the blanket. Rusty stayed back in scorn and contempt, sure that the blame would somehow be pinned on him. He was the proper scapegoat; everything that happened was caused by his awkwardness.

Ray was stooping, shaking Spurlock's shoulder. His hand worked at the muffler around Spurlock's face. Then he straightened up fierce and ready and with so much power left that Rusty moved a step back, astonished. "The lantern!" Ray shouted, and lunged around the line of walkers to reach and take the lantern from Jesse's hand. Back at Spurlock, stooping to hold the lantern directly against the muffler, he said over his shoulder, "Rusty, unhitch yourself and rustle some wood. We're gonna have to stop and thaw out."

The knot was stiff with ice, his fingers like sticks, but he got loose and stumped around in the deep snow breaking dead stalks out of willow clumps. Slip appeared to help him, and Rusty said, pausing a second in his fumbling, "What's the matter with Spurlock?"

"Smotherin'," Slip said. "God damn muffler froze to his whiskers."

"Are we going to camp here?"

"Why?" said Slip in surprise. "Do you *want* to?"

Rusty floundered down the bank with his handful of twigs, watched Panguingue cone them on the ice and souse them with kerosene. The smell cut his nostrils, and he sniffed back the

wetness and spat in the snow. It was that drooling that had got
Spurlock in trouble. Drool and freeze fast. Dully curious, he
watched Ray moving the lantern glass around on the frozen
wool, while Buck pulled on the unfrozen ends. Spurlock's head
was pulled out of his collar; he looked like a fish on a hook.
Then Panguingue found a match and reached across Buck to
scratch it on the dry bottom of the lantern. The little cone of
sticks exploded in bright flame.

"More," Panguingue said thickly.

Little Horn, who had led the Clydes around in a half circle, was
already up over the endgate, unlashing the wagon cover. Stupidly
Rusty watched as he loosened it all across the windward side and
dropped it in the lee, and then, comprehending, he helped tie it
to the spokes to make a windbreak. The fire had burned out its
splash of kerosene, and was smoldering in the snow until Panguingue swished it again and it blazed up. "More!" he said. "We
need wood."

"In the wagon," Jesse said. "What do you think I chopped all
that wood for yesterday?"

He climbed the wheel to burrow into the uncovered load, and
his face with its bowed mustaches emerged from under the
tangled tent like a walrus at a waterhole and he winked in
Rusty's face, handing him out wood two and three sticks at a
time. His manner was incredible to the boy. He acted as if
they were out on a picnic or a berry-picking and were stopping
for lunch. Buck and Ray were holding Spurlock's face close to
the little fire and working away at the muffler. The wind, here,
was only a noise: they squatted in their bivouac with the fire
growing and sputtering in the water of its melting, and they
gathered close around it, venturing their faces a little out of their
coverings.

Spurlock cursed clearly for the first time, the muffler came
loose in Buck's hands. Ray set the lantern aside while Spurlock
breathed deeply and passed his hands around on his face.

"Stick her right in," Jesse said. "That's the quickest way to thaw
her. Set those weeds on fire."

They sat knee to knee, they put their mittens on sticks of wood
in the snow and held stiff red hands in the very flames, they
opened collars and exposed smarting faces. Life returned as

pain: far down his legs Rusty felt a deep, passionate ache beginning in his feet. He knew from the burn of his cheeks and the chilblain feel of his fingers that he would have some frostbite to doctor. But he loved the snug out-of-the-wind shelter, the fire, even the pain that was beginning now and would get worse. For no matter how they came out, or whether they camped here to wait out the storm or went on after a rest to Bates, which couldn't be more than another mile or two, he would go with a knowledge that warmed him like Jesse's lantern under the robe: it hadn't been *he* that cracked. And what a beautiful and righteous and just thing it was that the one who did crack should be Spurlock! In triumph and justification he looked across the fire at the sagging figure, but he couldn't make the restless reddened eyes hold still. Spurlock hadn't said a word since they released him from the smothering scarf.

A half hour later, when Ray said they must go on, Rusty received the words like a knife in his guts. He had been sitting and secretly willing that they should stay. But he glanced again across the fire and this time caught Ed Spurlock's moving eyes, and the eyes ducked like mice. He told himself that if he was unwilling, Spurlock was scared to death. When they lashed the wagon cover back on and tied themselves together again and hooded the Clydes in the red Hudson's Bay blanket and Little Horn and Ray swung them by the bits and the forlorn night pony stretched his neck and came unwillingly, Rusty had a feeling that the moving line literally tore Spurlock from the side of the fire, now sunk into the crust and sizzling out blackly at the edges in steam and smoke.

The river swung, and the wind got at them. It swung wider, and they were plucked and shoved and blinded so that they walked sideward with their backs to the bar and their faces turned to the fantastic pagoda-roof of snow along the cutbank. In fury and anguish they felt how the river turned them. Like things with an identical electrical charge, their faces bent and flinched away, but in the end there was no evading it. The wagon stopped and started, stopped and started. The feet that by the fire had felt renewed life began to go dead again, the hands were going back to wood, the faces, chafed and chapped and sore, were pulled deep into the wool and fur. Gasping, smelling wet sheepskin and the tallowy smell of muskrat fur, feeling the ice at their very beards and the wind hunting for their throats, they hunched and struggled on.

Rusty, bent like a bow, with every muscle strained to the mindless plod, plod, plod of one foot after the other, and his eyes focused through the blanket's crack on Spurlock's heels, saw the feet turn sideward, the legs go out of sight. Apparently Spurlock had simply sat down, but the rope, tightening on him, pulled him over. Sliding on the ice, hauled after the backward-walking, braced, and shouting Panguingue, he was trying to untie the rope around his waist with his mittened hands.

Again their yells were torn away downwind, voices to blend with the blizzard's crying, or thaw out to haunt hunters or cowboys in some soft spring. They dragged Spurlock a hundred feet before those up in front heard. Then Rusty stood furiously over him and cursed him for his clumsiness and cried for him to get up, but Spurlock, straightening to sit with his arms hung over his knees, neither looked up nor stood up. He mumbled something with his head down.

"Lone," he mumbled, "rest minute."

Rusty's leg twitched: he all but kicked the miserable bundle. Slip and Jesse or both were shouting from the wagon seat, Ray Henry was coming back—for the how many'th time? They were utterly exposed, the wind whistled and the drift blinded them. He dropped his mouth again to Spurlock's ear, shouted again. Panguingue was hauling at Spurlock's armpits. "Can't sit down," he said. "Got to keep him movin'."

Not until then did the understanding grow into Rusty's mind, a slow ache of meaning like the remote feeling in his feet. Spurlock was done. It wasn't just awkwardness, he wasn't just quitting, he was exhausted. The danger they had been running from, a possibility in which Rusty had never thoroughly believed, was right among them. This was how a man died.

His hands found an arm under blanket and coat, and he and Panguingue helped Spurlock's feeble scrambling until they had him on his feet. They held him there, dragged down by his reluctant weight, while Ray peered grimly into his face. "He's played out," Panguingue said, and Rusty said, "Couldn't we put him in the wagon? He can't walk any farther."

Ray said, "Put him in the wagon he'd be froze stiff in twenty minutes." His hands went out to Spurlock's shoulders and he shook him roughly. "Ed! You hear? You got to keep movin'. It's only another mile. Just keep comin'."

" 'mall right," Spurlock said. "Just rest minute."

"Not a damn minute," Ray said. "You rest a minute and you're dead."

Spurlock hung between Rusty and Panguingue until they were holding almost his whole weight. "You hear, Ed?" Ray said, glaring from his visor like a hairy animal. "You stop to rest, you're dead. Come on now, stand up and walk."

Somehow he bullied strength into the legs and a glitter of life into the eyes. Then he drove back against the wind to take the bridle of the off horse, and the halting, laborious crawl moved on. But now Rusty and Panguingue had hitched their ropes around and walked one on each side of Ed Spurlock, each with a hand under the rope around his waist to haul him along, and to support him if he started to go down. He came wobbling, and he murmured through the blanket they had wrapped over his whole head, but he came.

Rusty's shoulder ached—he ached all over, in fact, whenever he had any feeling at all—and the strain of half supporting Spurlock twisted his body until he had a stabbing stitch in his side. The hand he kept in Spurlock's waist rope was as unfeeling as an iron hook.

A mile more, Ray said. But the river led them a long time around an exposed loop. He had all he could do to force himself into the blast of snow and wind that faded and luffed only to howl in their faces again more bitterly than ever. When Spurlock, stumbling like a sleepwalker, hung back or sagged, trying to sit down, Rusty felt Panguingue's strength and heard Panguingue's stout cursing. His own face was so stiff that he felt he could not have spoken, even to curse, if he tried; he had lost all feeling in his lips and chin. His inhuman hook dragged at Spurlock's waist rope, he threw his shoulder across to meet Panguingue's when the weight surged too far forward, and he put foot after foot, not merely imbecilic now with cold and exhaustion, but nearly mindless, watching not the feet ahead, for there were none now, with three of them abreast and Buck trailing them behind, but the roll of the broad iron tire with the snow spume hissing from it. He watched it hypnotically, revolving slowly like the white waste of his mind where a spark of awareness as dim as the consciousness of an angleworm glimmered. His body lived only in its pain and weariness. The white waste on which the wheel moved broke into dark angles, was overspread by blackness that somehow rose and grew, strangely fluid and engulfing, and the air was full of voices wild and desolate and terrible as the sound of hunting wolves. The led pony reared and broke its halter rope and vanished somewhere. Then Rusty felt himself yanked sideward, falling into Spurlock and Panguingue in an encumbered tangle, seeing even as he fell, shocked from his stupor, that the endgate was clear down, the hub drowned in black water that spread across the snow. Kicking crabwise, he fled it on his back, helped by someone hauling on the rope behind, until they stood at the edge of the little shallow rapid and saw Jesse and Slip in the tilted wagon ready to jump, and the round wet heads of stones among the broken ice, and the Clydes struggling, one half down and then up again, Little Horn hanging from the bits, hauled clear of the ice as they plunged. There was a crack like a tree coming down, the stallions plunged and steadied, and then Ray was working back along the broken tongue to get at the singletrees and unhook the tugs and free them.

Ray was standing on the broken tongue and calming the stallions with a hand on each back while he yelled downwind. Rusty pulled at his cap, exposed one brittle ear, and heard the foreman shouting, "Get him on up to the cabin . . . two or three hundred yards . . . right after you."

So with hardly a pause longer than the pause of their falling sideward away from the crunch of ice and the upwelling of water from the broken shell of the rapid, he and Panguingue were walking again, cast free from the rope and supporting Spurlock each with one arm around his shoulders, the other hands locked in front of him. He drooped and wobbled, mumbling and murmuring about rest. He tricked them with sudden lurches to left or right; when he staggered against them his weight was as hard to hold as a falling wall. Twice he toppled them to the ice. Compelled to watch where he walked, Rusty had to let the blanket blow from head and face, and without its protection he flinched and gasped, blinded, and felt the ice forming stickily along his eyelashes, and peered and squinted for the sight of the dugway that would lead them out of the channel and up the cutbank and across a little flat to the final security, so close now and so much more desperately hard to reach with every step.

The river bent, they dragged their burden along, they yielded to his murmurings and to their own exhaustion and let him sag a minute onto the ice, and then hauled and dragged him onto his feet and staggered on. The right bank was low and brushy; the wind came across it so that they leaned and fought across its whipping edge. Rusty freed his left hand and scoured the wrist of the mitten across his eyes and looked into the blast for the slant of the dugway, and saw nothing but the very throat of the blizzard. It was more than muscle and will could endure; panic was alive in his insides again. Even a hundred yards was too much; they could fall and die before the others could overtake them, right here within a few rods of safety. He gasped and sucked at his drooling lip, lost his hold on Panguingue's hand, felt with anguish how Spurlock slid away and went down.

Somehow they got him up again; somehow they struggled another hundred feet along the ice, and now a cutbank curving into a left-hand bend cut off some of the wind, and Rusty heard Panguingue grunt and felt the veer and stagger as he turned in toward the bank. Rusty still could not see it, but starting up, slipping, he put a hand down to stay himself and felt the dugway. Strengthless, they leaned into the bank; Spurlock tried to lie back; they held him with difficulty, and lifting the blanket to look into his face Rusty saw his eyes frozen wholly shut with teardrops of ice on the lashes. Above the dark beard the cheekbones were dead white.

When they tried to move him again, he sagged back against the bank and gave them his limp arms to haul at, and their combined strength was not enough to get him onto his feet, much less to start him up the steep dugway. They tried to drag him and stopped exhausted after six feet. The glare of uncertainty, fear, helplessness, was in Panguingue's glimmer of eyes and teeth. Rusty understood him well enough. Leave him? The others would soon come along. But if they didn't come in a few minutes he would be dead. Again they lifted and hauled at Spurlock, got him halfway, and felt him slip and go comfortably down again. Panguingue let go. "We better try to get up to the cabin. Schulz might be there."

"Suppose he isn't?"

He heard the forlorn, hopeless sound of Panguingue's snuffing. The face looked at him, bearded clear to the eyes.

"You go," Rusty said. "I'll wait here with him."

A snuffle, a momentary look, and Panguingue ducked away, scrambling with hands and feet, to disappear over the dugway edge.

For a while Rusty lay beside Spurlock on the slope, his blanket huddled over to cover both their faces, and simply waited, without mind or thought, no longer afraid, not hopeful, not even aware or sentient, but simply waiting while the gasp of breath and hammer of heart labored toward some slowing-point. He could not feel his feet at all; his hands were clubs of wood. Driven inward from its frontiers, his life concentrated itself in his chest where heart and lungs struggled.

A little later there was a stage in which his consciousness hung above him, like the consciousness in a dream where one is both actor and observer, and saw him lying there, numb already nearly to the knees, nearly to the elbows, nose and lips and forehead and the tender sockets of the eyes gone feelingless, ears as impersonal as paper ears pinned to his head. What he saw was essentially a corpse huddling over another corpse. He recognized the fact without surprise or alarm. This was the way it ended, this was the way they would be found.

Under the blanket's hood was a darkness and stillness. He felt how absurd it was, really. Absurd for men to chase around an arctic prairie wearing themselves and their cattle to death. Absurd. Take a rest, now, and . . .

Coming? Who? *Qu'appelle?* Old wolf, old walker of the snow, old windigo, *qu'appelle?* He smiled. It was a joke between them.

He heard now neither the wind nor the dry rustle of his mind. Inside the blanket the air was still, red-dusky, not cold. But as he moved to make his legs more comfortable the hillside toppled, a dull anguish of unwilling sensation spread in his throat, and he struggled back up, straightening the elbow that had given way and let him fall across Spurlock's up-jutting face. A powder flash of terror lighted up his whole head. The imprint of Spurlock's chin, unyielding as stone, ached in his Adam's apple. The face of a corpse—his too? But it was not his own pain so much as the appalling rigidity of Spurlock's jaw that shocked him. The man was dying, if not dead. Something had to be done, he couldn't just wait for help from Panguingue or the others.

His hands clutched and shook the stiffening bundle, the unfeeling hooks tried to close, to lift. "Ed! Ed, come on! We're almost there, man! Get up, you can't lie here. Only a little way farther. Ed! *Ed!* You hear? God damn it, Ed, get up! Come on, move!"

His eyes were full of catastrophic tears; he dashed them away with a fold of the blanket and threw a look up the dugway and gulped a burning throatful of the wind. He heard the voices wail and howl around the eaves of the riverbank, and he bent and slapped and pounded and tugged, screaming at the clownish, bearded, ice-eyed, and white-cheekboned face that turned and whimpered under his attack.

Gasping, he stopped a moment, threw another look upward. The top of the bank was less than thirty feet above him. Beyond that, within two hundred feet, should be the cabin. Five minutes, no more than ten even on hands and knees. He looked in anguish for the outfit, possibly coming up the river ice, and saw only trails of drift vanishing around the bend. The boys rendering their fantastic duty to the horses could not possibly come in time. And Panguingue must have found the shack deserted or he would have been back by now. Was he stopping to build a fire, or was he too exhausted to come back? Or was he lying in the snow himself, somewhere between the cutbank and the cabin?

"Ed! Wake up! Get up and walk! It's only a little way!"

Hopeless; inert and hopeless. He could not help the tears, though he knew they would be his blindness and his death. "Please, Ed! Please, come on!"

In a clumsy frenzy he hauled and yanked and dragged; his frantic strength skidded Spurlock a yard or two up the dugway, and when Spurlock began mumblingly to resist with arms and legs, Rusty attacked him with three times more fury and by slaps and kicks and blows reinforced his resistance until, miraculously,

Spurlock was on his feet. With hooks and shoulder Rusty helped him, braced him, shoved him upward, moved him a step, and another; and crying encouragement, panting, winded and dead-armed and dead-legged, forced the man foot by foot up the dugway path until he felt the ground level off and the wind fling itself full against them.

They toppled and almost fell. Spurlock sagged and started to sit down and Rusty barely managed to hold him. He could not see more than a bleared half-light—no objects at all. His tears were already ice, his lashes stitched together, and he could make no move to clear his sight without letting Spurlock slip away, probably for the last time. Savagely he rasped his face across the snow-slick wool of Spurlock's blanketed shoulder; with what little vision he could gain he glared straight into the wind for the dark wall or icicled eaves that would be the cabin. The wind drove down his throat; his shouting was strangled and obliterated; it was like trying to look and shout up a waterfall. The wilderness howled at him in all its voices. He was brought to a full stop, sightless, breathless, deafened, and with no strength to move and barely enough to stand, not enough—frantically not enough—to hold the weight of Ed Spurlock that despite every effort he could make slid away and down.

With a groan Rusty let him go. Both hands rose to rub the wristlets of his mittens across his sealed eyes. Pain stabbed through his eyeballs as if he had run across them with sandpaper, but he broke the threads of ice that stitched him shut, and looked again into the gray and howling wind, saw a square darkness, a loom of shadow in the murk, and thought in wonder, My God, we've been right against the shack all the time, and then the darkness moved and the wind's voice fell from whine and howl to a doglike barking, and Panguingue was there shouting in his face.

Relief was such pure bliss to him that he was rendered imbecilic by it, and stood mouth open and cheeks stretched to force open his eyes, watching Panguingue try to pull Spurlock erect. He loved Panguingue, the stoutest and decentest and bravest and most dependable man alive. Merely his presence brought not only hope but assurance. It would be no trouble now. And even while he was bending to help he heard the unmistakable dig and clump of the Clydes behind him, and turned to see them clear the dugway with tennis balls of ice rattling in their fetlocks and Jesse hanging to the lines behind them, and then the others—one, then another, then another, leading the pony.

What had been impossible was suddenly easy, was nothing. Among them they hoisted Spurlock to his feet. Rusty felt an arm around him, the urge of someone else's undiminished strength helping him along through a thigh-deep drift that gave way abruptly to clear ground. His head sounded with hollow kickings and poundings and with one last defeated howl of wind, and he saw icicles under the shack's eaves like yard-long teeth, and the wind stopped, the noises fell, the light through his sticky eyelids darkened, his nostrils filled with smells of mice, kerosene, sheepskins, ham rind, sardines, and a delirious tropical odor of cinnamon and cloves like his mother's spice cupboard, and someone steered him and turned him and pushed on his shoulders, and Ray Henry's whisper said, "O.K., kid, take a load off your feet." He felt safety with his very buttocks as he eased himself down on the rustly hay-stuffed tick of a bunk.

Later he sat with his aching feet in a dishpan of snow and water, and when the pain in his hands swelled until it seemed the fingers would split like sausages, he stooped and numbed the ache into bearability in the same dishpan. His eyes were inflamed and sore; in each cheek a spot throbbed with such violence that he thought the pulse must be visible in the skin like a twitching nerve. His ears were swollen red-hot fungi, his nose that had run and drooled incontinently all the way through the blizzard was now so stuffed and swollen that he gurgled for air. He knew how he looked by looking at Little Horn, who had got wet to the knees when the Clydes went through the rapid, and who sat now on an apple box with first one foot and then the other in a bucket of snow. Little Horn's skin showed like a flaming sunburn through his reddish beard. He had innocent blue eyes like Jesse's, and the same blunt chin. When he was twenty years older he would look a good deal like Jesse—they were members of the same tribe. Now he lifted one tallowy foot from the deep snowprint in the pail and set it tenderly on the floor and lifted the other into its place, and looked across at Rusty

with his mild ironic eye and shook his head in acknowledgment
of something.

Ray and Jesse were squatting by the bunk against the side wall
where Spurlock lay. Each had a blotched foot in his hands, each
was massaging it and sousing it with snow. At the head of the
bunk Buck worked on Spurlock's hands. Spurlock's fiery face
looked straight upward; his teeth were set; he said nothing. Back
by the door Slip and Panguingue had just finished washing each
other's faces with snow. All of them, emerged from their cum-
bersome wrappings, looked disheveled as corpses dredged from a
river. Rusty marveled at their bony hairless feet, their red hands,
their vulnerable throats. They were making a good deal of talkative noise, their skins were full of the happiness of rescue, and
not yet quite full of pain.

Little Horn looked at Panguingue's wet face. He said to Rusty,
"Ain't that the way it goes? Of all the people that might of froze
their feet and got a good wash out of it, who is the one God
damn boy in the outfit without even a frozen toe but old Pan?"

Jesse said from the end of Spurlock's bunk, "Cold couldn't get
through that crust."

"B.S.," Panguingue said. "I'm just tougher than you. And besides, I froze my face damn good."

"Snow washed some of the protective layer off," Little Horn
said. "No, more I think of it, more I think you shouldn't make
any mistake and wash them feet till spring, Pan. We'll need
somebody around to do the chores while we get well."

"Hey, by God," Panguingue said. "How about my face?"

"Just leave it go. A little proud flesh would improve it."

"B.S.," said Slip, in imitation of Panguingue's growl, and he
and Panguingue threatened each other with pans of snow. From
the other bunk Ray Henry said, "Feelin' 'em yet?"

"You're damn right," Ed Spurlock said through his teeth.

"Better let 'em set in the water for a while," Ray said. "The
slower they come back the better." He stood up, looking at
Rusty. "Rusty, you needin' that dishpan for a while?"

"No, take it." He moved his feet carefully out onto the dirty
board floor, and the foreman shoved the pan under Spurlock's
dangling feet. Standing over Rusty, burly, matted-haired, grave-

eyed, totally enigmatic to the boy but restored to his position of authority and respect, he said, "How you doin'? Feelin' yours?"

"Enough," Rusty said. He raised his head a little. "What's the cure for frostbite?"

"Whiskey," Jesse said from beside Spurlock.

"Fine," said Little Horn. "Just what we ain't got."

"If we had some rocks we could have some rock and rye," Slip said. "If we had some rye."

"No particular cure," Ray said to Rusty. "Thaw it out slow, keep away from heat, little arnica if you get sores, cut it out if you get gangrene. And wait."

"How long?"

"Depends how bad you are. You and Little Horn, maybe a week, ten days. Ed maybe two-three weeks. It's the hands and feet that lay you up."

"What do we do, stay here till we're well?"

"I expect we'll cobble up that tongue and beat it for the ranch soon as it clears off."

"Vacation with pay," Little Horn said. "Peach pies. Whiskey every hour, while Panguingue does the chores. I tell you, Rusty, there's no life like a cowboy's."

But Rusty was thinking of the two weeks they had just gone through, and of the cattle that had gone streaming miserably downwind from the Horse Camp corrals, the gaunt exhausted horses that had hung around the tent and wagon until the wind literally blew them away. "What about the calves?" he asked. "And what about the horses?"

"Horses we'll have to round up, some of them anyway. They'll winter out all right, but we need work ponies."

"You mean—ride out there and hunt through all that country and drive them on back to the ranch?"

"Uh-huh."

"I tell you," Little Horn said, and lifted his left foot out of the bucket and raised his right tenderly in, "there's no business like the cow business to make a man healthy and active. There's hardly a job you can work at that'll keep you more in the open air."

Rusty smelled the coffee that Jesse had put on the fire as soon as he got it going. He saw the flaw of moisture the spout cast on the stovepipe, and he moved his pain-distended hands cautiously, cradling them in his lap. The shack's growing warmth burned in his cheeks. Over on the other side of the stove Slippers' face, purple in the bare patches, black where the beard grew, brooded with its eyes on the floor. This was the leathery little man who would ride out to bring the ponies back across sixty miles of rough country. And maybe one or two others—maybe himself—with him. The very notion, at that moment, moved the boy to something like awe.

"What about the calves?" he said.

For the first time expression—disgust? anger? ironic resignation?—flickered across Ray's chapped, bearded mouth. "The calves. Well, the ones that ain't dead by the time this one blows out may find some willows to gnaw in a coulee, and if we get a chinook they'll have feed and come through all right. If we don't get a chinook the wolves are gonna be very fat by spring."

"But we aren't going to try rounding them up again."

Ray turned away with the flicker widening momentarily on his mouth. "I wouldn't worry about it," he said.

"Don't be impatient," Little Horn said, and hissed sharply as he moved his foot and bumped the pail. He set the heel on the floor and looked at the swollen toes, looked at his sausage-like fingers, shook his head. On the bunk Spurlock raised one foot from the dishpan. "Wait a minute," Jesse said. "Got enough of that footbath for a while?"

He helped the legs with their rolled-up pants to straighten out in the bunk. In the silence that came down as the pain of returning blood preoccupied them Rusty heard the undiminished wind shriek along the icicled eaves of the shack and swoop away. Smoke puffed out around the rings of the stove lids, lay there for a minute like fat white circular worms, and was sucked in again. Shaggy as cavemen, weather-beaten and battered, they huddled back against the walls and away from the stove and contemplated each in his own way the discomforts of the outraged flesh. Each retired within his skinful of pain and weariness, and among them Rusty Cullen, as weary as any, as full of pain as any—pain enough to fill him to the chin and make him lock his jaw for fear of whimpering. He made note that none whimpered, not even Spurlock; the worst was an occasional querulous growl when one moved too fast. Jesse, the old-timer, the knowing one, Nestor and patriarch, unfrozen except for a touch on the fingers and ears, moved between them in stockinged feet and flipped the coffeepot lid with the edge of his palm, saving his tender fingertips, and looked in. The mystic smells of brotherhood were strong in the shack. The stove lids puffed out worms of smoke once more, and once more sucked them inward. The wind went over and around them, the ancient implacable wind, and tore away balked and shrill.

The Rusty Cullen who sat among them was a different boy, outside and inside, from the one who had set out with them two weeks before. He thought that he knew enough not to want to distinguish himself by heroic deeds: singlehanded walks to the North Pole, incredible journeys, rescues, what not. Given his way, he did not think that he would ever want to do anything alone again, not in this country. Even a trip to the privy was something a man might want to take in company.

The notion insinuated itself into his head, not for the first time, that his sticking with Spurlock after Panguingue left was an act of special excellence, that the others must look upon him with a new respect because of it. But the tempting thought did not stand up under the examination he gave it. Special excellence? Why hadn't anyone praised him for it, then? He knew why: because it was what any of them would have done. To have done less would have been cowardice and disgrace. It was probably a step in the making of a cowhand when he learned that what would pass for heroics in a softer world was only chores around here.

Around him he heard the hiss of air drawn between clenched teeth, he saw the careful, excruciating slowness of hands and feet being moved in search of more comfortable positions, he saw and smelled and felt how he was indistinguishable from the other seven. His greenness did not show, was perhaps not quite so green as it had been. And he did not take it ill, but understood it as a muffled acceptance of acknowledgment, when Spurlock sniffed thickly and said to the sagging springs above his nose, "Is that coffee I smell, Jesse, or is it only fawncy?"

3

Carrion Spring

Often in Saskatchewan a man awakens on a winter night hearing a great wind, and his heart sinks at the prospect of more shut-in days, more cold, difficulty, discomfort, and danger. But one time in ten, something keeps him from burrowing back under his blankets, something keeps him suspiciously on his elbow, straining his ears for the sounds of hope. Repudiating his hope even while he indulges it, he may leave the warmth of bed and go to the door, bracing himself for the needles of thirty below. And one time in ten, when he opens door and storm door against the grab and bluster of the wind, the air rushes in his face as warm as milk, all but smelling of orange blossoms, and he dances a caper on his cold floor and goes back to bed knowing that in the two or three days that the chinook blows it will gulp all the snow except the heaviest drifts and leave the prairie dry enough to sit down on Dozing off, he hears the crescendo of drip, the slump of heavied snow on the roof, the crash of loosened icicles under the eaves.

Several times every winter the harsh Saskatchewan weather is relieved by that beautiful mild wind that can raise the temperature in a half hour from zero to fifty above. It is the chinook that makes Saskatchewan bearable in winter, the chinook that clears the prairies periodically and allows cattle to feed. It was a chinook that the cattle outfits on the Whitemud waited for in vain during the winter of 1906-07.

In vain, or nearly. November, December, January, brought

them only blizzards, cold snaps, freezing fogs, snow. A forkful at a time, the T-Down boys fed the hay they had stacked at Bates and Stonepile. They broke down their ponies trying to drag clear patches of hillside where the cattle could feed, only to see new snow cover their work, or the cattle flinching back from the wind to gnaw willows and starve in the snowy bottoms. Not until the end of January did the punchers at Bates and Stonepile feel on their faces that soft and strengthening blast from the southwest. They went to bed drunk on it, assured that though hundreds of cattle were dead along the river, something could be saved. When they awoke in the morning the air was still, the abortive chinook had died, the snow that had been thawed mushy was frozen hard again, the prairie was sheathed in four inches of solid ice, and cattle that had lain down in the snow were frozen in, unable to move. They dragged free as many as they could reach, threw open the gates on whatever scraps of hay were left, and retreated to the ranch, which was hoarding its few stacks for the ultimate emergency. The emergency arrived, or rather continued. Storm and cold through February; then a chinook that gave the scarecrow survivors a few days of relief; then more blizzards and cold that locked them in ice until May. During the last six weeks they could do nothing but skin out the dead.

Their story goes on too long; it is nothing but unrelieved hardship, failure, death, gloom. Even the wolfer Schulz, who had no concern about cattle, shared the ruin of that winter. The wolves that he would ordinarily have run down with his hounds on the flats were all down in the deep snow of the bottoms, where the cattle were and where their big pads would let them run while a hound floundered. They sat just out of rifle range and laughed; they were so well fed and so smart they never went near the traps Schulz set. In February, furious and frustrated, without a single wolf to show for months of effort, Schulz locked up his hounds in the Stonepile stable and poisoned a dozen carcasses up and down the river. But his great staghound, Puma, was too much of a pet to stay locked in. He broke out one afternoon when Schulz was gone, followed his master's tracks several miles up-river, stopped on the way to feed on one of the poisoned carcasses, and came upon Schulz in the middle of a white-out, a dense freezing fog, where the wolfer had built a fire on the ice to keep warm until he could get his bearings. For an hour or two the hound padded back and forth with the man as he walked to keep from freezing around the little fire of willows. Then the dog began acting strange, rolling, gaping; and at some moment during the night, lost in the whiteness of that lost river, sick and furious at his winter's failure, the wolfer looked up and saw the hound coming for him. He jumped to his gun, stuck butt down in the snow, and killed the dog with one shot in the mouth.

No one saw Schulz again. He simply vanished, disappointed or crazy or fed up. Several months later the T-Down boys, conducting their pitiful spring roundup of survivors, heard how he drowned swimming his horse across the Milk River in the spring break-up.

A casualty, a wild man defeated by the wild. But the civilized did no better. And especially Molly Henry, who on her wedding day in late October had said goodby to whatever civilization was offered by her home town of Malta, Montana, and who except for the Christmas blowout had enjoyed neither fun nor the company of another woman since. She was a tough and competent little body; she believed in work as a cure for the doldrums, and she had married with the full intention of being a good wife to a cattleman. Among the things she and Ray had talked about on their buckboard honeymoon were the future settlement of that country and the opportunities open to the young and industrious.

But six months is a long time to be shut in, too long a stretch of desperate work and hardship and shortages and unmitigated failure. The brief dream of Indian Summer would not have lasted through all that disastrous winter. In spite of the work she used as therapy, hope would have festered in her. When the long agony finally broke, and the thaw began, and the sun that had seemed gone forever came back in spells of unbelievable warmth, she would have greeted release with a tight mouth, determined to take her man and her marriage back where there was a chance for both.

The moment she came to the door she could smell it, not really rotten and not coming from any particular direction, but sweetish, faintly sickening, sourceless, filling the whole air the way a river's water can taste of weeds—the carrion smell of a whole country breathing out in the first warmth across hundreds of square miles.

Three days of chinook had uncovered everything that had been under snow since November. The yard lay discolored and ugly, gray ashpile, rusted cans, spilled lignite, bones. The clinkers that had given them winter footing to privy and stable lay in raised gray wavers across the mud; the strung lariats they had used for lifelines in blizzardy weather had dried out and sagged to the ground. Muck was knee deep down in the corrals by the sod-roofed stable, the whitewashed logs were yellowed at the corners from dogs lifting their legs against them. Sunken drifts around the hay yard were a reminder of how many times the boys had had to shovel out there to keep the calves from walking into the stacks across the top of them. Across the wan and disheveled yard the willows were bare, and beyond them the flood-plain hill was brown. The sky was roiled with gray cloud.

Matted, filthy, lifeless, littered, the place of her winter imprisonment was exposed, ugly enough to put gooseflesh up her backbone, and with the carrion smell over all of it. It was like a bad and disgusting wound, infected wire cut or proud flesh or the gangrene of frostbite, with the bandage off. With her packed trunk and her telescope bag and two loaded grain sacks behind her, she stood in the door waiting for Ray to come with the buckboard, and she was sick to be gone.

Yet when he did come, with the boys all slopping through the mud behind him, and they threw her trunk and telescope and bags into the buckboard and tied the tarp down and there was nothing left to do but go, she faced them with a sudden, desolating desire to cry. She laughed, and caught her lower lip under her teeth and bit down hard on it, and went around to shake one hoof-like hand after the other, staring into each face in turn and seeing in each something that made it all the harder to say something easy: Goodbye. Red-bearded, black-bearded, gray-bristled, clean-shaven (for her?), two of them with puckered sunken scars on the cheekbones, all of them seedy, matted-haired, weathered and cracked as old lumber left out for years, they looked sheepish, or sober, or cheerful, and said things like, "Well, Molly, have you a nice trip, now," or "See you in Malta maybe." They had been her family. She had looked after them, fed them, patched their clothes, unraveled old socks to knit them new ones, cut their hair, lanced their boils, tended their wounds. Now it was like the gathered-in family parting at the graveside after someone's funeral.

She had begun quite openly to cry. She pulled her cheeks down, opened her mouth, dabbed at her eyes with her knuckles, laughed. "Now you all take care," she said. "And come see us, you hear? Jesse? Rusty? Slip? Buck, when you come I'll fix you a better patch on your pants than that one. Goodbye, Panguingue, you were the best man I had on the coal scuttle. Don't you forget me. Little Horn, I'm *sorry* we ran out of pie fixings. When you come to Malta I'll make you a peach pie a yard across."

She could not have helped speaking their names, as if to name them were to insure their permanence. But she knew that though she might see them, or most of them, when Ray brought the drive in to Malta in July, these were friends who would soon be lost for good. They had already got the word: sweep the range and sell everything—steers, bulls, calves, cows—for whatever it would bring. Put a For Sale sign on the ranch, or simply abandon it. The country had rubbed its lesson in. Like half the outfits between the Milk and the CPR, the T-Down was quitting. As for her, she was quitting first.

She saw Ray slumping, glooming down from the buckboard seat with the reins wrapped around one gloved hand. Dude and Dinger were hipshot in the harness. As Rusty and Little Horn gave Molly a hand up to climb the wheel, Dude raised his tail and dropped an oaty bundle of dung on the singletree, but she did not even bother to make a face or say something provoked and joking. She was watching Ray, looking right into his gray eyes and his somber dark face and seeing all at once what the winter of disaster had done to him. His cheek, like Ed's and Rusty's, was puckered with frost scars; frost had nibbled at the lobes of his ears; she could see the strain of bone-cracking labor, the bitterness of failure, in the lines from his nose to the corners of his mouth. Making room for her, he did not smile. With her back momentarily to the others, speaking only for him, she said through her tight teeth, "Let's git!"

Promptly—he was always prompt and ready—he plucked whip from whipsocket. The tip snapped on Dinger's haunch, the lurch of the buggy threw her so that she could cling and not have to turn to reveal her face. "Goodbye!" she cried, more into the collar of her mackinaw than to them, throwing the words over her shoulder like a flower or a coin, and tossed her left hand in the air and shook it. The single burst of their voices chopped off into silence. She heard only the grate of the tires in gravel; beside her the wheel poured yellow drip. She concentrated on it, fighting her lips that wanted to blubber.

"This could be bad for a minute," Ray said. She looked up. Obediently she clamped thumb and finger over her nose. To their right, filling half of Frying Pan Flat, was the boneyard, two acres of carcasses scattered where the boys had dragged them after skinning them out when they found them dead in the brush. It did not seem that off there they could smell, for the chinook was blowing out in light airs from the west. But when she let go her nose she smelled it rich and rotten, as if it rolled upwind the way water runs upstream in an eddy.

Beside her Ray was silent. The horses were trotting now in the soft sand of the patrol trail. On both sides the willows were gnawed down to stubs, broken and mouthed and gummed off by starving cattle. There was floodwater in the low spots, and the sound of running water under the drifts of every side coulee.

Once Ray said, "Harry Willis says a railroad survey's coming right up the Whitemud valley this summer. S'pose that'll mean homesteaders in here, maybe a town."

"I s'pose."

"Make it a little easier when you run out of prunes, if there was a store at Whitemud."

"Well," she said, "we won't be here to run out," and then immediately, as she caught a whiff that gagged her, "Pee-you! Hurry up!"

Ray did not touch up the team. "What for?" he said. "To get to the next one quicker?"

She appraised the surliness of his voice, and judged that some of it was general disgust and some of it was aimed at her. But what did he want? Every time she made a suggestion of some outfit around Malta or Chinook where he might get a job he humped his back and looked inpenetrable. What *did* he want? To come back here and take another licking? When there wasn't even a cattle outfit left, except maybe the little ones like the Z-X and the Lazy-S? And where one winter could kill you, as it had just killed the T-Down? She felt like yelling at him, "Look at your face. Look at your hands—you can't open them even halfway, for calluses. For what? Maybe three thousand cattle left out of ten thousand, and them skin and bone. Why wouldn't I be glad to get out? Who *cares* if there's a store at Whitemud? You're just like an old bulldog with his teeth clinched in somebody's behind, and it'll take a pry-bar to make you unclinch!" She said nothing; she forced herself to breathe evenly the tainted air.

Floodwater forced them out of the bottoms and up onto the second floodplain. Below them Molly saw the river astonishingly wide, pushing across willow bars and pressing deep into the cutbank bends. She could hear it, when the wheels went quietly—a hushed roar like wind. Cattle were balloonily afloat in the brush where they had died. She saw a brindle longhorn waltz around the deep water of a bend with his legs in the air, and farther on a whiteface that stranded momentarily among flooded rosebushes, and rotated free, and stranded again.

Their bench was cut by a side coulee, and they tipped and rocked down, the rumps of the horses back against the dashboard, Ray's hand on the brake, the shoes screeching mud from the tires. There was brush in the bottom, and stained drifts still unmelted. Their wheels sank in slush, she hung to the seat rail, they righted, the lines cracked across the muscling rumps as the team dug in and lifted them out of the cold, snowbank breath of the draw. Then abruptly, in a hollow on the right, dead eyeballs stared at her from between spraddled legs, horns and tails and legs were tangled in a starved mass of bone and hide not yet, in that cold bottom, puffing with the gases of decay. They must have been three deep—piled on one another, she supposed, while drifting before some one of the winter's blizzards.

A little later, accosted by a stench so overpowering that she breathed it in deeply as if to sample the worst, she looked to the left and saw a longhorn, its belly blown up ready to pop, hanging by neck and horns from a tight clump of alder and black birch where the snow had left him. She saw the wind make catspaws in the heavy winter hair.

"Jesus," Ray said, "when you find 'em in *trees!*"

His boots, worn and whitened by many wettings, were braced against the dash. From the corner of her eye Molly could see his glove, its wrist-lace open. His wrist looked as wide as a doubletree, the sleeve of his Levi jacket was tight with forearm. The very sight of his strength made her hate the tone of defeat and outrage in his voice. Yet she appraised the tone cunningly, for she did not want him somehow butting his bullheaded way back into it. There were better things they could do than break their backs and hearts in a hopeless country a hundred miles from anywhere.

With narrowed eyes, caught in an instant vision, she saw the lilac bushes by the front porch of her father's house, heard the screen door bang behind her brother Charley (screen doors!), saw people passing, women in dresses, maybe all going to a picnic or a ballgame down in the park by the river. She passed the front of McCabe's General Store and through the window saw the counters and shelves: dried apples, dried peaches, prunes, tapioca, Karo syrup, everything they had done without for six weeks; and new white-stitched overalls, yellow horsehide gloves, varnished axe handles, barrels of flour and bags of sugar, shiny boots and workshoes, counters full of calico and flowered voile and crepe de chine and curtain net, whole stacks of flypaper stuck sheet to sheet, jars of peppermints and striped candy and horehound . . . She giggled.

"What?" Ray's neck and shoulders were so stiff with muscle that he all but creaked when he turned his head.

"I was just thinking. Remember the night I used our last sugar to make that batch of divinity, and dragged all the boys in after bedtime to eat it?"

"Kind of saved the day," Ray said. "Took the edge off ever'-body."

"Kind of left us starving for sugar, too. I can still see them picking up those little bitty dabs of fluff with their fingers like tongs, and stuffing them in among their whiskers and making faces, *yum yum*, and wondering what on earth had got into me."

"Nothing got into you. You was just fed up. We all was."

"Remember when Slip picked up that pincushion I was tatting a cover for, and I got sort of hysterical and asked him if he knew what it was? Remember what he said? 'It a doll piller, ain't it, Molly?' I thought I'd die."

She shook her head angrily. Ray was looking sideward at her in alarm. She turned her face away and stared down across the water that spread nearly a half-mile wide in the bottoms. Dirty foam and brush circled in the eddies. She saw a slab cave from an almost drowned cutbank and sink bubbling. From where they drove, between the water and the outer slope that rolled up to the high prairie, the Cypress Hills made a snow-patched, tree-darkened dome across the west. The wind came off them mild as milk. Poisoned! she told herself, and dragged it deep into her lungs.

She was aware again of Ray's gray eye. "Hard on you," he said. For some reason he made her mad, as if he were accusing her of bellyaching. She felt how all the time they bumped and rolled along the shoulder of the river valley they had this antagonism between them like a snarl of barbed wire. You couldn't reach out anywhere without running into it. Did he blame her for going home, or what? What did he expect her to do, come along with a whole bunch of men on that roundup, spend six or eight weeks in pants out among the carcasses? And then what?

A high, sharp whicker came downwind. The team chuckled and surged into their collars. Looking ahead, she saw a horse—picketed or hobbled—and a man who leaned on something—rifle?—watching them. "Young Schulz," Ray said, and then here came the dogs, four big bony hounds. The team began to dance. Ray held them in tight and whistled the buggywhip in the air when the hounds got too close.

Young Schulz, Molly saw as they got closer, was leaning on a shovel, not a rifle. He had dug a trench two or three feet deep and ten or twelve long. He dragged a bare forearm across his forehead under a muskrat cap: a sullen-faced boy with eyes like dirty ice. She supposed he had been living all alone since his father had disappeared. Somehow he made her want to turn her lips inside out. A wild man, worse than an Indian. She had not liked his father and she did not like him.

The hounds below her were sniffing at the wheels and testing the air up in her direction, wagging slow tails. "What've you got, wolves?" Ray asked.

"Coyotes."

"Old ones down there?"

"One, anyway. Chased her in."

"Find any escape holes?"

"One. Plugged it."

"You get 'em the hard way," Ray said. "How've you been doing on wolves?"

The boy said a hard four-letter word, slanted his eyes sideward at Molly in something less than apology—acknowledgment, maybe. "The dogs ain't worth a damn without Puma to kill for 'em. Since he got killed they just catch up with a wolf and run alongside him. I dug out a couple dens."

With his thumb and finger he worked at a pimple under his jaw. The soft wind blew over them, the taint of carrion only a suspicion, perhaps imaginary. The roily sky had begun to break up in patches of blue. Beside her Molly felt the solid bump of Ray's shoulder as he twisted to cast a weather eye upward. "Going to be a real spring day," he said. To young Schulz he said, "How far in that burrow go, d'you s'pose?"

"Wouldn't ordinarily go more'n twenty feet or so."

"Need any help diggin'?"

The Schulz boy spat. "Never turn it down."

"Ray . . ." Molly said. But she stopped when she saw his face.

"Been a long time since I helped dig out a coyote," he said. He watched her as if waiting for a reaction. "Been a long time since I did anything for *fun*."

"Oh, go ahead!" she said. "Long as we don't miss that train."

"I guess we can make Maple Creek by noon tomorrow. And you ain't in such a hurry you have to be there sooner, are you?"

She had never heard so much edge in his voice. He looked at her as if he hated her. She turned so as to keep the Schulz boy from seeing her face, and for just a second she and Ray were all alone up there, eye to eye. She laid a hand on his knee. "I don't know what it is," she said. "Honestly I don't. But you better work it off."

Young Schulz went back to his digging while Ray unhitched and looped the tugs and tied the horses to the wheels. Then Ray took the shovel and began to fill the air with clods. He moved more dirt than the Fresno scrapers she had seen grading the railroad back home; he worked as if exercising his muscles after a long layoff, as if spring had fired him up and set him to running.

The soil was sandy and came out in clean brown shovelfuls. The hounds lay back out of range and watched. Ray did not look toward Molly, or say anything to Schulz. He just moved dirt as if dirt was his worst enemy. After a few minutes Molly pulled the buffalo robe out of the buckboard and spread it on the drying prairie. By that time it was getting close to noon. The sun was full out; she felt it warm on her face and hands.

The coyote hole ran along about three feet underground. From where she sat she could look right up the trench, and see the black opening at the bottom when the shovel broke into it. She could imagine the coyotes crammed back at the end of their burrow, hearing the noises and seeing the growing light as their death dug toward them, and no way out, nothing to do but wait.

Young Schulz took the shovel and Ray stood out of the trench, blowing. The violent work seemed to have made him more cheerful. He said to Schulz, when the boy stooped and reached a gloved hand up the hole, "She comes out of there in a hurry she'll run right up your sleeve."

Schulz grunted and resumed his digging. The untroubled sun went over, hanging almost overhead, and an untroubled wind stirred the old grass. Over where the last terrace of the floodplain rolled up to the prairie the first gopher of the season sat up and looked them over. A dog moved, and he disappeared with a flirt of his tail. Ray was rolling up his sleeves, whistling loosely between his teeth. His forearms were white, his hands blackened and cracked as the charred ends of sticks. His eyes touched her—speculatively, she thought. She smiled, making a forgiving, kissing motion of her mouth, but all he did in reply was work his eyebrows, and she could not tell what he was thinking.

Young Schulz was poking up the hole with the shovel handle. Crouching in the trench in his muskrat cap, he looked like some digging animal; she half expected him to put his nose into the hole and sniff and then start throwing dirt out between his hind legs.

Then in a single convulsion of movement Schulz rolled sideward. A naked-gummed thing of teeth and gray fur shot into sight, scrambled at the edge, and disappeared in a pinwheel of dogs. Molly leaped to the heads of the horses, rearing and wall-eyed and yanking the light buckboard sideways, and with a hand in each bridle steadied them down. Schulz, she saw, was circling the dogs with the shotgun, but the dogs had already done it for him. The roaring and snapping tailed off. Schulz kicked the dogs away and with one quick flash and circle and rip tore the scalp and ears off the coyote. It lay there wet, mauled, bloody, with its pink skull bare—a little dog brutally murdered. One of the hounds came up, sniffed with its neck stretched out, sank its teeth in the coyote's shoulder, dragged it a foot or two.

"Ray . . ." Molly said.

He did not hear her; he was blocking the burrow with the shovel blade while Schulz went over to his horse. The boy came back with a red willow stick seven or eight feet long, forked like a small slingshot at the end. Ray pulled away the shovel and Schulz twisted in the hole with the forked end of the stick. A hard grunt came out of him, and he backed up, pulling the stick from the hole. At the last moment he yanked hard, and a squirm of gray broke free and rolled and was pounced on by the hounds.

This time Ray kicked them aside. He picked up the pup by the tail, and it hung down and kicked its hind legs a little. Schulz was down again, probing the burrow, twisting, probing again, twisting hard.

Again he backed up, working the entangled pup out carefully until it was in the open, and then landing it over his head like a sucker from the river. The pup landed within three feet of the buckboard wheel, and floundered, stunned. In an instant Molly dropped down and smothered it in clothes, hands, arms. There was snarling in her very ear, she was bumped hard, she heard Ray yelling, and then he had her on her feet. From his face, she thought he was going to hit her. Against her middle, held by the scruff and grappled with the other arm, the pup snapped and slavered with needle teeth. She felt the sting of bites on her hands and wrists. The dogs ringed her, ready to jump, kept off by Ray's kicking boot.

"God a'mighty," Ray said, "you want to get yourself killed?"

"I didn't want the dogs to get him."

"No. What are you going to do with him? We'll just have to knock him in the head."

"I'm going to keep him."

"In Malta?"

"Why not?"

He let go his clutch on her arm. "He'll be a cute pup for a month and then he'll be a chicken thief and then somebody'll shoot him."

"At least he'll have a little bit of a life. Get *away*, you dirty, murdering . . . !" She cradled the thudding little body along one arm under her mackinaw, keeping her hold in the scruff with her right hand, and turned herself away from the crowding hounds. "I'm going to tame him," she said. "I don't care what you say."

"Scalp's worth three dollars," Schulz said from the edge of the ditch.

Ray kicked the dogs back. His eyes, ordinarily so cool and gray, looked hot. The digging and the excitement did not seem to have taken the edge off whatever was eating him. He said, "Look, maybe you have to go back home to your folks, but you don't have to take a menagerie along. What are you going to do with him on the train?"

But now it was out. He did blame her. "You think I'm running out on you," she said.

"I just said you can't take a menagerie back to town."

"You said *maybe* I had to go home. Where else would I go? You're going to be on roundup till July. The ranch is going to be sold. Where on earth *would* I go but home?"

"You don't have to stay. You don't have to make me go back to ridin' for some outfit for twenty a month and found."

His dark, battered, scarred face told her to be quiet. Dipping far down in the tight pocket of his Levis he brought up his snap purse and took from it three silver dollars. Young Schulz, who had been probing the den to see if anything else was there, climbed out of the ditch and took the money in his dirty chapped hand. He gave Molly one cool look with his dirty-ice eyes, scalped the dead pup, picked up shotgun and twisting-stick and shovel, tied them behind the saddle, mounted, whistled at the dogs, and with barely a nod rode off toward the northeastern flank of the Hills. The hounds fanned out ahead of him, running loose and easy. In the silence their departure left behind, a clod broke and rolled into the ditch. A gopher piped somewhere. The wind moved quiet as breathing in the grass.

Molly drew a breath that caught a little—a sigh for their quarreling, for whatever bothered him so deeply that he gloomed and grumped and asked something impossible of her—but when she spoke she spoke around it. "No thanks for your digging."

"He don't know much about living with people."

"He's like everything else in this country, wild and dirty and thankless."

In a minute she would really start feeling sorry for herself. But why not? Did it ever occur to him that since November, when they came across the prairie on their honeymoon in this same buckboard, she had seen exactly one woman, for one day and a night? Did he have any idea how she had felt, a bride of three weeks, when he went out with the boys on late fall roundup and was gone ten days, through three different blizzards, while she stayed home and didn't know whether he was dead or alive?

"If you mean me," Ray said, "I may be wild and I'm probably dirty, but I ain't thankless, honey." Shamed, she opened her mouth to reply, but he was already turning away to rummage up a strap and a piece of whang leather to make a collar and leash for her pup.

"Are you hungry?" she said to his shoulders.

"Any time."

"I put up some sandwiches."

"O.K."

"Oh, Ray," she said, "let's not crab at each other! Sure I'm glad we're getting out. Is that so awful? I hate to see you killing yourself bucking this *hopeless* country. But does that mean we have to fight? I thought maybe we could have a picnic like we had coming in, back on that slough where the ducks kept coming in and landing on the ice and skidding end over end. I don't know, it don't hardly seem we've laughed since."

"Well," he said, "it ain't been much of a laughing winter, for a fact." He had cut down a cheekstrap and tied a rawhide thong to it. Carefully she brought out the pup and he buckled the collar around its neck, but when she set it on the ground it backed up to the end of the thong, cringing and showing its naked gums, so that she picked it up again and let it dig along her arm, hunting darkness under her mackinaw.

"Shall we eat here?" Ray said. "Kind of a lot of chewed-up coyote around."

"Let's go up on the bench."

"Want to tie the pup in the buckboard?"

"I'll take him. I want to get him used to me."

"O.K.," he said. "You go on. I'll tie a nosebag on these nags and bring the robe and the lunchbox."

She walked slowly, not to scare the pup, until she was up the little bench and onto the prairie. From up there she could see not only the Cypress Hills across the west, but the valley of the Whitemud breaking out of them, and a big slough, spread by floodwater, and watercourses going both ways out of it, marked by thin willows. Just where the Whitemud emerged from the hills were three white dots—the Mountie post, probably, or the Lazy-S, or both. The sun was surprisingly warm, until she counted up and found that it was May 8. It ought to be warm.

Ray brought the buffalo robe and spread it, and she sat down. One-handed because she had the thong of the leash wrapped around her palm, she doled out sandwiches and hard-boiled eggs. Ray popped a whole egg in his mouth, and chewing, pointed. "There goes the South Fork of the Swift Current, out of the slough. The one this side, that little scraggle of willows you can see, empties into the Whitemud. That slough sits right on the divide and runs both ways. You don't see that very often."

She appraised his tone. He was feeling better. For that matter, so was she. It had turned out a beautiful day, with big fair-weather clouds coasting over. She saw the flooded river bottoms below them, on the left, darken to winter and then sweep bright back to spring again while she could have counted no more than ten. As she moved, the coyote pup clawed and scrambled against her side, and she said, wrinkling her nose in her Freckleface smile, "If he started eating me, I wonder if I could keep from yelling? Did you ever read that story about the boy that hid the fox under his clothes and the fox started eating a hole in him and the boy never batted an eye, just let himself be chewed?"

"No, I never heard that one," Ray said. "Don't seem very likely, does it?" He lay back and turned his face, shut-eyed, into the sun. Now and then his hand rose to feed bites of sandwich into his mouth.

"The pup's quieter," Molly said. "I bet he'll tame. I wonder if he'd eat a piece of sandwich?"

"Leave him be for a while, I would."

"I guess."

His hand reached over blindly and she put another sandwich into its pincer claws. Chewing, he came up on an elbow; his eyes opened, he stared a long time down into the flooded bottoms and then across toward the slough and the hills. "Soon as the sun comes out, she don't look like the same country, does she?"

Molly said nothing. She watched his nostrils fan in and out as he sniffed. "No smell up here, do you think?" he said. But she heard the direction he was groping in, the regret that could lead, if they did not watch out, to some renewed and futile hope, and she said tartly, "I can smell it, all right."

He sighed. He lay back and closed his eyes. After about three minutes he said, "Boy, what a day, though. I won't get through on the patrol trail goin' back. The ice'll be breakin' up before to-night, at this rate. Did you hear it crackin' and poppin' a minute ago?"

"I didn't hear it."

"Listen."

They were still. She heard the soft wind move in the prairie wool, and beyond it, filling the background, the hushed and hollow noise of the floodwater, sigh of drowned willows, suck of whirlpools, splash and guggle as cutbanks caved, and the steady push and swash and ripple of moving water. Into the soft rush of sound came a muffled report like a tree cracking, or a shot a long way off. "Is that it?" she said. "Is that the ice letting loose?"

"Stick around till tomorrow and you'll see that whole channel full of ice."

Another shadow from one of the big flat-bottomed clouds chilled across them and passed. Ray said into the air, "Harry Willis said this railroad survey will go right through to Medicine Hat. Open up this whole country."

Now she sat very still, stroking the soft bulge of the pup through the cloth.

"Probably mean a town at Whitemud."

"You told me."

"With a store that close we couldn't get quite so snowed in as we did this winter."

Molly said nothing, because she dared not. They were a couple that, like the slough spread out northwest of them, flowed two ways, he to this wild range, she back to town and friends and family. And yet in the thaw of one bright day, their last together up here north of the Line, she teetered. She feared the softening that could start her draining toward his side.

"Molly," Ray said, and made her look at him. She saw him as the country and the winter had left him, weathered and scarred. His eyes were gray and steady, marksman's eyes.

She made a wordless sound that sounded in her own ears almost a groan. "You want awful bad to stay," she said.

His tong fingers plucked a strand of grass, he bit it between his teeth, his head went slowly up and down.

"But how?" she said. "Do you want to strike the Z-X for a job, or the Lazy-S, or somebody? Do you want to open a store in Whitemud for when the railroad comes through, or what?"

"Haven't you figured that out yet?" he said. "Kept waitin' for you to see it. I want to buy the T-Down."

"You *what?*"

"I want us to buy the T-Down and make her go."

She felt that she went all to pieces. She laughed. She threw her hands around so that the pup scrambled and clawed at her side. "Ray Henry," she said, "you're crazy as a bedbug. Even if it made any sense, which it doesn't, where'd we get the money?"

"Borrow it."

"Go in debt to stay up *here?*"

"Molly," he said, and she heard the slow gather of determination in his voice, "when else could we pick up cattle for twenty dollars a head with sucking calves thrown in? When else could we get a whole ranch layout for a few hundred bucks? That Goodnight herd we were running was the best herd in Canada, maybe anywhere. This spring roundup we could take our pick of what's left, including bulls, and put our brand on 'em and turn 'em into summer range and drive everything else to Malta. We wouldn't want more than three-four hundred head. We can swing that much, and we can cut enough hay to bring that many through even a winter like this last one."

She watched him; her eyes groped and slipped. He said, "We're never goin' to have another chance like this as long as we live. This country's goin' to change; there'll be homesteaders in here soon as the railroad comes. Towns, stores, what you've been missin'. Women folks. And we can sit out here on the Whitemud with good hay land and good range and just make this God darned country holler uncle."

"How long?" she said. "How long have you been thinking this way?"

"Since we got John's letter."

"You never said anything."

"I kept waitin' for you to get the idea yourself. But you were hell bent to get out."

She escaped his eyes, looked down, shifted carefully to accommodate the wild thing snuggled in darkness at her waist, and as she moved, her foot scuffed up the scalloped felt edge of the buffalo robe. By her toe was a half-crushed crocus, palely lavender, a thing so tender and unbelievable in the waste of brown grass under the great pour of sky that she cried out, "Why, good land, look at that!"—taking advantage of it both as discovery and as diversion.

"Crocus?" Ray said, bending. "Don't take long, once the snow goes."

It lay in her palm, a thing lucky as a four-leaf clover, and as if it had had some effect in clearing her sight, Molly looked down the south-facing slope and saw it tinged with faintest green. She put the crocus to her nose, but smelled only a mild freshness, an odor no more showy than that of grass. But maybe enough to cover the scent of carrion.

Her eyes came up and found Ray's watching her steadily. "You think we could do it," she said.

"I know we could."

"It's a funny time to start talking that way, when I'm on my way out."

"You don't have to stay out."

Sniffing the crocus, she put her right hand under the mackinaw until her fingers touched fur. The pup stiffened but did not turn or snap. She moved her fingers softly along his back, willing him tame. For some reason she felt as if she might burst out crying.

"Haven't you got any ambition to be the first white woman in five hundred miles?" Ray said.

Past and below him, three or four miles off, she saw the great slough darken under a driving cloud shadow and then brighten to a blue that danced with little wind-whipped waves. She wondered what happened to the ice in a slough like that, whether it went on down the little flooded creeks to add to the jams in the Whitemud and Swift Current, or whether it just rose to the surface and gradually melted there. She didn't suppose it would be spectacular like the break-up in the river.

"Mumma and Dad would think we'd lost our minds," she said. "How much would we have to borrow?"

"Maybe six or eight thousand."

"Oh Lord!" She contemplated the sum, a burden of debt heavy enough to pin them down for life. She remembered the winter, six months of unremitting slavery and imprisonment. She lifted the crocus and laid it against Ray's dark scarred cheek.

"You should never wear lavender," she said, and giggled at the very idea, and let her eyes come up to his and stared at him, sick and scared. "All right," she said. "If it's what you want."

IV

TOWN AND COUNTRY

My native town was a mining town in the Sierra Nevada —a place five or six years older than myself. My earliest recollections include the very frequent wonder as to what my elders meant when they said that this was a new community. I frequently looked at the vestiges left by the former diggings of miners, saw that many pine logs were rotten, and that a miner's grave was to be found in a lonely spot not far from my own house. Plainly men had lived and died thereabouts. I dimly reflected that this sort of life had apparently been going on ever since men dwelt in that land. The logs and graves looked old. The sunsets were beautiful. The wide prospects when one looked across the Sacramento Valley were impressive, and had long interested the people of whose love for my country I had heard much. What was there then in this place that ought to be called new, or for that matter, crude? I wondered, and gradually came to feel that part of my life's business was to find out what all this wonder meant.

JOSIAH ROYCE, *The Hope of the Great Community*

1

The Town Builders

Until after the turn of the century—until after the winter of 1906-07, in fact—the population of the Cypress Hills country was thin and mobile. The typical ranch was a little home place and a big lease, the typical way of life a calculated movement between summer and winter range and between range and railroad. But something new came in with the owners of the Lazy-S.

Though they began as ranchers, they were not wanderers; and very early in their residence in the valley of the Whitemud they started the drift that could lead only to permanence and people. One of them in particular had the Myth of the Garden bad, but he had it in a special way, for he was no homesteader bent on hewing out a family home in the wilderness, but a town-builder with a manorial imagination. Though he would not have recognized himself in literary form, he is a common figure in our novels, from Cooper's Judge Temple, who gave Leatherstocking so much trouble with his settlement law, to Captain Forrester, who declines so symbolically in Willa Cather's *A Lost Lady*. He was literally the father of our town. He did not want to be merely a tenant of Eden, he wanted to be its founder, creator, landlord, and patron.

Call the partners Martin and Fisher. Their money came from a business in Butte that some said was restaurant, some saloon, some gambling joint, and some whorehouse. All the descriptions may have had validity, for all I know. In any case there was

241

plenty of money, and along with the money a compulsion to dream big. Fisher I never knew, but I have a 1906 photograph of him on horseback and in a Chihuahua hat, with Schulz's great staghound beside him, under the flume that crossed the eastern reach of the Whitemud. He is only a name and a somewhat theatrical picture. But Martin was the rich man of my boyhood, his son Homer the rich boy, his wife Nellie the *grande dame*. Because Pop Martin shaped much of the structure of the town of 'Whitemud, he shaped my perceptions and recollections; because he blew in a certain way, my vane turned to match his wind.

The Martins lived in the big Lazy-S ranch house surrounded by screened verandas. They had a Chinese cook (Mah Li's brother Mah Jim) and an English maid, and on moonlit winter nights there was sometimes a team and a bobsled full of straw, with a ranch hand to drive, and the word went through town like the news of an exposed nerve in a tooth, so that we came laboring and slipping, panting smoke into the iron air, and flopped behind the belly-flopping sled last in line, and caught ankles and hung on, and felt our ankles caught in turn, and so strung out, a black line with the moon pouring on us and the trailside snow touched with red from the lantern on the endgate, until we reached the Swift Current hill where the best coasting was.

Eheu. They are the material for a sermon on the vanity of human wishes. The last time I saw Homer Martin he was jerking soda in a Hollywood drugstore; his mother was running a beauty parlor that catered to the stars; his father was long dead and longer bankrupt. By that time, twenty years or so after Pop Martin founded our town, half its population had drifted out or been driven out; Mah Jim had taken Mah Li's body back to China for burial among his ancestors; the English maid Irene, married for a while to one of the cowpunchers, had divorced him out of love of a married man. After we left Whitemud she lived with us for a while in Salt Lake City: I helped pump her out one night when she swallowed a handful of sleeping pills. Later she returned to Whitemud, married again, bought our old house in the west end, and lived there in apparent content until she died of cancer.

So far off and long ago, so wavering across time like rain on a windowpane! Poor Irene did not find contentment easily. Nearly a half century ago she scared me half out of my skin when, sent to her house on some errand, I found her drinking with friends at her kitchen table. She had a crying jag well begun, and when I arrived unseen in the doorway she was telling the others, through angry tears, that she was *not* ashamed of her shape. While they laughed, she started yanking at her clothes. Her skirt was kicked against the wall, her shirtwaist came off. She was down to her high laced shoes and the frilled pants that the British call knickers before she saw me. "Peeping little bugger!" she said, and came for me with her big breasts bobbing. I looked back once, in time to see her friends catch and hold her at the ditchbank, but by that time I was a block away, and gaining. That is one of the saddest memories I carry with me from that town. It was a hard town on women.

But for men, or at least men of a certain gambler kind, it opened up into the future with the triumphant certainty of a pat flush picked up card by card.

Martin and Fisher bought the Lazy-S brand in 1902, and moved it to the bottomlands at the east edge of the hills. They stocked it with whitefaces the next spring, and the year following, taking advantage of the territorial law which permitted acquisition at low cost of lands brought under irrigation, they completed a dam —really a weir—across the Whitemud a couple of miles west of the ranch. With the diversion planks in, the weir raised the level of the river enough to send water down the main ditch to irrigate about 500 acres. In winter the planks were removed, so that in the spring breakup floodwater could carry the ice smoothly over the whole structure.

Eheu again. I loved that dam and the main ditch. Almost as much as the river they defined my world of town. For a reason I never understood, the pilings of the dam's anchoring buttresses were a place much liked by weasels. I caught four prime ermine in that one spot in the winter of 1918, and the only mink my brother and I ever succeeded in trapping came out of the ice-shelled little rapid below. As for the ditch, I learned to swim in it, I walked its welted banks to school and Sunday School and town, I played shove-your-neighbor on its narrow plank foot-bridges. When there was a gopher to be drowned out anywhere in the town area, we ran to and from the ditch with lard pails, leaving our old dog Caesar trembling at the mouth of the burrow, ready to snap on any slicked-down drowned-rat head if it popped out of the guggle and sink of the hole. There was a lovely summer sound the ditch made, flowing softly against its banks and waving the long grasses like hair; at the weirs that diverted it off into side ditches the water poured curves of amber glass. In winter the dry channel drifted full of snow and made a place for forts and entrenchments. And there was always, whenever we got over into the east end of town, the flume. What the children of Whitemud got out of Martin's irrigation system was not the thing he built it for, but I can't help thinking it important.

Martin and Fisher were not seriously hurt by the winter of 1906-07, for they had good bottom hay land. And anyway, cattle were not their true business. They were horse men, and being gamblers they liked horses that could run. They leased and fenced three entire townships—nearly 70,000 acres, 48 miles of fence—on the southern flank of the hills and stocked that princely pasture with a band of brood mares and a champion trotter stud. They imported several sulkies and laid out a trotting track inside the western bend. By the time we arrived, the dream of feudal grandeur had altered to a dream of unearned increment, and the racetrack was gone, but there was still something. Every time we stopped along the trail for lunch on our racking sixteen-hour drive to the homestead in the spring, those wild range horses used to come with a rush and a drive and a flow of manes and tails to stand prick-eared on the ridge and send our team into nervous whickerings. Perhaps Martin never made a dollar from his horses, perhaps he made them profitable selling them as remounts to the Mounted Police; in any case I owe him something for that part of his dream too. To see two or three hundred horses as wild as antelope, shining black and blood bay and sorrel and chestnut, pour across that apparently limitless pasture under that big sky—beautiful wild creatures born to run, and a country made to run in—that was something to catch at the breath. I have seen my mother watch them with tears in her eyes. I hope Pop Martin got as much as we did out of his horse ranch.

Without the coming of the branch railroad, Martin and Fisher might have remained for a long time lords of a free and enviable domain. But they had been counting on the railroad, and had probably helped promote it. Like other pioneers, they would have believed in Progress, and would have realized no better than others how surely Progress destroys what makes a frontier satisfying. I do not know that any record exists of the deal they made with the Canadian Pacific to guarantee themselves a townsite. If they had offered the railroad a block of lots they would not have been entirely out of line with common practice. In any event they assured themselves not merely a townsite but a division point, and in 1913, when the line began building out from Moose Jaw, they surveyed their bottomland into lots and formed the Whitemud Townsite Company. Thus the accidental huddling of people that had begun with Cowie's Hudson's Bay Company post, and had later become a mutually helpful ranch, post office, and Mountie detachment, was ready to move on toward the system, the legal structure, the permanence, and the density of population that both town-father fantasies and the profit motive suggested.

2

Whitemud, Saskatchewan

It began crude, but it began strenuous. The first meeting of the Village Council was held on March 30, 1914, when the population was 117. Its first act was to establish the town nuisance ground on land donated by Pop Martin. In doing so it corroborated a truth known wherever men have gathered into permanent communities: we are the dirtiest species, and must make provision for our wastes. At the end of May, when we arrived, Whitemud was a straggle of shacks, a general store, a frame hotel, a railroad boarding house, and some derailed dining and box cars rigged for housekeeping. In wet weather the town's one street was gouged and furrowed; in dry it was a river of gray powder, with saddle horses and teams dozing at the hitching bars and flies rising and settling over mounds of dung.

By July 9 a live-wire Board of Trade had opened bids for plank sidewalks, thereby earning the gratitude of every woman in the place. It was not merely mud and dust that women found troublesome. My mother complained that one of the worst things was the way we all wore our shoes out at the toes, kicking through the weeds and sweet clover. Until we took up moccasins, she solved the problem for my brother and me by letting us run barefoot in good weather, and by having our shoe-toes capped with sheet copper. But for a lady there were no such alternatives. I remember, as a rueful commentary on how the amenities suffered among us, the lopped-over high laced shoes in her cupboard, with their heels worn down and their toes whipped and roughened.

On July 17 we had our first stampede, down in the bend where Martin's racetrack had been. That was the stampede at which I adopted Slivers, who won the saddle bronc competition, as my guide in life. (As for me, my brother and I took fourth in a three-legged race for boys seven and under, and I finished out of the money, trussed and humiliated, unable even to get up without help, in the children's sack race.)

By September we had street lights—about a half dozen as I remember—hanging globes of popping radiance between blocks of absolute blackness along Main Street. Off that street we still groped along footpaths by moonlight or starlight or the light of coal-oil lanterns that threw blobs of shadow around a walker's feet and confused more than they illuminated. The lighting of the town illustrated how rigid a pattern habit can impose on a new community. To do any good, the lighting system should have strung itself out along the paths that spoked and took shortcuts through the bottoms, instead of reaching out a road where nobody lived and nobody walked at night.

Before the village was anything but a shack camp, the press and type of the Whitemud *Leader,* having served one tour of duty in another forming Saskatchewan town, arrived from Gull Lake by wagon. By June 11 the first issue was on the street, full of oil prospects, clay prospects, glass prospects, filings and pre-emptions, opportunities, and suggestions to the Board of Trade. Shortly it could add patriotism to its normal frontier frenzy of practical optimism, for on August 4, honoring her treaty with invaded Belgium, England declared war on Germany, and Canada acquired the double duty of providing cannon fodder and growing bread to feed the cannon fodder. The Dominion sent around recruiters, the Province dispatched a Better Farming Train to teach Cockneys and Ukrainians how to grow wheat. A man without funds could get a government loan of Marquis seed wheat, specially developed in Manitoba for the short growing season of northern latitudes. There was still plenty of land for the filing, though it might be, like ours, fifty miles from a town or a railroad, and though the man who filed on it might find himself in a Flanders trench before he could get a crop in the ground.

Church and school arrived almost simultaneously with the press. During Whitemud's first summer a pair of vacationing seminary students, one a Presbyterian and the other a Methodist, camped together out by the dam, living an idyl and pooling their rival theological systems for Sunday services in the room above Christenson's pool hall. When they returned to school in September the pool hall's loft became the town's first school, where fifteen of us learned to read and write and cipher to the click and mutter of farmers playing rotation pool in the billiard hell below. If we needed to go out we raised one or two fingers and were excused to visit the pool hall's privy, whose walls taught us reading faster than the school blackboard did. If we wanted a drink we got to go down to the pool hall itself, a place that smelled of lignite smoke and wet boots and the sweetness of pop and the sour-yeasty smell of beer, and ask one of the men sitting arou .̣ to reach us down a dipperful from the pail of river water on a shelf in the corner.

During the month of Indian Summer following the first blizzard people were busy banking their houses with dirt and putting on storm windows and slaughtering steers and hogs and putting eggs down in waterglass and getting the cellars full of potatoes and rutabagas. Except for the twice-a-week train there was no connection with the outside. As a community and as individuals we braced ourselves for the long dark shut-in time. My mother sewed my brother and me into red flannel in November, and regularly thereafter unsewed us every two weeks for a bath in the tin washtub on the dining-car floor. In the intervals of decent weather my father was building us a house in the west end, on the river. He may have bought the lot from Pop Martin, but my understanding always was that he won it in a poker game.

In nearly every way we were a typical sagebrush village. Though we could not, since Saskatchewan had no counties, reproduce the bitter county-seat battles of the American Midwest, we did have rivalries of a comparable kind with the town of Shaunavon. As elsewhere, too, the town's founders were of every stripe and spot—farmers, shopmen, sharpies, *métis* squatters, Texas cowboys, Syrian and Jewish peddlers, and Cockneys straight out of London's East End. It was a far from unanimous town, and the probity of some parts of it was questionable. Essentially Whitemud drew three kinds of people. One group was made up of sober farmers, family men, members of the Grain

Growers Association who had accounts—or mortgages—in the Grain Growers Bank. Many of these were Scandinavians who had begun their North American experience on the plains of North Dakota, and acquired a Populist tinge in the process. A lot of them were still in Whitemud after the other kinds had diminished or disappeared. A second group included the boosters and land speculators, the "service" people, the merchants, the editor of the *Leader*, the members of the Board of Trade, the priests of Progress. The third group was the gamblers, at best demi-respectable and at worst lawless. For a while these carried on into the tamed agricultural community some of the violence that had marked the Cypress Hills when they were the hideout of whiskey traders and border-jumpers. And there was of course Pop Martin, allied in some ways to all three groups but running his own show.

The gambling crowd, inevitably, struck the sober farming element as a menace. They should have. All through the winter of 1916, I remember, there was a non-stop poker game going in Joe Knight's hotel. When the hotel burned down the game adjourned to Christenson's pool-hall loft which had once served as church and school, and as soon as the hotel was rebuilt it moved back. During the winter the gamblers emptied a lot of relatively empty pockets, but they also took out of one retired rancher the full $16,000 he had realized from the sale of his land and stock. I know, for my father was one of the card players, and a part of that rancher's stake helped pull us out of our starving time. I know too that at least part of the time in that game the cards were marked.

The gamblers gave up reluctantly before the Progress-and-Probity campaign pressed by the *Leader* and the Board of Trade. They had the sympathy of the displaced cattlemen, though they did not especially deserve it. In 1917 and 1918 one of the gambling crowd (and his wife too was a casualty, trying suicide with half a cupful of gopher poison one winter day) allied himself with two hard-case ladies of the region and did a brisk business in rustled stock. I knew him well, and also one of the ladies, who had an adopted son about my age. He died in the flu epidemic of 1918, and she never properly recovered. And yet she was the least sentimental-appearing woman I ever saw. She went around in overalls and riding boots run over at the heels, or in a set of tan coveralls full of pockets. Being naturally ample, she bulged the coveralls in fascinating ways—from a little distance she looked quilted. She had a hoarse, ribald voice and a laugh that threw her into coughing fits and left her glassy-eyed; she swore like a mule driver and she would shoot at anything that moved. Rabbits, stray cats, low-flying geese, muskrats, beaver, meadow-larks—she carried to extremities the destructiveness common to the place and time. Once I saw her staggering back from the dam burdened under two enormous sandhill cranes, which she had shot not because she thought them edible, nor because she wanted their feathers, but because they were standing there in the water. As soon as she had shown them to us, her interest in them was exhausted, and she threw them into the river.

That was the Bad Element, distrusted by the Sober Citizens and abused, not so justly, by the sharpies and speculators who thought them bad for business. But the Bad Element had little to do, really, with the making of Whitemud; it only threatened to frustrate those who wanted to dream this flea-bitten, false-fronted burg into another Chicago.

Floods of settlers, thousands of cattle and horses, millions of bushels of wheat, a busy and beneficent railroad, all figured in the dream, as did lignite coal, oil, pottery clay, glass sand, and other vaguely realizable resources upon which the restless pro-motional eye fell. Towns such as Whitemud have always been floated on the rising gas of great expectations. And true enough—the high benches and the short-grass flanks of the Cypress Hills were horse heaven, and though most of the range out on the prairie had been broken up into homesteads, the protected ranches in the Hills themselves continued every spring to send long trains of cattle cars down the river. And there was some dig-ging of kaolin from a pit northwest of town, and some cars went out to the potteries in Medicine Hat. And wheat? The year 1914 was cold, and the crop mediocre, but 1915 produced a bumper—hardly a field anywhere produced less than forty-five bushels to the acre, and some went nearly to sixty. The town did not ship any lignite, but we all dug our winter fuel from the sidehill, and where else but in the Garden of the World could you do that? As for oil, the wildcat well that went down out by the railroad bridge did not hit anything, and was abandoned, but the derrick was still there for years, a reminder of a hope that might still be realized.

Progress? It is impossible not to believe in progress in a frontier town. Every possibility is open, every opportunity still untested. In the shadowless light before sunup, no disappointments or failures show. And everybody, everybody, is there for the new start. Not one of them would recognize failure if it was in front of him as tall as an elevator.

So Pop Martin sold many lots, including whole blocks of them to speculators who could only become, in the circumstances, additional press agents of growth. He could not have liked the Sober Citizens too much, for if rumor was true he had been run out of Butte by just such pious middle-class people as they. But he could cooperate with them, for they were clearly the hope of the new community. He could with a large gesture donate his old race course as a sports ground for the town, he could give the land for the town dump. He may even, though I was never sure of this, have provided the site of the cemetery, which, once it was established, was promptly—supply following demand—fulfilled with its first grave. (*Ugh*, my mother used to say. *No matter what I've done, no matter if they hang me, don't bury me out there!*)

Benefactor, *padrone*, Pop Martin commanded respect because of his money and power, and owned a good many people because when homesteaders desperate for house-money or machinery-money came around, he would issue them loans, with their land as security. What came in from the sale of town lots he reinvested in farm mortgages; though he seemed to be disposing of his landed holdings, he was actually spreading like an ink-blot over the whole eastern end of the Hills. But not graspingly, not for the odd dollar in it; he was far more interested in his position as town father than in money. And he vastly enhanced his status by his handling of the first two crises that confronted him. The first challenge came from the railroad, supposed to be his ally; the second from the Village Council, supposed to be in his pocket. The first had happened just before we came, the second happened just after.

It is hard to imagine what may have been in the mind of the railroad's engineers and construction men. Maybe only an error, a misapprehension. In any case, grading their beeline up past South Fork, they first cut across the little pond that drained to two oceans, and so committed a small crime against geography, and then cut across Martin's irrigation ditch. When Martin protested, the CPR told him to move his ditch. But Martin was, though a small man, not a man who wilted before a show of arrogance. He is a long way back in my memory, but I remember a cold eye under his ranch Stetson, and a bulldog jaw complete with a slight dewlap. He would have shoved the jaw an inch or so forward and tightened the dewlap by a forward thrust of his head. He sued the CPR, and collected, whereupon the CPR, though it could not move its townsite, since there was no way to get through the Hills except straight up the river valley, decided that it *could* move its division point, and did—to rival Shaunavon. In actuality it was a blow to the town, for it removed one steady resource. But how I heard it first was how Pop Martin made the CPR back down. His belligerence, and its success, enhanced him in everyone's eyes, for even before it got steel into Whitemud the railroad was doing more to demonstrate the economics of Henry George than to prove itself the farmer's friend. There was already, all over western Canada, a growing protest straight out of the Populist agitation of the 1890's; a protest aimed both at the railroad and at the elevator companies with whom the farmers thought the railroad was in cahoots. To put the CPR down, to sue it and collect, was to become a popular hero.

But then in the next year, right in the midst of an era of good feeling, right after his donations of dump ground and sports ground and maybe burying ground, Pop Martin found himself nose to nose with the Sober Citizens of the Village Council, and here the Populist feelings that had applauded his victory over the CPR were quaintly at odds with him.

Many of them came from the Dakotas, many lived and died by Henry George. Here in a new country, starting anew in Eden, they exercised their democratic prerogatives and organized as a single-tax town. It took a little while before Pop Martin, amiably indulgent to his new dependents, discovered that in a single-tax town the landowner pays the taxes. When he comprehended his tax bill, he demurred with considerable heat. The Village Council said, But that's how the law reads. Well change the law, said

Pop Martin. But, they said. Come on, hurry up, said Pop Martin. Or would you like me to give you all my town property, and the taxes along with it?

Reluctantly they altered the tax structure, but it was a long time before they got over saying what a splendid thing it would have been for the little man and how good for the future of the town, if the single-tax system could have been made to stick. But single-tax or not, the town's cheerfulness and energy were unchecked, its hope almost millennial, in the year when we came into it, built a house in it, and began to use it as a base for our suitcase farming.

3

The Garden of the World

If you do not learn from history, George Santayana once remarked, you will have to repeat it. But history on the Plains took a lot of learning. For one thing, the frontier was discontinuous. Half-adapted plainsmen were always being overtaken, out-numbered, or replaced by newcomers and tenderfeet whose notions, learned in countries of plentiful rain and moderate weather, were a long time wearing out. The agrarian optimism that broke the Plains sod did not realize all the consequences of what it did until sixty or seventy years after the first dryland farmers edged out into Kansas in the 1860's. Some things the homesteaders learned, including summer fallowing and dust mulching, and if some of what they learned turned out to be wrong—as, for instance, deep plowing, which was eventually given up in favor of a mere stirring of the surface with a Noble blade or a Graham Hoeme or a rod weeder—at least it was subject to observation and gradual correction. But the lesson that the Plains settler could not learn, short of living it out, was that no system of farming, no matter how strenuously applied, could produce crops in that country during one of the irregular and unpredictable periods of drought and that the consequences of trying to force the issue could be disastrous to both people and land.

There were books that would have told him (though he might not have believed) that the reduction of the annual rainfall by a single inch, or a shift of the period of greatest precipitation from spring and summer to fall, could mean the difference between a

good crop and a burned field. The winds, hail, and cyclones he
would believe as soon as he experienced them once. But the large
lesson that he would have found most useful—the marginal nature of agriculture on the arid Plains—was precisely the one that
as a pioneer he found unacceptable, because it denied his hope.

His hope was involved with the myth of the Garden West.
Franklin and Jefferson had formulated it, politicians and speculators and railroads had promoted it, the ignorant faith of hundreds of thousands of home-seekers had kept it alive well into the
industrial age and out into the dry country where it had little
chance of coming true. The dream that circulated vaguely in the
heads of people like my parents had something to do with the
corncribs and pigpens of Illinois and Iowa, but little to do with
the arid Plains furred with their curly grass and seared by blowtorch winds. If the frontier had been continuous either as to people or as to experience, Kansas might have taught them something, the Dakotas where they had tarried briefly might have
given them a hint. But apparently no matter how hard a time
hope may have had in earlier settlements, the opening of any
new frontier, even a marginal one, revives it intact and undiminished. In the midst of the worst drouth until then experienced
on the Plains, people burned out in the Dakotas turned their
teams south toward Indian Territory to give her another whirl.

So Whitemud, though some of its founders had had experience
in Manitoba, Montana, or the Dakotas, and though some of them
remembered the dry '90's, simply had to repeat history. What is
more, the pioneers unquestionably passed on to their children,
including me, some of their faith in the future. At least until the
memory of free land fades, hope, it turns out, is heritable.

Yet the fact is, failure was woven into the very web of Whitemud. It was the inevitable warp, as hope was the woof, of that
belated frontier. Our lawyers and doctors, for instance. Once in a
while pioneering enthusiasm or a real medical-missionary ideal-
ism draws good doctors into the hinterlands, but more often the
cause of their coming is incompetence or venality, and what applies to doctors applies double to lawyers. One of Whitemud's
two barristers had lost his license in England and could not get
a new one in Canada. He did clerk jobs for the other, a boozer
and incompetent who lost papers, tangled titles, irritated clients,

and offended the whole town during the flu epidemic by developing an incontinent diarrhea while a patient in the sixth-and-seventh-grade room of the schoolhouse. They said it was just like him. After a few years he simply disappeared, leaving behind him his hopelessly scrambled papers—another frontier casualty, *spurlos verloren*.

Of the doctors, the earliest and probably the best, an enthusiastic youngster from Saskatoon, practiced only briefly before he enlisted in the army, never to return. His successor also enlisted, and shortly died of drinking wood alcohol in training camp. The third, a Frenchman who appeared to the town brilliant and well trained, and who may have been both, got into trouble for dispensing drugs (to Pop Martin's wife—that town was hard on women), and died a suicide, of strychnine poisoning, in 1920. The fourth died, accidentally or on purpose, of an overdose of opiates.

And not merely the professional men. Witness Sid Crane, for a time the postmaster, a heavy drinker who in deference to his public responsibilities used to gargle rose water, and through his little wicket send abroad, along with stamps and money orders, a mingled rum-and-flowers breath that could daunt the most hardened post-office sitter.

Or old Hugh McGuire, a gangling scarecrow in a celluloid collar, a lonely bachelor dying of spiritual cold. He was the victim of the practical jokers, a butt more universal and more ridiculed than even Mah Li. And he was the first to fall when a traveling group of hootchie-kootchie dancers pitched a tent in the brush and sent their impresario through town advertising "performances." If Whitemud was hard on women, it was also hard on unmarried men, who in the face of an actual woman shortage put the virtue of the town girls under constant harassment and rallied like a band of winter-gaunted coyotes to every visiting opportunity. The fullest acceptance Hugh McGuire achieved, probably, came when he contributed to the town's biggest scandal. A moronic girl from the North Bench came to town one day and let it be known that she was willing. Let it be known? She pranced it, tittered it; she couldn't have walked down an empty boxcar without bruising both hips. She was more than willing. So, it developed, was Hugh, who was always ardent, and so were a half dozen of the town's solidest citizens. They lined up for her in the brush, and within an hour discovered that she was not only willing, she was mouthy. She showed the money and trinkets they had given her, and named all their names. The tale got around at approximately the speed of light. Within an hour it had leaked down even into the school yard. I have a memory of a couple of girls my age red with shame because their fathers were among the delinquents.

Old Hugh McGuire. He limped in from Ireland wistfully looking for something, maybe love, and finding little of it he limped back to Ireland to die. There were plenty in substantially his fix, like the barrister with his red, stunned face and his thickened speech and his scrambled papers—I have seen him sitting bewilderedly among them at midmorning, stirring them with his finger as if to discover what they were about—and like the doctors with their drink and their dope, and like the defeated and desperate women. The weak and the hard-luck prone could hardly be expected to make it when practical and hard-working men had trouble doing so. That they did have trouble is evident from some rudimentary statistics I once gathered on the early settlers. Of sixty-five that I was able to trace, forty-nine left Whitemud within six years. The only one of them who seems to have left with any money was one of the land sharks. He left with about three thousand dollars. People said it was about what he had honestly earned in his six years there.

If is a big word in the history of a town like Whitemud. If it had happened to have its beginnings in a wet cycle rather than at the beginning of a cycle of drouth. If the war had not persuaded people, for mixed patriotism and profit, to plow up a lot of prairie that was either too dry or too far from a railroad to be decent wheat land. If cattlemen in and around the Cypress Hills had been able in some way to prevent the breaking up of the bench hay lands on which most of them depended for winter feed. If Pop Martin hadn't quarreled with the CPR. If a series of natural catastrophes, including the flu epidemic and the spring flood of 1918, had not hit the town just when it could least stand discouragement. But there *was* a drouth, there *was* a war, the farmers *did* plow up too much submarginal land, the cattlemen *did* get caught without enough hay, Martin *did* have his row with the CPR, there *were* natural catastrophes. Year by year, through 1916, 1917, 1918, the *Leader* pumped harder at its leaky bellows, and one by one the resources on which it proposed to build the future went flat. As children, we knew the shrinking prospects of Whitemud not as they were, but for a certain salvage that boys could take out of even the resources on which their fathers went broke.

Our oil was a dry hole, but its abandoned derrick made a splendid trapeze on which we could perform acrobatics to impress girls who pretended always to be unimpressed; and for a while, during a fall or two when someone cut the hay in the field down below, we had a lovely Freudian play-cycle going, alternating between the exposed and rigid derrick and dark tunnels under the haystack.

The whitemud that was much in the town's consciousness as a source of riches did not, during our years there, get dug very much. A few cars did go out to Medicine Hat, but almost as much came home with us by the pailful, to be wet to the right consistency and rolled between the palms and baked in the oven to make marbles. They were not very good marbles, being irregular and easily broken, but they had the great advantage of being in inexhaustible supply. A boy could be cleaned out at afternoon recess and be in business again by morning.

From the fading cattle industry we derived much in the way of attitude and pose, but little in the way of economics beyond the dollar a month we could earn by driving the town herd to pasture in the morning and bringing it back at night. The cattle trains from ranches west of us in the Hills provided a game of collecting boxcar numbers and the names of exotic railroads, but from the immediate area of Whitemud, within little more than a year of our arrival, the cattle were gone because the range was gone into homesteads.

From wheat we got certain fringe benefits. When we could sneak by the elevator man, the elevator bins were fine places to play in, a good deal like enormous clean sandpiles. We were constantly being warned about the danger of drowning in the grain, but we discovered early that only flax could really suck you down. In wheat we deliberately started avalanches and buried one another. We found also that wheat made a good substitute for gum if it was chewed hard until it formed a glutinous, sweet-tasting mass. Wheat for that purpose was always available, even when the year was bad and even when the elevator man was vigilant, for under the spouts by the tracks there was always a cone of spilled grain. We never went by the elevators without grabbing up a handful. Probably we lengthened our lives with the vitamins we unknowingly absorbed, and not even the word that it was healthful would have stopped our chewing it.

Nothing, either, could have prevented us from hunting, fishing, trapping, and generally fulfilling ourselves as predators. I think there was not a boy who did not have a .22 by the time he was ten or eleven; my brother at ten was shooting a twelve-gauge shotgun, picking off cottontails and snowshoe hares, an occasional duck, an even more occasional grouse, which he sold to a lath-like woman who was anemic and had been told to eat wild game. Though she was a market, she gave us the creeps; we had seen her break a raw egg into a glass of beer and drink it down.

Without anemia to justify us, we had our own savage feasts out in the willows, dining upon sage hen or rabbit broiled on sticks over the fire. When larger game failed we netted bullfrogs, or caught them on a fish hook baited with a scrap of red flannel, and hacked off their legs and roasted them. We stole old frying pans and cached them in our hideouts in the brush so that when occasion offered we could fry up a panful of chubs or a big intricately boned sucker. I remember one whole day below Martin's dam when we waded the shallow clear water hunting for the tracks of clams in the sandy bottom; and the saltless, emetic chowder we cooked up and bravely ate; and the distorted little knob of a pearl that one of us found in a clam smashed open on a rock, and the instant dream of fortune it aroused, and the decimation that resulted as we employed against the clams the mass destruction that our fathers and grandfathers had employed against placer gravels and buffalo and virgin timber and free land. We had it in us to be as blindly destructive as any in the history of North America. Only our opportunities were limited.

Occasionally a minor bonanza came our way. During the war the price of furs rose until a good slough muskrat brought three dollars in the hardware store, and even more if sent direct to one of the fur houses in St. Louis. The river rats were smaller and less valuable, but more within our reach, and the traps that in summer we used for gophers would serve for muskrats quite as well. From the time I was nine until I was nearly twelve, my brother and I trapped the river with a good deal of persistence, and when we bundled up our take one spring I remember that we had fifteen muskrats, nine ermine, one mink, and a beaver that we had mistakenly skinned closed instead of open so that he brought us next to nothing. But he was full of holes anyway, having been shot in the water when the spring flood washed him out of wherever he lived. As a miser remembers his hoard I remember those dried skins inside-out on their stretchers of shaped shingle and bent red osier, and the glove-like, excruciating opulence of pushing a hand up inside the fur. The money we made trapping, my mother put carefully away for the purchase of Victory Bonds to be a nest egg for our future. They may have helped win the war, but they never lasted until our future. Some family emergency swallowed them, which was just as well. It would have been inappropriate to take anything out of that country when we left it.

Actually, our juvenile money-making resources were about as lean as those of our parents. In summer we could make some small change, if we happened to be in town, picking saskatoons, pin-cherries, or gooseberries for home-canning housewives. Picking gooseberries at ten cents a quart, even when the berries hang on the underside of the prickly stems in heavy rows, is not a way to get rich. The meagerness of our total earning power was an analogue of the ways our fathers worked and the rewards they got, and the expedient we were frequently put to—to crawl under the plank sidewalk in front of the hotel and search among the dirt and papers and tinfoil and old spit for coins that had fallen through the cracks—was an even more wistful analogue of their dreams of getting rich quick and easy.

It is strange, after nearly half a century, to read the files of the Whitemud *Leader* and find in them scraps of my own life as unexpected as those I sometimes found on the dump. I discover, for instance, that my father was for a while a deputy sheriff— a sure sign that he must have been desperate, for he was natu-

rally unsympathetic to the law. His spell of serving the enemy
may explain two or three vaguely remembered times when he
took me with him on all-day trips to the North Bench. I am sure
he did not take me for my company, for he was never very fond
of it. Probably he took me to open gates. Our mare Daisy was
a hysteric (he had won *her* in a poker game, too), and could
spook at a squeaky gate and pull old phlegmatic gelding Dick
into a runaway in the twinkling of an eye. He was generally
asleep when she spooked, and anything that happened suddenly
to upset his slumbers unsettled his mind. Sometimes he fell
asleep walking, and happening to break wind while plodding
along, awoke wall-eyed and plunging as if someone had set off a
firecracker under his tail.

I discover too that when Joe Knight's hotel burned down in
1916, it had in its basement seven hundred bushels of potatoes
that belonged to us. That helps to explain another stretch of hard
times, harder than any we ever had, when Christmas dinner was
bacon and potatoes and canned-saskatoon pie, and my brother
and I fell silent and ashamed when on Christmas morning other
kids came around to show off their presents. We had each got a
pencil box and a pair of home-knit stockings and homemade shirts
made out of the lining of an old coat of my mother's. Lacking any
other resources at all, she had sat up nights to make them, and
sacrificed a coat she still wore. But we would never wear the shirts
—they looked homemade. During that bad spell "Jew" Meyer
stopped our credit, and for a while we literally had difficulty getting enough to eat. We blamed his Jewishness, naturally. After
that miserable Christmas my father swore, and kept his oath, that
Meyer would be the last of his creditors to get paid. As soon as
he had recouped a little by helping to skin the well-heeled retired rancher in the hotel's poker game, he went out of his way to
pay off everybody but Meyer. Him he let wait for over a year,
and only paid him then because Meyer, who was getting out,
threatened to attach our house for payment of his debt.

Meantime the town that Pop Martin had founded went on, in
spite of hard times and isolation and wartime shortages, building
itself into a future that no one yet had given up on. Most of what
the *Leader* reported in 1916, 1917, and 1918 could have been

interpreted as Progress, or preparation for Progress. Even the fifty-one below, eighty-mile-an-hour blizzard of 1916, which marooned teachers and children in the schoolhouse for a day and a night and part of the next day before my father and others could beat their way in on a long string of lariats and lead us home along that lifeline with our stocking caps pulled down over our faces and our hands up the sleeves of our mackinaws—even that had the exhilarating quality of shared and successfully passed trial that helps make a village a community. The same with the influenza epidemic: at no time in Whitemud's history was it ever so united. On Hallowe'en, 1918, I was assisting in a project aimed at installing Hazards' backhouse on the steps of the hospital, which was three beds in an abandoned false-front restaurant building. We were interrupted by a buckboard which drove up with a patient; within an hour, in response to somber adjurations from the druggist, we were all distributing gauze flu masks and bottles of eucalyptus oil, which was supposed to be a protection. Before another two days had passed, all four rooms of the schoolhouse were filled with beds, and everyone in town had been enlisted, either as patient or victim or helper. A tenth of the town died, besides a lot of farmers who had crowded in to be near help. The cemetery was a less lonesome place thereafter, and the bonds between the survivors were stronger.

But Whitemud was weaker, too. The war had already taken out of the district more than a hundred of the youngest and most vigorous men; now the flu bled us from the same vein, for it seemed to kill, by preference, the biggest and strongest. By the time spring finally came, there were a good many farms abandoned, a good many families leaving for the States. Every such defection lessened the town economically and psychologically, deepened its mistrust of the future, diluted its hope. And what it did to the town it did most particularly to Pop Martin, for he had loaned a lot of homesteaders money with their land as security, and now he found, when they gave up and quit, that most of them had never proved up on their land. They had no title, not even any equity, and he had no lien; he couldn't even claim the land and put whitefaces back on it. Having become a promoter of the New Jerusalem, he had put himself at the mercy of agencies outside of the weather. The *Leader* might still welcome

visitors from Shaunavon with ironic courtesy, pointing out that
they lived out on the bald flats far from the swimming, picnic
spots, and coasting hills that the fortunate citizens of Whitemud
took for granted. But Shaunavon nevertheless was the division
point, and could subsist on the railroad business that came to it,
and we had not even that. As one bad year succeeded the next,
Whitemud's promise, and along with it Martin's expectations,
passed with a gust and a spatter, like a summer shower that
hardly settles the dust.

Corky Jones, who is the closest thing that country has to a
local historian, has a theory that those who came there with the
greatest resources went broke the fastest because they were deluded into extending themselves. I am not sure that the theory is
entirely dependable—certainly Martin lasted a good deal longer
than many others, including ourselves. But the country broke him
just as surely as it broke the dirt farmer with 320 acres, a tar-
paper shack, and a borrowed team and plow—broke him a leg
or an arm at a time until he didn't have a sound bone in him. I
was a witness to one of the major blows, though it took us all
a while to realize how major it was.

Just north of the school yard, beyond the basketball standards
and the lumpy region where for a couple of springs we had all
hoed and raked at Victory Gardens that by June were withered
rectangles of dust, the river ran in a straight smooth reach against
the foot of the hills. Sometimes we caught a muskrat incautiously
swimming up that stretch, and gave him a warm time. Thirty or
forty boys with rocks, even if they are not accurate, have an
effect like shrapnel. We used to scout the water at recess, hopeful
of sport. And in very early spring the cutbank there was a good
place from which to watch the ice go out.

We were all there at recess one day at the end of April, 1917.
The quiet little creek that we knew in summer was swollen out
of all recognition. Its coffee-colored current, streaked with dirty
foam and spinning in whirlpools, scoured nearly to the lip of the
cutbank; on the far bank the tips of the flooded willows sawed
like buggywhips in the stream. We had heard the ice booming
and cracking all morning, but after such a winter as we had
had, it was reluctant to let loose. Now it began to come, the

edges of big thick cakes pushing through the surface, tipping and breaking and bumping. The glint and show and cover again of the ice was like a showing of teeth.

We went along kicking sections of undermined clay off the cutbank, and throwing rocks at things that floated by, and just before the bell the word came from somewhere that the railroad bridge was in danger of going out. Instantly recess became a holiday. We lit out westward in a streaming mob, and as we went we were joined by men and women and all the happy dogs of Whitemud. As we passed the last house, Van Dam's, we could see the derrick, with little black figures on it. When we eased off to a walk to get our wind we could hear the big steady sound of the river. Then from up ahead the air came at us with a sound as rich and heavy as a smoke-ring: dynamite. We forgot the stitches in our sides and sprinted again.

There was still room on the derrick. We squirmed and clambered until we were wedged in angles of the timbers near the top. For a good half mile the river spread out across the willows, clear to the edge of the hills beyond Carpenters', and clear downriver until it merged with the lake behind Martin's dam. I could see the Carpenter corrals all flooded, and the glitter of water coming down the big coulee behind, and the sagged and dirty snowbanks still left in the shaded hollows of the Hills, and the Hills themselves, bare and picked-looking, with a big blue-china sky back of everything.

Down below us, right at our feet, a section crew had derailed their speeder and were busy about something. The crowd down there edged back—edged back with its feet even while it leaned forward from the waist—and I saw the arm of one of the section crew swing and the stick of dynamite arch down into the ice backed up against the pilings of the bridge. I opened my mouth to be able to take the noise, but there was only a dull pop like a firecracker, and slivers of ice flew into the air and fell again. I thought I must be deaf. The boy next to me yelled something a foot from my face and I couldn't understand what he said. Then it dawned on me that the whole world was throbbing with sound: rush and tumble and hiss of water, crack and knock of big ice pans three feet thick and twenty square that kept coming from upstream and tilting and stacking against the bridge, and grinding higher, and toppling with their weight of tons, and occasionally squeezing sideways between the pilings and *swowshing* into open water below. Another stick of dynamite arched out and fell and popped its harmless pop and threw up its chips of ice. From the south, blowing across hundreds of miles of drying grassland, spring leaned against us a soft, exciting wind.

The bridge was tilted to the right, pushed by the ice jam that was now ten or fifteen feet high on the pilings. The rails across the open comb of the ties were bowed out of line. The leaning grew while I watched, the whole bridge bent downriver, the rails contorted themselves into an S curve. Everything upriver must have broken up, because the pans and cakes were coming hard and heavy, damming the water back until the level above the bridge was several feet higher than that below, and the dirty flood squirted and flowed through and between and over the ice and the straining piles.

Just at the water level, at the upstream meeting of ice and bridge, a piling crumpled like a wet match. The bridge leaned more, cakes mounted up the sloping timbers. And suddenly it went. One of the rails snapped free and hummed out over the tormented web of wood and steel, and the air was crystallized with its gong-sound. We felt it in the roots of our teeth. In one ponderous, rotating motion the bridge bowed and went down, and the backed-up ice and water pushed over it and buried it in a wash of yellow foam, spit it up again and floated it, poles and ties and braces in a bound-together tangle, and wrenched it loose from its roots and washed it away downriver.

Somebody above me stepped on my fingers, I kicked the boy below me accidentally in the head. We were all scrambling and falling off the derrick, hitting ground and running, racing the crest of ice and timbers to watch it go over the dam's smooth spillway slope. But it didn't go over. The snaggle of timbers caught in the weir, jammed between planks and pilings, and locked itself into a barricade behind which the ice again began to build up. It kept on building up all that afternoon, and the water kept rising. I saw Pop Martin standing with a group of men, watching it and not talking, a little man in a ranch Stetson with his vest open and the wind fluttering the Bull Durham tag in the pocket, but it did not occur to me then that the danger to the dam was any different to him than to me: an excitement.

By the time darkness and cold drove us home, there was a great lake behind the dam, held by an ice pack a hundred yards from bank to bank. They had opened the spillway to the ditch, and floodwater was flowing down that in a scouring stream, but it did not seem to ease the pressure or lower the flood above. When I went to bed that night I stood for a minute at the window and put my ear to one of the three round ventilator holes in the frame of the storm window, and felt the icy flow of night air against my eardrum and heard the steady sound of water. But whether it was the river just behind us, or the irrigation ditch pouring its full stream over its weirs, or the spring thaw still emptying more water down out of the Hills, I could not tell.

The sound ran through my sleep, so that it seemed completely proper that I should be awakened by yelling. I rushed to the window at the back gable and here came Martin's dam with the CPR bridge entangled in it, wallowing in a second disastrous crest past our house. The water was so high that things went by at the cutbank level as if on a road, and some ice and timbers even washed over the cutbank edge and stranded on our lot. People with ropes and pikepoles were running to snatch timbers from the river for firewood. Before long women came out with coffee pots. A man fell in, reaching too far, and my father hooked a pikepole in his coat and pulled him out. We built a big bonfire and turned it into a picnic, and nobody thought much about what Pop Martin was going to do.

What he did was characteristic, and showed he was a long way from dead. He sued the CPR again, this time on the ground that its bridge had been so badly engineered that it prevented passage of the ice, and that only the going-out of the bridge could have brought about the destruction of the dam. That suit, too, he won; within a year I heard men talking with incredulity and admiration of the $11,000 damages he had been awarded. It seemed to me a fabulous fortune. But he did not use it to rebuild his weir across the Whitemud. He must already have been farther down than anyone suspected, over-extended, tied up in frozen real estate and defaulted debts and unsecured loans, trapped in the things he himself had created. He must already have been in trouble with his bored and discontented wife, and she in trouble with drugs. That fall the Whitemud Townsite Company disbanded, Martin dividing its assets with his absent partner Fisher, wherever *he* had gone. There still were a few assets; there may have still been a few expectations. The full dissolution of Martin's little empire would take a few more years.

So it was not quite Götterdämmerung that we witnessed when his dam went out in the spring of 1917. He did not have the satisfaction of a dramatic and crushing defeat such as many ranchers suffered in 1906-07. He was whittled away. Shortly after the doctor swallowed strychnine, Nelly Martin took her private troubles and her son Homer and left for California, a place where promises were reported to pay off rather oftener, and where a bored capable woman had more opportunities for action.

When Pop Martin finally left Saskatchewan after twenty years of effort, he left a town behind him in the bends of the Whitemud, but he left stony broke, bankrupt. When he died in the mid-twenties the town was hanging on by its eyebrows, barely surviving, and the prairie all around was a dust bowl. Martin himself, for the two or three years before his death, had been living in California on the charity of his divorced but pitying wife.

4

The Making of Paths

They felt how far beyond the scope
Of elder Europe's saddest thought
Might be the New World sudden brought
In youth to share old age's pains—
To feel the arrest of hope's advance,
And squandered last inheritance;
And cry—"To Terminus build fanes!
Columbus ended earth's romance:
No New World to mankind remains!"

HERMAN MELVILLE, *Clarel*

At least Martin left something behind him—a town, a cemetery. Even a dump ground is an institution of permanence. But what we did on the homestead was written in wind. It began as it ended—empty space, grass and sky. I remember it as it originally was, for my brother and I, aged eight and six, accompanied my father when he went out to make the first "improvements." Except for the four-foot iron post jutting from the prairie just where our wagon track met the trail to Hydro, Montana, and for the three shallow holes with the survey stake at their apex that marked the near corner of our land, there was nothing to distinguish or divide our land from all other, to show which 320 acres of that wind and grass were ours.

That was our first experience of how flat land could spread

from the wagon and tent by which we attempted to demonstrate ownership—flat to the horizon and beyond, wherever we looked, except that, halfway to our western line, a shallow, nearly imperceptible coulee began, feeling its way, turning and turning again, baffled and blocked, a watercourse so nearly a slough that the spring runoff hardly flowed at all, its water not so much moving as pushed by the thaw behind it and having to go somewhere, until it passed our land and turned south, and at the border found another coulee, which carried in most seasons a little water—not enough to run but enough to seep, and with holes that gave sanctuary to a few minnows and suckers. It was called Coteau Creek, a part of the Milk-Missouri watershed. In good seasons we might get a swim of sorts in its holes; in dry years we hauled water from it in barrels, stealing from the minnows to serve ourselves and our stock. Between it and our house we wore, during the five summers we spent vainly trying to make a wheat farm there, one of our private wagon tracks.

Coteau Creek was a landmark and sometimes a hazard. Once my father, gunning our old Model T across one of its fords, hit something and broke an axle. Next day he started walking the forty miles into Chinook, Montana, leaving me with a homesteader family, and two days later he came back carrying a new axle on his back and installed it himself after the homesteader's team had hauled the Ford out of the creek bed. I remember that high, square car, with its yellow spoke wheels and its brass bracing rods from windshield to mudguards and its four-eared brass radiator cap. It stuck up black and foreign, a wanderer from another planet, on the flats by Coteau Creek, while my father, red-faced and sweating, crawled in and out under the jacked-up rear end and I squatted in the car's shade and played what games I could with pebbles and a blue robin's egg. We sat baldly on the plain, something the earth refused to swallow, right in the middle of everything and with the prairie as empty as nightmare clear to the crawl and shimmer where hot earth met hot sky. I saw the sun flash off brass, a heliograph winking off a message into space, calling attention to us, saying "Look, look!"

Because that was the essential feeling I had about that country —the sense of being foreign and noticeable, of sticking out. I did not at first feel even safe, much less that I was helping to take charge of and make our own a parcel of the world. I moped for Whitemud, nearly fifty miles north and east on its willowed river, where all my friends were and where my mother was waiting until we could get a shack built. Out here we did not belong to the earth as the prairie dogs and burrowing owls and gophers and weasels and badgers and coyotes did, nor to the sky as the hawks did, nor to any combination as meadowlarks and sparrows and robins did. The shack that my father built was an ugly tarpaper-covered box on the face of the prairie, and not even its low rounded roof, built low and round to give the wind less grip on it, could bind it into the horizontal world.

Before the shack was finished we lived in a tent, which the night wind constantly threatened to blow away, flapping the canvas and straining the ropes and pulling the pegs from the gravelly ground. And when, just as we were unloading the lumber to start building, a funnel-shaped cloud appeared in the south, moving against a background of gray-black shot with lightning forks, and even while the sun still shone on us the air grew tense and metallic to breathe, and a light like a reflection from brass glowed around us, and high above, pure and untroubled, the zenith was blue—then indeed exposure was like paralysis or panic, and we looked at the strangely still tent, bronzed in the yellow air, and felt the air shiver and saw a dart of wind move like a lizard across the dust and vanish again. My father rushed us to the shallow section holes at the corner, and with ropes he lashed us to the stake and made us cower down. The holes were no more than a foot deep; they could in no sense be called shelter. Over their edge our eyes, level with the plain, looked southward and saw nothing between us and the ominous bent funnel except gopher mounds and the still unshaken grass. Across the coulee a gopher sat up, erect as the picket pin from which he took his nickname.

Then the grass stirred; it was as if gooseflesh prickled suddenly on the prairie's skin. The gopher disappeared as if some friend below had reached up and yanked him down into his burrow. Even while we were realizing it, the yellow air darkened, and then all the brown and yellow went out of it and it was blue-black. The wind began to pluck at the shirts on our backs, the hair on our heads was wrenched, the air was full of dust. From the third section hole my father, glaring over the shallow rim, yelled to us to keep down, and with a fierce rush rain trampled our backs, and the curly buffalo grass at the level of my squinted eyes was strained out straight and whistling. I popped my head into my arms and fitted my body to the earth. To give the wind more than my flat back, I felt, would be sure destruction, for that was a wind, and that was a country, that hated a foreign and vertical thing.

The cyclone missed us; we got only its lashing edge. We came up cautiously from our muddy burrows and saw the tent collapsed and the sky clearing, and smelled the air, washed and rinsed of all its sultry oppressiveness. I for one felt a little better about being who I was, but for a good many weeks I watched the sky with suspicion; exposed as we were, it could jump on us like a leopard from a tree. And I know I was disappointed in the shack that my father swiftly put together. A soddy that poked its low brow no higher than the tailings of a gopher's burrow would have suited me better. The bond with the earth that all the footed and winged creatures felt in that country was quite as valid for me.

And that was why I so loved the trails and paths we made. They were ceremonial, an insistence not only that we had a right to be in sight on the prairie but that we owned and controlled a piece of it. In a country practically without landmarks, as that part of Saskatchewan was, it might have been assumed that any road would comfort the soul. But I don't recall feeling anything special about the graded road that led us more than half of the way from town to homestead, or for the wiggling tracks that turned off to the homesteads of others. It was our own trail, lightly worn, its ruts a slightly fresher green where old cured grass had been rubbed away, that lifted my heart. It took off across the prairie like an extension of myself. Our own wheels had made it: broad, iron-shod wagon wheels first, then narrow democrat wheels that cut through the mat of grass and scored the earth until it blew and washed and started a rut, then finally the wheels of the Ford.

By the time we turned off it, the road we followed from town had itself dwindled to a pair of ruts, but it never quite disappeared; it simply divided and subdivided. I do not know why the last miles, across buffalo grass and burnouts, past the shacks we called Pete and Emil, across Coteau Creek, and on westward until the ruts passed through the gate in our pasture fence and stopped before our house, should always have excited me so, unless it was that the trail was a thing we had exclusively created and that it led to a place we had exclusively built. Here is the pioneer root-cause of the American cult of Progress, the satisfaction that *Homo fabricans* feels in altering to his own purposes the virgin earth. Those tracks demonstrated our existence as triumphantly as an Indian is demonstrated by his handprint in ochre on a cliff wall. Not so idiotically as the stranded Ford, this trail and the shack and chicken house and privy at its end said, "See? We are here." Thus, in the truest sense, was "located" a homestead.

More satisfying than the wagon trail, even, because more intimately and privately made, were the paths that our daily living wore in the prairie. I loved the horses for poking along the pasture fence looking for a way out, because that habit very soon wore a plain path all around inside the barbed wire. Whenever I had to go and catch them, I went out of my way to walk along it, partly because the path was easier on my bare feet but more because I wanted to contribute my feet to the wearing process. I scuffed and kicked at clods and persistent grass clumps, and twisted my weight on incipient weeds and flowers, willing that the trail around the inside of our pasture should be beaten dusty and plain, a worn border to our inheritance.

It was the same with the path to the woodpile and the privy. In late June, when my mother and brother and I reached the homestead, that would be nearly overgrown, the faintest sort of radius line within the fireguard. But our feet quickly wore it anew, though there were only the four of us, and though other members of the family, less addicted to paths than I, often frustrated and irritated me by cutting across from the wrong corner of the house, or detouring past the fence-post pile to get a handful of cedar bark for kindling, and so neglected their plain duty to the highway. It was an unspeakable satisfaction to me when after a few weeks I could rise in the flat morning light that came across the prairie in one thrust, like a train rushing down a track, and see the beaten footpath, leading gray and dusty between grass and cactus and the little orange flowers of the false mallow that we called wild geranium, until it ended, its purpose served, at the hooked privy door.

Wearing any such path in the earth's rind is an intimate act, an act like love, and it is denied to the dweller in cities. He lacks the proper mana for it, he is out of touch with the earth of which he is made. Once, on Fifty-eighth Street in New York, I saw an apartment dweller walking his captive deer on a leash. They had not the pleasure of leaving a single footprint, and the sound of the thin little hoofs on concrete seemed as melancholy to me as, at the moment, the sound of my own steps.

So we had an opportunity that few any longer can have: we printed an earth that seemed creation-new with the marks of our identity. And then the earth wiped them out again. It is possible that our dam still holds a reservoir behind it, that our family effort has endowed the country with one more small slough for which nesting ducks and thirsty coyotes may bless us. It may be that some of the ground cherries my mother brought as seed from Iowa and planted in the fireguard have grown and fruited and been spread by wind and birds. If so, field mice opening the papery husks and dining on the little yellow tomatoes inside may bless us too. There is not much else that we can be blessed for. Because of us, quite a lot of the homestead's thin soil lies miles downwind. Because of us, Russian thistle and other weeds that came in with the wheat have filled the old fields and choked out the grass and made much more difficult the job of bringing back the old natural range. But with those exceptions, we are erased, we are one with Fort Walsh. Though it established itself permanently in more favored parts of the region, the wheat frontier never got a foothold in "Palliser's Triangle," at whose base our homestead lay, and we ourselves helped corroborate Palliser's 1858 prediction that agriculture would prove impracticable there. Our dream of a wheat bonanza, or failing that, of a home, is as lost as the night wind that used to blow across the prairie's great emptiness and, finding a little human box in its way, moan and mourn under the eaves and through the screens.

The homestead, though it was a stead of sorts, was never a home. There was only a handful of real homes on either side of the Line. Most houses were like ours, shacks made to be camped in during the crop season; and some were like Pete and Emil, never meant to be lived in at all, but only to satisfy the law's requirement. (The grass grows more sweetly on Pete and Emil than on our place, for during their simple-minded effort to cheat the government out of title to 320 acres their owners plowed no prairie, imported no weeds, started no dust bowl.) Those of us who really tried to farm lived on the prairie as summerers, exact opposites of the *métis* winterers who knew that country first, and anyone who tries to farm there now will still be a summerer. Nobody, quite apart from the question of school, wants to risk six hard lonely months thirty or forty miles from fuel, supplies, medical care, and human company.

As agriculturists we were not inventive. We used the methods and the machinery that were said to be right, and planted the crops and the varieties advised by rumor or the Better Farming Train. At least once, tradition did well by us. Because my parents had brought from Dakota the notion that flax is the best crop in a newly broken field, we endowed our prairie briefly, in 1916, with twenty acres of bluebells. I remember the pleasure their beauty brought us all; that was a green and rainy summer, and the sight of lush grass and wildflowers and the blue wave of flax persuaded us for a little while that we did indeed live in the Garden of the World. But I remember them also for the evidence they give me now of how uneventful and lonesome the homestead must have been for two boys who had read everything in the shack ten times, had studied the Sears Roebuck catalog into shreds, had trapped gophers in increasing circles out from the house until the gopher population was down to bare survivors, had stoned to death the one badger they caught in a gopher trap, had lost in a big night windstorm their three captive weasels and two burrowing owls, and had played to boredom every two-man game they knew. We couldn't even take our .22's and go killing things, for we had no money for cartridges, not even shorts, not even the despised BB's.

To keep us from our interminable squabbling, my father said we could reap as our own crop all the flax that had grown up too close to the pasture fence for machinery. We cut our flax with butcher knives and threshed it by beating it against the inside of a washtub. It took half an hour to realize a cupful, but we kept at it until we had filled two flour sacks. It brought us, as I recall, about four dollars—memorable money. But I have a more lasting souvenir of that piece of bored laboriousness. Cutting at flax stalks with my knife, I slammed my hand into a cactus clump and drove a spine clear through my middle finger. There was no pulling it out, for it was broken off at the skin, and so I waited for it to fester out. It never did. It is there in the X-rays yet, a needle of authentic calcified Saskatchewan, as much a part of me as the bones between which it wedged itself.

When he first broke sod, my father took pride in plowing a furrow six inches deep, as straight as a string, and nearly a mile long. He started at our pasture fence, plowed straight south to the Line, turned east, plowed a few rods along the border, and turned north again to our fence, enclosing a long narrow field that in a demonic burst of non-stop work he plowed and disked and harrowed and planted to Red Fife wheat.

It was like putting money on a horse and watching him take the lead at the first turn and go on pulling away to the finish. That first summer, 1915, the wheat came up in thin rows—a miracle, really, considering that we ourselves had done it, and in so short a time. Rains came every few days, and were followed by long hot days with sixteen hours of sun. The earth steamed, things grew like plants in trick photography. We looked away from the field for a minute and looked back to find the wheat ankle high, looked away again, and back, and found it as high as our knees. Gophers mowed big swaths, cutting it to get at the tender joints, and so we went up and down the mile-long field with traps and .22's and buckets of sweet-smelling strychnine-soaked wheat. That summer, according to the prize they gave us, my brother and I collected more gopher tails than anybody in southern Saskatchewan.

We lived an idyl of miniature savagery, small humans against rodents. Experts in dispensing death, we knew to the slightest kick and reflex the gophers' ways of dying: knew how the eyes popped out blue as marbles when we clubbed a trapped gopher with a stake, knew how a gopher shot in the behind just as he dove into his hole would sometimes back right out again with ridiculous promptness and die in the open, knew how an unburied carcass would begin within a few hours to seethe with little black scavenger bugs, and how a big orange carrion beetle working in one could all but roll it over with the energy of his greed, and how after a few days of scavengers and sun a gas-bloated gopher had shrunk to a flattened wisp of fur.

We were as untroubled by all our slaughter as early plainsmen were by their slaughter of buffalo. In the name of the wheat we absolved ourselves of cruelty and callousness. Our justification came at the end of that first summer when my father, who was just six feet tall, walked into the field one afternoon and disappeared. The wheat overtopped and absorbed him. From a field of less than thirty acres he took more than twelve hundred bushels of Number One Northern.

It was our last triumph. The next spring my father went out early to prepare another field and plant the old one. We joined him late in June, after driving all day in a drenching downpour—load soaked, us soaked, horses streaming, old Red the cow splashing along behind with her hipbones poking up under her slicked wet hide like a chairback under a sheet. My father had barely got the crops in—thirty acres of wheat, twenty of flax. Then we sat for two weeks in the mouse-smelling shack, playing checkers and reading, while the rain continued to come down. We wondered if the seed would be washed out of the ground, it rained so. The cat prowled unhappily and lost his reputation for being house-broken, because he would not go out in the wet.

Between soakers we inspected the fields. A thin combing of green, then sturdy rows, then ankle high—it grew like weeds. Though I trapped for gophers, I caught few; they had drowned in their holes. The cat grew thin for lack of field mice. Going to the vegetable garden for our usual summer job of picking off potato bugs and piling them at the ends of the rows and burning them with kerosene, we found hardly a bug on the vines. Nothing throve on that rainy prairie but wheat and flax. Rich farmer's sons, we grew lavish in our selection of next Christmas's gifts from the Sears Roebuck catalog. For weeks on end water stood in the burnouts; every low spot was a slough; the rezavoy lapped the top of the dam. Like effete visitors to a summer resort area, we swam in water over our heads. We had no hot winds, no hail-storms, no twisters, no grasshoppers. Every natural pest and hazard was suspended. Except one. Rust. We got a flax crop, but no wheat at all, not a bushel. In town, where my father had planted his potato field and hired the Chinese to look after it, we had a bumper crop of spuds, so big that storage had to be found for a good part of it. Those were the potatoes that were in the cellar of Joe Knight's hotel when it burned down.

Bad luck, surely. And yet if bad luck had not begun for us in 1916 we would simply have been a year or so longer on the hook. As it was, 1917 gave us our seed back, 1918 gave us only a little better, and 1919 served us up such blistering hot winds that we didn't even bother to call in the threshers. One more year and we would have proved up on the homestead and been Canadians all the way instead of only halfway. But when you have stood for three summers in a row turning from the rainy east to the windy southwest, and propitiated one and cursed the other, and every time, just when you have been brought to the point of hope by good spring rains, have felt that first puff out of the southwest, hotter by far than the air around you, you are not likely to require further proofs. My father did not grow discouraged; he grew furious. When he matched himself against something he wanted a chance to win. By 1920 he was already down in Montana scouting around for some new opportunity, and we had stopped walking the paths and making our marks on the face of the prairie.

But how much of my remembering senses is imprisoned there where I would not for a thousand dollars an hour return to live! I retain, as surely as a salmon returning to its spawning grounds after six years at sea knows its native stream, and turns in unerringly from salt water, the taste and smell of the rezavoy when we swam in it among the agitated garter snakes and frogs. (Where *they* came from, God alone knew. There were none in that semi-desert when we built the dam, but next spring there were pollywogs. My mother firmly believed it rained them). I could detect just as surely, if someone offered me a cup of it now, the clay-tasting, modified rezavoy water that we drank—the water from a well-hole dug eight or ten feet from shore so that the seepage from the open slough would be filtered by earth. It took a good amount of earth and earth flavors with it in passage, and it was about as full of wigglers as the rezavoy itself. In late summer we boiled it, but it never lost its taste. The water of Coteau Creek, by contrast, had a slick, soapy taste of alkali about it, and if we had to drink it for any length of time, as we did the last two summers, it gave us the trots.

There was a whole folklore of water. People said a man had to make a dipperful go as far as it would. You boiled sweet corn, say. Instead of throwing the water out, you washed the dishes in it. Then you washed your hands in it a few times. Then you strained it through a cloth into the radiator of your car, and if your car should break down you didn't just leave the water to evaporate in its gullet, but drained it out to water the sweet peas.

We learned to drink with an eye on the dipper so as to keep from sucking down wigglers. When we went on a day's visit to some farm and had a good clean drink out of a deep well, we made jokes that the water didn't seem to have much *body* to it. All we lacked to put us into the position of the surveyors and hunters who had drunk slough water in that country in the 1870's was a few buffalo to fill our tank with urine and excrement.

As much as we starved for a decent drink we starved for shade. No one who has not lived out on a baking flat where the summer days are eighteen hours long and the midday temperatures can go up to a hundred and five degrees has any business talking about discomfort from heat. The air crisps the skin and cracks the lips. There is not a tree for fifty miles in any direction, not even a whisker of willows, to transpire moisture into the air or shade one inch of the scorched ground. The wind that hundreds of miles to the west started up the mountains warm and wet had dropped its moisture on the heights and come down our side wrung dry—dry and gaining temperature at the rate of one degree for every four hundred feet of altitude lost. It hits the Plains and comes across Alberta and Saskatchewan like the breath of a blowtorch. There is no cloud, not one, to cut off the sun and relieve the glare even for a minute. The horizons crawl with mirages. Maybe, far back along the crest of the mountains, out of the straining sight of Plains dwellers as far east as ourselves, there may lie the pearly bank called the Chinook Arch, but that would be no comfort to us even if we could see it—only a confirmation of the foehn wind.

Searing wind, scorching sky, tormented and heat-warped light, and not a tree. The band of shade thrown by the shack narrows as the sun climbs, until at noon it is gone. It will be two hours before it is wide enough on the other side to shelter a boy's body. There is no refuge except inside. The green blinds are drawn, the canvas flaps are rolled down over the screens of the sleeping porch; the light is dusky and comforting to the eyes. But the still air is hotter, if anything, than that outside. Outside, the wind dries sweat before it ever bubbles through the little wells of the pores; inside we are sticky and labor for breath. The wind bellies the canvas in the porch, leaks past. Driven from the still heat of the shack, we look out the door into the white glare of the yard and the hallucinatory writhing of the horizon, and are driven back in again.

On such a day my mother would not try to cook anything on the Florence kerosene stove. She would have milk, butter, eggs, anything perishable, down in the semi-cool hole under the trap-door in the floor, down among the spiders. Bacon, ham, dried beef, about the only meats we can use because they are the only ones that will keep more than a day, are buried deep in a box of oats to keep them cooler and moister. Hung in the air they would grow rancid, be blown by the flies, harden like rock. During the hot-wind days the gingersnaps that are our standard cookies are so dry and hard they fly into fragments when we take a bite; if they should grow soft we would take it as an almost certain sign of coming rain.

At meal time the trapdoor is raised and up come crocks of tepid milk, often "on the turn," and the dish of butter. We dine, these days, primarily on homemade bread and butter, sometimes with peanut butter, sometimes with brown sugar, sometimes with a slather of Karo syrup or molasses. But eating, ordinarily our purest pleasure, is no fun. There is a headachy crankiness around the table, the flies are infuriating. Before it has been on the table five minutes, the butter is ghee, yellow liquid that we scoop up with spoons to spread our bread. Put down into the hole again, it will harden into a flat, whitish, untasty-looking sheet sprinkled with a rime of salt like an alkali flat. When spread, it is coarse and crumbly, without buttery consistency and with a rancid taste. Sometimes, in spite of the twists of flypaper hanging in a dozen places from the ceiling, and the big treacherous sheets spread around on tables and boxes, all of them murmurous with trapped flies, we will find in the melted-and-congealed-again butter a black kinked leg or a transparent wing.

And what of the insects caught in that heat-softened, incredibly sticky fly paper? I used to watch for minutes at a time as some fly, gummed and stuck with glue, his wings plastered to his body, his legs fused, dragged himself with super-fly effort toward the edge of a sheet, and made it, and rested there, slimed with the death he had dragged with him, and then tried with his stuck-together forefeet to wipe his head and clean himself. A fly could often drag himself a good way through the warmed glue, but even if he made it to the edge he didn't have a chance. I used to put pencil circles around some struggler still hopefully mopping his head with his slimed feet, and come back later to see if he had got clean and got away. He never had. Once I caught my mother watching *me,* and together, for a while, we stared at the sheet of gummed paper loud with the buzzing of flies whose feet were caught but whose wings were still free. We watched a few get their wings caught too, so they could only slide and crawl. My mother's lips drew up as if she tasted something nasty. "What's the matter, sorry for the old flies?" I said. "It's a parable," she said, and crumpled the sheet up and stuck it in the sheep-wagon stove we used in chilly weather.

A parable, indeed. In spite of my mother's flimsy pretense that we were farmers of the kind her Iowa parents were, drawing our full sustenance from the soil and tending the soil as good husbandmen should; in spite of her cow and her dasher churn and her cloths of cottage cheese dripping from the clothesline; in spite of her chickens and eggs and vegetable garden, she was not fooled. It was not a farm, and we were not farmers, but wheat miners, and trapped ones at that. We had flown in carelessly, looking for something, and got ourselves stuck. The only question now was how to get free.

She knew it was failure we were living; and if she did not realize, then or ever, that it was more than family failure, that it was the failure of a system and a dream, she knew the family failure better than any of us. Given her choice in the matter, she might have elected to go on farming—get some better land somewhere, maybe in the Cypress Hills, and become one of the stickers. She had the character and the skills for it as my father did not. But she likewise had impulses toward a richer and more rewarding life, and ambitions for her sons, and she must have understood that compared to what a Saskatchewan homesteader considered his opportunity, five years of Siberian exile would have been a relatively comfortable outing. She had gone to school only through the sixth grade. It would never have occurred to her to think that her family and thousands of others had been betrayed by homestead laws totally inapplicable on the arid Plains; or that she and hers had been victimized by the folklore of hope. She had not education enough to know that the mass impulse that had started her parents from Ulvik on the Hardanger Fjord, and started her and my father from Iowa into Dakota and on across the border, had lost its legitimacy beyond the hundredth meridian. She knew nothing about minimal annual rainfall, distribution of precipitation, isohyetal lines. All she knew was that we were trapped and licked, and it would not have helped her much to be told that this was where a mass human movement dwindled to its end.

For her sake I have regretted that miserable homestead, and blamed my father for the blind and ignorant lemming-impulse that brought us to it. But on my own account I would not have missed it—could not have missed it and be who I am, for better or worse. How better could a boy have known loneliness, which I must think a good thing to know? Who ever came more truly face to face with beauty than a boy who in a waste of characterless grass and burnouts came upon the first pale primrose on the coulee bank, or on some day of great coasting clouds looked across acres of flax in bloom? Why, short of exile, would anyone ever submit to the vast geometry of sky and earth, to the glare and heat, to the withering winds? But how else could he have met the mystery of nights when the stars were scoured clean and the prairie was full of breathings from a long way off, and the strange, friendly barking of night-hunting owls?

There may be as good ways to understand the shape and intensity of the dream that peopled the continent, but this seems to me one good one. How does one know in his bones what this continent has meant to Western man unless he has, though briefly and in the midst of failure, belatedly and in the wrong place, made trails and paths on an untouched country and built human living places, however transitory, at the edge of a field that he helped break from prairie sod? How does one know what wilderness has meant to Americans unless he has shared the guilt of wastefully and ignorantly tampering with it in the name of Progress?

One who has lived the dream, the temporary fulfillment, and the disappointment has had the full course. He may lack a thousand things that the rest of the world takes for granted, and because his experience is belated he may feel like an anachronism all his life. But he will know one thing about what it means to be an American, because he has known the raw continent, and not as tourist but as denizen. Some of the beauty, the innocence, and the callousness must stick to him, and some of the regret. The vein of melancholy in the North American mind may be owing to many causes, but it is surely not weakened by the perception that the fulfillment of the American Dream means inevitably the death of the noble savagery and freedom of the wild. Anyone who has lived on a frontier knows the inescapable ambivalence of the old-fashioned American conscience, for he has first renewed himself in Eden and then set about converting it into the lamentable modern world. And that is true even if the Eden is, as mine was, almost unmitigated discomfort and deprivation.

I saw the homestead just once after we left it to go back into town in the bitter fall of 1919. In the spring of 1920 we came past it on our way to Montana and camped in the shack for one night. We did not even take the boards off the windows or roll up the canvas blinds, but went about in the familiar, musty place, breathing the heavy air, in a kind of somnambulism. Our visit was not meant to change anything, or restore for an instant the hope we had given up. We merely passed through, picked up a few objects that we wanted, touched things with our hands in a reminding way, stood looking from the doorway down across the coulee. My brother and I walked up the pasture and saw where a badger had been busy, but did not get out our traps. Our pasture fence was banked high as the posts with tumbleweed blown in from the next farm, two miles west. Our own fields were growing, in addition to spears of volunteer wheat, a solid mat of Russian thistle that by fall would be bounding and rolling eastward ahead of the frolic winds, to scatter their seed broadcast and lodge eventually in someone else's fences. The gophers that our wheat had allowed to increase prodigiously, and that our traps and poison had kept artificially in check, would thrive a year or two on whatever wheat volunteered in old fields, and then shrink gradually back to a population in balance with the hawks, owls, coyotes, badgers, and weasels that lived on them. And our house would begin—had already begun—its process of weathering and rusting and blowing away.

When we drove away we closed the gate carefully on our empty pasture, shutting in shack and privy and chickencoop and the paths connecting them, hooking shut three strands of barbed wire around the place we had made there, enclosing our own special plot of failure from the encroaching emptiness. We congratulated ourselves that it was such a tight, firm fence. Wandering stock couldn't get in and camp in the chicken house, or rub anything down scratching off winter hair. We told ourselves that some day we would be back. We memorized the landmarks of five years.

But we knew, we all knew, that we wouldn't be back any more than the families of our acquaintance who had already left; and I imagine we obscurely felt that more than our personal hope had died in the shack that stayed in sight all the time we were bumping down along the field to the border. With nothing in sight to stop anything, along a border so unwatched that it might have been unmapped, something really had stopped there; a crawl of human hope had stopped.

As we turned at the Line, headed for the county road that began at Hydro, we could still see the round roof of the shack lifting above the prairie north of us. There was nothing else in sight up there but empty prairie. My mother drew in her breath and blew it out again with a little laugh, and said the words that showed us how such a departure should be taken. "Well," she said, "better luck next time!"

EPILOGUE:
FALSE-FRONT
ATHENS

She looked across the silent fields to the West. She was conscious of an unbroken sweep of land to the Rockies, to Alaska; a dominion which will rise to unexampled greatness when other empires have grown senile. Before that time, she knew, a hundred generations of Carols will aspire and go down in tragedy devoid of palls and solemn chanting, the humdrum inevitable tragedy of struggle against inertia.

SINCLAIR LEWIS, *Main Street*

Once nostalgia has been stirred and placated by the sight of old places and the corroboration of the ineradicable images, I have no personal excuse for extending my return to Whitemud. But I do extend it for several days, reading old files of the *Leader* and talking with Corky Jones and going back and forth through the town to see what, in its less than fifty years, it has become. Has it anything, by now, that would recommend it as a human habitat? The question ought to be answered without the scorn of a city intellectual or the angry defensiveness of a native son; and it is not easy.

From one point of view Whitemud is an object lesson in the naïveté of the American hope of a new society. It emphasizes the predictability and repetitiousness of the frontier curve from hope to habit, from optimism to a country rut, from American Dream to Revolt against the Village—in Clarence King's phrase, the pilgrimage from savagery through barbarism to vulgarity. That curve is possible anywhere in America, but nearly inevitable on the Plains, because on the Plains the iron inflexibilities of low rainfall, short growing season, monotonous landscape, and wide extremes of temperature limit the number of people who can settle and the prosperity and contentment of the ones who manage to stick.

The drouth of the 1930's suggested not only that a large part of the semi-arid Plains country was over-populated, but that those who continue to live there are probably doomed to a lower standard of living than most parts of the country enjoy. And there are corollaries of a non-economic kind. Whitemud, a generation past its pioneering stage, demonstrates all over again how much of amenity and the refined intelligence is lost when civilized men are transplanted to a wilderness. It raises the question, unthinkable to pioneers but common enough among their expatriate sons, whether any Whitemud can hope to develop to a state of civilization as high as that which some of its founders abandoned—whether those pioneers who were educated men did not give up a heritage of some richness to become part of a backwater peasantry incapable of the feeblest cultural aspiration. If the answer to that question is yes, if generations of children are to grow up without architecture, art, theater, dance, music, or conversation, and if at the same time the charm of savagery is systematically reduced by the uglifications we call progress, then the only alternatives for the intelligent and talented young will be frustration (see *The Story of a Country Town, The Damnation of Theron Ware, The Spoon River Anthology, Winesburg Ohio, Main Street, One of Ours*) or escape. These are not quite the alternatives that the dream of the new world promised.

Obviously it is unfair to demand that Whitemud demonstrate itself a rural Athens, or even a Syracuse. Few gods came along into this Latium; one of the conditions of settlement was that old gods be lost and new ones developed, appropriate to the time and place. And these are hard to discern, slow to make themselves apparent. Still, precisely because it is belated and a backwater, the Cypress Hills country tempts one into a trial balance between what was given up on the frontier and what the new town has regained or created since. Implicit in any such trial balance is the testing of what was once an American faith: that a new society striking boldly off from the old would first give up everything but axe and gun and then, as the pioneering hardships were survived, would begin to shape itself in new forms. Prosperity would follow in due course. A native character would begin to emerge, a character more self-reliant and more naturally noble than any that could be formed in tired and corrupt Europe, and new institutions would spring from the new social compact among free and classless men. After an appropriate interval this society ought to find its voice in unmistakably native arts.

What came? A whole baggage of habits, customs, tendencies, leanings, memories, political and religious affiliations, codes of conduct, educational practices. Pioneers always try to use the past as a template by which to cut the future. The most viable imports, because the commonest, were associated with democratic-cooperative politics, the English language, and Protestantism, but there were other elements in the mixture, and by no means all of the English-democratic-Protestant baggage survived.

In my years there, Whitemud had one Jewish family, one Syrian family, one Greek Orthodox bachelor, and two Chinese, who could have been Confucian, Taoist, or Buddhist without its making the slightest difference. For the isolates there were only two alternatives: join or be excluded. And joining, which would have had to be both religious and social, was not always practicable. The Jews, the Greek, and the two Chinese stuck to their own traditions and were never really a part of the town. On the contrary the Syrians, despite a glutinous Middle-Eastern accent, were actively and completely a part of it because they sent their children to the United Presbyterian Sunday School, and their children, who were lively, bright, and about nine in number, made the transition for them.

Other religious divisions made no transitions, but maintained their separateness. The Anglicans were a faintly superior group of exclusives, especially after they had a church built for them as a war memorial by the Girls Friendly Society of Huntley, diocese of Chichester, Sussex. The Catholics, who had inaugurated Christianity in the area through the labors of Father Lestanc, limped along for seven years having Mass celebrated in the Pastime Theater by a visiting priest from Dollard, until in 1921, after we left Whitemud, they got a parish church and a resident priest of their own. The United Church, following the amiably non-sectarian precedent established by the two camping seminarians in 1914, served a collection of Presbyterians, Methodists, Baptists, Lutherans, Congregationalists, Dutch Reformeds, and others who, like the Syrians, were not denominationally choosy. Religiously, Whitemud became the counterpart of ten thousand little American and Canadian towns. Of all the habits and customs imported, its religious traditions were least modified by the frontier.

In other ways, too, it tried to tie itself to the forms of what it had left behind, and to bend immigrants from other cultures to those patterns. Within two months of the first meeting of the Village Council, a group was agitating for the formation of a Masonic Lodge, and within two years they had it. Nine years later they let the ladies in by getting a charter for a chapter of the Order of the Eastern Star. In 1917 the all-seeing eye of the I.O.O.F. began looking up Main Street from the false front of Christenson's pool hall, which had once housed the school.

The school itself, though it had to make early concessions as to quarters, was from the beginning a stabilizing and traditional element in the town's life. From the loft above the pool hall it moved briefly to a shop next to Jakey Klein's butcher shop. Though the official town history, compiled for the 1955 Jubilee, does not mention that stage in the school's development, I know it existed. That was where I first saw colored crayons and plasticine, where I embroidered on a pre-stamped, pre-punched card a gorgeous yarn maple leaf, and where I fell in love for the first time—with a girl whom I later cruelly jilted because some of my friends pointed out she was bowlegged. The butcher-shop temple of learning must have been a very temporary makeshift, for in 1915 the town built the first two rooms of a new brick school, and in 1917 finished two more. There we spent the hours from eight to four, five days a week, ten months a year. The classrooms tied us to the past, the school yard to the present and future.

If my memory is reliable at all, the teachers were at least average, and made up in enthusiasm and dedication whatever they may have lacked in training. In particular I remember Miss Birch, a delicate, rather pretty girl who always shrank from me a little after I put my dirty bare hoof on her desk to show her where I had shot myself through the toe. Also Miss Mitchell, a city slicker from Kingston, Ontario, for whom I nourished a sullen, implacable hatred because she once made me stand from recess to noon bent over the water fountain. The object was to cure me of stopping for a drink after the bell. It cured me. But Miss Mitchell got hers. In the flu epidemic, when she was in bed in her old schoolroom, one of the volunteer nurses found a quart of bootlegged rye whiskey between her knees. Over in the first-and-second-grade room where I was lying at death's door with deliriums and nosebleeds and a fever of a hundred and four, I heard that story as it spread, and I swear it made me well.

I remember also Mr. McGregor, a young and active principal whom we liked as universally as we disliked Miss Mitchell, probably because for the first time in our experience he was a male in the schoolroom. And his maleness was real. He was a mighty swimmer and ball player, a great hand at a frolic or masquerade, a promoter of town entertainments, and a firm but not harsh judge of schoolboy delinquencies. God rest him, where-ever he is. I do not recall his intellectual attainments, but I know he praised mine, and so I must think he was a good teacher.

Our curriculum was out of joint with our life, but it did tie us into Western civilization; if it told us little about who we were, it taught us something of who we had been. Along with the arithmetic, reading, writing, geography, and history that had all been made for other children in another world, we got a heavy steeping in the growth-and-progress gospels that were peculiarly our own. The success story, however dubious it may look later, is the inevitable literature, because it is the unquestioned faith, of a frontier. And if part of our education was indoctrinating us with assumptions that we would shortly have to unlearn, that was of the very essence of the frontier experience. As I snoop around my old town I do not find evidence that the urge toward success has been chastened since my time. I hear a good deal about people I grew up with, and most of it concerns how they married an American millionaire, or made it big as a geologist for Standard Oil, or tour the country every year giving piano recitals, or have become contractors in Calgary, bankers in Victoria, newspaper publishers in Regina, teachers or doctors or executives somewhere else. It even seems that in the town's own terms the children of Whitemud have had more than their share of honors and success. But always somewhere else. Instead of developing as a land of opportunity, Whitemud has become an exporter of manpower to the places where real opportunity exists.

I find myself ruminating on the kind of manpower it has been able to export, the kind of people that the children I knew might have grown into. Frontiers, like wars, are said to break down established civilizing restraints and to encourage demorali-

zation. They are also sometimes said to engender in people, by
freeing them from artificial restraints and throwing them into
contact with clean nature, a generosity, openness, independence,
and courage unknown to the over-civilized. We were all sensuous
little savages. Was that good or bad for us in the long run? Did
it encourage depravity or promote natural goodness?

According to Leslie Fiedler, "There is a sense, disquieting to
good Montanans, in which Montana is the product of European
literature." So there is; some of what Whitemud was, and some
of the image I learned to have of myself, derived from words
spoken and attitudes struck by romantic philosophers and poets.
But I doubt that the fact is as disquieting to good Montanans as
Mr. Fiedler thinks, nor to good Saskatchewanians either, who
are the same breed, only more backward. Like all westerners,
they are prone to glorify the pioneer time (after all, what other
history and what other mythic figures are so intimately theirs?)
and to applaud in themselves the perhaps phantasmal echoes of
Noble Savagery. It has its ridiculous aspects when Frontier Days
come around and the boys start growing beards. But it also has
its salutary aspects, in that it provides models of conduct that
may be limited but are never ignoble. It likewise may give a
child a faith in life by teaching him what it means to be a
healthy animal. Finally, I doubt that self-deception is as wide-
spread in Montana or the West at large as Mr. Fiedler thinks it
is, or natural goodness (western brand) so universally assumed.
I think none of the people I grew up with would deny that a
snake grew in the pioneer garden, and found it as much to his
liking as any Noble Savage ever did. As frontier children, we
demonstrated just about as much natural goodness as would balance our old Adam.

On one side we were junior Boones and Bumppos, self-reliant
individualists with nothing between us and the lightnings except
our own unparted hair. We swam without lifeguards, hiked without scoutmasters, carried deadly weapons before we had reached
the age of discretion, came and went as we pleased except when
school kept us hobbled. On the other hand we had mothers,
most of us, who became all the more aware of the proprieties as
the proprieties suffered slippage; and we were Sunday Schooled,

reproved, jawed, and licked almost as much as if we had grown up in Eton jackets. Altogether, it amounted to a stand-off.

Only one of my Whitemud generation, so far as I know, grew up corrupt or criminal, but his example must be accounted for. He was the Town Bull of our later years in the village. Some years after we left, he took a girl to an abandoned shack in the hills and kept her there three days, feeding her Spanish fly. She died and he went to jail, and there were many, I am sure, who ran back over T.B.'s career and said I told you so, he was a bad one all the way. And yet not unrecognizably different from the rest of us. I knew that shack, for I had raided it with my gang once or twice, had once helped steal a .44 pistol and some dynamite caps from it, and had once tried to burn it down just for the hell of it. We were not well-bred young gentlemen, and not all our young ladies were ladies. All of us were guilty of juvenile thefts; in the face of our envious wants and lacks no property was really safe. Likewise we grew up killing things, and that might have matured in violence. The boys (I was one) who hunted down every stray cat and shot it for its fifty-cent hide could have come to any of several bad ends. As for the ugly sort of crime that T.B. committed, it might have been expected of more of us. Our sexual environment was a combination of conventional prudery and barnyard freedom. Perhaps our infantile sexual investigations did not differ much from those that go on in any rural and unchaperoned place, but we were more unchaperoned than most. No boy was a man if he did not indulge in backhouse pornography, we had our show parties in haylofts, gang diddling of complaisant little girls happened now and then, and at least once a group of us witnessed a public exhibition of brother-sister incest.

All this is sufficiently barbarous or natural, depending on the point of view. But it is important that it went on in conjunction with an official adult prudery to which we all tacitly subscribed. Psychiatrists would call it most unhealthy. Sometimes I wonder if it was as unhealthy as it is supposed to be. Random historical investigations will not tell us how many of my Whitemud companions have been driven to repent their hypocritical upbringing on the couch, but I would guess very few. For one thing, even if we had been warped by the lack of frankness in our sexual education, going to a psychiatrist about it would strike most of us, I imagine, as both crybabyish and mouthy. We discussed sexual matters frankly enough, and with frank sniggers, when we got the chance; but on the subject of our personal hurts our morality told us to be as taciturn as stones.

It was not only Pop Martin, with his attempt to create a gentleman's seat in the Whitemud Valley, who lost everything he brought in. Conventions also suffered decay and disintegration in our backwoods community. And the amenities suffered even worse than the conventions. In particular, the educated and the English, who were often but not invariably synonymous, found that it was impossible to keep alive on the frontier the things that made life agreeable. Many made the most strenuous efforts to naturalize their old life on new soil, but a great deal of what they transplanted has died, and some of the survivals are surprising.

Tennis, for example. A group of English found that the silty clay of the bottoms made a smooth firm surface. They scraped and leveled a court, erected backstops, bought rackets, balls, and net by mail order, and one morning sallied out in their flannels, ignoring the ill-bred snickering of the village. They formed a club, held a tournament every Victoria Day, had club matches with Gull Lake, Shaunavon, Swift Current, and Maple Creek. But soon some of them went off to the war, and others drifted away, and tennis waned. It was a game for die-hards. In its whole history in Whitemud it does not seem to have been learned by a single Whitemud child, or played by a single adult who had not learned it elsewhere. Simply, it did not take. And what happened to the tennis crowd happened in identical terms to the golfers who used to knock balls around the sports ground. I look carefully, but I see not a sign of either golf or tennis now; when I inquire, I find that no one has attempted to revive them for years.

The local pride so noticeable in the early files of the *Leader*, the peppy competitiveness of the Board of Trade, has evidently grown tired. There is no longer a town baseball or rugby team to play for the town's honor against Shaunavon. Now and then

one is organized, but shortly dwindles away for lack of interest.
Even the swimming hole, which on a spring Sunday in my time
used to have the whole town and a lot of outside visitors either
in it or lined up on the cutbank watching, is obviously used now
almost exclusively by the children. A Tattooed Man could make
his appearance, as he once did to us, without drawing a crowd
or a gasp. It wouldn't be worth his while to show up, now, but in
my time he was a sensation. He appeared one Sunday morning
coming down to the footbridge. His arms and legs were covered
with designs, his body was ringed with blue and white stripes.
Some of the ladies on the cutbank grew terrified that he was *all*
tattoo, that he wore only ink. While the whole town watched
with hung jaw he lowered himself from the footbridge into water
shoulder deep and launched into a dignified, froglike breast-
stroke down around the bend under the editor's high board.
Like people on a ship moving to the opposite rail to watch some
passing sight, the crowd moved up along the cutbank; you could
almost feel the ground list under their weight. Then it listed back,
and here came the Tattooed Man breast-stroking upriver again.
The jitter of splashing and diving boys parted to let him through.
As he mounted the footbridge men craned and ladies averted
their eyes. Disappointingly, his blue and white stripes turned
out to be cotton. When he walked up the dugway to the bath-
house, about forty of us followed and watched him dress: we
wanted to see how far his pictures extended. We saw, but he
was not communicative otherwise. He covered his art work and
stepped to the door, and only then pulled down the whole right
side of his face in a wink. We adored him; he had us behind him
as the Pied Piper had rats, and when he climbed into his buggy
tied in front of the hotel, and smacked the lines on the team's
rumps and started off toward South Fork, we watched him out of
sight as we might have watched the departing Quetzalcoatl.

He was a nine-day wonder, as notable as the albino traveling
salesman who sported among us and palpitated girlish hearts for
a day. We followed *him* into the bath house too—we wanted to
see if his pubic hair was as white as the hair on his head. It was.

Alas, these marvels now would go unnoticed. There is nobody
but a rabble of children at the river. Aquatic sports, I learn, are
no longer organized. Nobody now tries to set town records down

the stretch between footbridge and high board, nobody tries to walk a greased pole braced out from the cutbank. There is an annual school sports day, but it is an outing rather than an athletic event, and nobody trains or practices for it.

The wheat-mining economy might explain this summer apathy, for many of the boys and young men are off living in tents or trailers or farm shacks during the crop season. But in winter it is not much different, I hear. Neither the hockey team nor the basketball team enlists much enthusiasm, and neither has a coach. Only one sport does get people out, and that is the one that no one would ever have predicted would have a future: curling.

I remember the first curling ever attempted in Whitemud. Some Scotchmen flooded a shed next to the livery stable and undertook to teach the town a real game. The rink was forty feet shorter than regulation, but the reception for some reason was enthusiastic, and curling did not dwindle like golf, tennis, baseball, rugby, even hockey. It grew. By now Whitemud has rinks with waiting rooms and twenty sheets, it has men's, women's, and students' curling clubs, it has club competitions and bonspiels from New Year to the spring thaw. And why that should be—why that odd game, a cross between bocci ball and sweeping the front porch, should catch on when every other imported game curled up and died—is one of the mysteries. It is more expensive in its facilities and equipment than most sports, it has none of the vigorous exercise or the exhilaration of body contact that a tough frontier town should like. I can understand why this softer generation prefers indoor rinks to our old system of shoveling off a stretch of bumpy river ice and skating with a big bonfire to warm up by. But I should have expected the youth of Whitemud to be whipping a puck up and down those indoor rinks, instead of sliding a chunk of tombstone with a handle on it down the ice while someone else performs witchcraft with a big besom to steer or hurry or impede it. Recruiters for the professional hockey leagues needn't come to Whitemud.

From all the obvious symptoms, it would be as hard to find any cultural stir in my old town as to find any vigorous games. Dead, dead, dead, says the mind contemplating the town's life. Dead in the poolroom, dead in the licensed premises of the hotel, where the Mountie comes in periodically to check up and to count empties, dead in the lace-curtained parlors, slack-jawed in feed store and elevator, vacant-faced before the flickering screen of the Pastime Theater, where boys and girls still tend, as in my time, to sit on different sides of the house, and where the aisle seats on both sides are double width for patrons especially broad in the beam. A dull, dull little town where nothing passes but the wind, a town so starved for excitement that a man's misfortune in losing his false teeth in the river can enliven a whole winter's pool-room and hardware-store conversation.

There is still no library in Whitemud, though now any six families may form a reading society and borrow as many as thirty books at a time from the Provincial Library in Saskatoon. That is an acceptable way of making books serve the largest possible public. The trouble is, the initiative comes from Saskatoon, a university town, and not from Whitemud. Moreover, there are few reading circles, and within the reading circles few young people. By and large, these borrow cultural collapse from the United States, and read comic books.

Books a bare minimum. Music about the same. And here, as in so many other intellectual and cultural matters, the town can show less than it could have when it was two years old. In 1915 there were several good garden-variety musicians who could conduct the band and orchestra and give lessons to boys and girls whose mothers thought them worth a cultural investment. (My mother was one. One year she inherited a thousand dollars from an Iowa uncle and promptly, despite the fact that we were hard up, invested more than half of it in a mail-order piano. For perhaps half a year my brother and I made half-hearted assaults on the mysteries of music, but in the end the only achievement was my mother's. She eavesdropped on our lessons, learned them much faster than we did, and eventually worked out perhaps a dozen popular songs, a bar at a time, from the sheet music. In the deprived little hole that Whitemud was in 1917, aspiration could burn as hot as in Florence or Siena. I wonder if it could now.)

In those early years, when the town gave a dance it could choose among three local dance orchestras. Now, Corky Jones tells me, it has not even one. Neither does it have a band, and the occasional child who really wants to study music has difficulty finding teachers or knowing how to proceed. Among the several distinctions of Corky Jones was a certain craftsmanly knack which for a time he indulged by making violins. He made several, one of which his brother used to play over the BBC Third Program, and another of which a *métis* fiddler used to borrow with enthusiasm. But Corky couldn't sell any of his violins in Whitemud, and so he finally gave the last two to two boys, brothers, who were anxious to learn to play. They did learn, a little, and as soon as they could make bearable noises they put the homemade fiddles aside and invested in shiny store-bought ones from T. Eaton.

Someone always brings the life of the mind into towns like Whitemud; the dream of the founders is often the dream of the full life as well as the dream of material success. But it can seldom maintain itself—certainly cannot without some sort of academy or college to keep renewing it. Without an academy, by a sort of cultural Gresham's Law, lower tastes drive out higher. During the pioneering years there are nearly always people of intelligence and education whose skills are at the service of the community, and whose eyes are sharp for the talented young to whom skill might be passed on. In early Whitemud, any children who could sing, recite, or play an instrument were dragooned for town entertainments, and so were the people who taught them, for such a town's amusements have to be homemade, and such a town's parents watch their children hopefully and with pride for manifestations of genius. As a town, Whitemud responded to what it thought culture with a hungry and unanimous Yea. At first.

I remember when the Chautauqua came. Its first manifestation was a lady named Miss Magowan who came through in May, 1917, and did a hard sell on the Board of Trade. Having agreed to guarantee a three-day Chautauqua in the fall, the Board felt its ambition quickened, and it in turn did a hard sell on the town. It was asserted that no parent dared deny his child this educational treat. The four rooms of school competed to see which could first reach a hundred per-cent sale of season tickets. Bull-headed parents without cultural impulses were put under such pressure that few could resist. The whole town was sold, and any farmer who came in for supplies was lucky to get away without season tickets for his whole family.

Then one fall morning a passion of excitement. A special car was shunted onto the siding by the elevators. Roustabouts swarmed out, a main tent went up, three smaller ones joined it, and by afternoon we were there, making agonized choices, for two or three things went on at once, and we couldn't see them all. There was a Harry Lauder imitator, a basso, a singing couple, an orchestra, a band, a theatrical troupe, a whole faculty of lecturers. The musical highlight was generally held to be the basso, who sang "Rocked in the Cradle of the Deep" so far down that he vibrated the folding chairs, and whose success so smote the local basso with envy that it was three weeks before the ladies could persuade him to come back to singing in the choir. The dramatic *pièce de résistance* was *The School for Scandal,* the first play that many of us had ever seen. The heavier intellectuals enjoyed the lectures, before which we children sat impressed and fidgety. I remember that one was concerned with How We See Colors, but I don't remember what the man said.

All in all, a monumental three days. We were all excused from school for the duration of Chautauqua, and we all agreed that not even the Cooper Brothers Circus was any better, and certainly not half so educational.

As I poke around through Whitemud, following the old ditchbank paths under the unfamiliar shade of big cottonwoods, and circling old Millionaire Row and curving with the river down along to Poverty Flat and so back up to the Catholic church at the end of Main Street, I wonder if any such cultural unanimity could be generated in this established town. The old-timers have lost any expectations they may once have had that Whitemud would become a sun-kissed prairie Athens, and the second generation, which is mine, is ninety per cent dispersed, and releasing whatever intellectual and cultural potential it has into other communities. The stickers who really built the town, and wore out their lives in the process, are still there, reinforced by other stickers who have moved in from prairie farms. The town now has a high school, and the level of education of those who grow up and stay there is undoubtedly higher than in my time. But only a limited number can make a living in Whitemud, and those who go hunting wider opportunities are nearly always the brightest and most energetic, as well as the most restless. Time acts like a great slow cream separator.

There is neither training nor a dependable audience for any of the arts in Whitemud, no way for any sort of intellectual or artist to make a living or even have adequate expression as an amateur. Not yet; maybe never. For unless a town like this acquires an academy or college—which by definition would itself have to be second or third rate—it is certain to remain a stagnant peasant society, a seedbed whose transplants will have to mature elsewhere. Now that the brief improbable dream has faded, what is left is a dead little country town which, thanks to radio, mail-order catalogs, and the other forms of communication, has not even the hope of an eventual Balkan color. Its distinguished sons, if any, will be able to contribute to their home town only an occasional visit and a free performance—to a full house, for pride in its sons remains even though the town cannot keep or use the boys it is proud of.

These are not particularly happy conclusions for me, for I like this town; it lives too compellingly in me for me to be indifferent to its subsidence into apathy. And that is why I feel a real and personal pleasure when I think I detect a few signs of native growth. The continued experimentation with methods of dry farming and the continued inventiveness with gang machinery and the continued development of harder and quicker-maturing varieties of wheat do not center in the Whitemud of the Plains region, but they affect the Whitemuds and may be fed from them. Likewise the evolving economic and political structure. Beginning with an individualism that on occasion was so complete as to be irritable, settlers soon enough found the semi-arid Plains a place where no man and no family could do it alone. I have seen those who tried—red-necked Swedes and Norwegians half crazy with hard work and loneliness who came riding or driving down to our shack on the prairie and could hardly bring themselves to leave again, who left with tears in their eyes for the glorious companionship of a day or an afternoon and a farm wife who could give them butter or a few eggs, and who, when their English failed, could talk with them in Norwegian. That single-handed assault on the wilderness might have worked in wooded country with plenty of water and game; nothing even approaching it should have been attempted on the Plains. So what began in individual effort remained—*if* it remained—to cooperate. The progress from the formation of the Grain Growers Association in 1915, and the gradual evolution of cooperative elevators, buying clubs, and banks, went its inevitable course to political flowering in a society militantly cooperative, even socialist. It is so because the country tolerated settlement on no other terms.

That is adaptation, human and institutional flexibility in the face of inflexible conditions, and is as truly a part of a forming native culture as the mobility of the suitcase farmers. There are a few other signs of life, too, and it surprises me, when I look into them, how many of them owe something to Corky Jones. If a community really is like a pile of kindling, inert and heatless until some accident of history or some great man touches it with fire, then Corky, in his humble and unpretentious way, is a sort of light-bringer. In more heroic dimensions and more heroic times, lives such as his get transformed into myth. He is no Prometheus, surely, and no Orpheus bringing music out of the Rhodopaeian mountains. But Saskatchewan gave him a Good Citizen award in 1955, the Jubilee year, and it had cause.

He is nobody important—an old-timer who lives in a little three-room house near the center of town and probably never made two hundred dollars a month in his life. But he has had all his life the best of all possible attitudes in a pioneer: he has never scorned learning, he has always been willing to try importing it, but when the imported varieties don't seem to take root he has hunted for native varieties that will.

He was the son of a doctor on the Isle of Wight. His father took care of Queen Victoria when she visited the island, and Corky's boyhood advantages were somewhat greater than those of the average Whitemud pioneer. But he abandoned them at eighteen and sailed for Canada and arrived in Maple Creek wanting to be a cowboy, in 1898. He was a cowboy, according to his wish, working for Dan Pollack, for Fisher and Martin, and finally for himself, with a ranch on Chimney Coulee almost exactly where Cowie's cabins and the *métis* village and the first Mountie post had stood. When the homesteading of the bench lands brought the application of fence-in herd law, he gave up his ranch to run a livery stable in Whitemud, and when the automobile began to shade out the livery-stable business he and a partner operated the town's first electric plant.

As one of the oldest citizens, antedating the town itself by sixteen years, Corky knows more about what has happened in the
valley than anyone else around. What is more, he cares what has
happened, and not many do. He is a mild and thinking man, with
a built-in, patient curiosity. By a lucky accident his ranch on
Chimney Coulee happened to contain all the archaeological relics
in those parts. Seeing the old foundations under the grass, Corky
measured them. He found a cemetery with six graves. Inquiring
around, he located an old *métis* named Jean Laframboise who
had lived there when a young man, and had known Fathers
Lestanc and de Corby. (De Corby is less well documented than
Lestanc—Corky's is the only reference I have found to him.)
Laframboise showed Corky how the *métis* built their villages in
long shed-like buildings fourteen feet wide and thirty to forty
long, partitioned into family cells every ten or twelve feet, with a
stone fireplace and chimney in each partition. So Corky knew,
when the rest of the town was content to guess, what had made
those lines of chimneys along the coulee. He had a knack for
knowing. Living his life, he picked up things. When Indians held
powwows nearby, he listened in, talked with them, went down
after they left to examine the blue and yellow streamers and the
packages and plugs of tobacco they had tied to the chokecherry
bushes for the departed. He dug up and read Cowie's *Company
of Adventurers*, he pumped passing Cree for stories of fights and
massacres, he knew the whole history of the Mounties in the
region.

None of his history-gathering had any particular purpose—he
just wanted to know. He made violins to see if he could; he
learned to play them a little because that seemed the natural next
step. And when, riding through the hills, he saw petrified bones of
great beasts weathered out of the soft rock, he began to collect
them, just as for a long time he had collected arrowheads and
medicine bags and spears and warclubs and other Indian artifacts.
Having the bones around, he could not be content until he got
books and learned what they might be. Whatever the defects of
his education, he knew the indispensable first step: how to go
about learning. Today his collection of dinosaur and Tertiary
mammal bones fills the whole basement of the school. It was
created entirely by Corky, but it contains several unique speci-

mens and it enlists the respectful attention of every trained paleontologist who comes to dig in the rich fossil beds of the Cypress
Hills.

It is a question whether or not the museum means anything in
particular, outside of an easily satisfied and idle curiosity, to the
pupils in the four rooms above it, though it offers them more
information on the history of their own place than anything else
in the school or the town either. But it is barely possible that
Corky's Indian relics and old bones are a cultural match. When
they and the proper kindling are brought close together, something might happen. And even if no Whitemud child ever
takes fire from Corky's collection and becomes an anthropologist
or paleontologist, something may still have been accomplished by
his example. Any child who knows Corky can see knowledge
being loved for its own sake—something not too common in
Whitemud, but not totally unknown.

There was another in Whitemud who had a little of Corky's
intellectual curiosity. He was Jack Wilkinson, a machinist and
general repair man. In 1949 he began to get interested in astronomy, and put together for his own edification a six-inch reflector
telescope. A hobby, we might say, half amused and half pitying.
A desperate effort of a starved spirit. Many must live and die
alone, even in Winesburg. But Wilkinson was so thrilled by his
first look at the heavens that he built a larger telescope, an eight-
incher, and a little observatory to house it, and he invited the
town to come in any time for a look. In 1953 he died, much respected. But his observatory did not die with him, because Corky
Jones, and a few others unwilling to see a light go out, formed—
how touching and how finally splendid—the Whitemud Astronomical Society, and sold memberships for funds to buy the
telescope and dome from Wilkinson's estate. It stands there now
across from the Pastime Theater, the Wilkinson Memorial Observatory, whose published intent is "to further the study of the
stars and perhaps some day to help develop a budding Newton."

Seeing it there, the weeds suspiciously tall and untrampled
around it, I don't know whether to be more struck by the difficulty of keeping the flame alive, or by the fact that in the occasional Corky Jones it is unquenchable.

During my childhood the principal thoroughfare we traveled was a footpath that led along the welt of the ditchbank toward town. At the first diversion weir and plank footbridge, a branch path led off right to the *Leader* office, and from the corner of that another branch led on to the United Church. A little farther up the ditch from the first weir, another branch turned off left to the school. And that was it, that was the town, essentially: public school, free press, Protestant church. The forked path articulated three of the basic institutions of Whitemud. Bath houses and sports ground defined another, and the dump was fundamental to them all. In forty years others have grown up around them; the modern Whitemud child has architecture other than grain elevators; the monuments of his tribe have had four decades to accumulate, and if they are not any of them Giotto's tower or Independence Hall, they are enough to tell him who he is. The several churches, the hospital, the enlarged school, the town memorial hall, are accomplishment against real odds, and they create a solidity and permanence that were notably lacking for us. Crude as it still is, this is a community, and a very much less ugly one than the bare, ditch-cut, shack-strewn, sweet-clover-smelling village of my youth.

My walk has brought me back around by the elevators and a vacant lot full of rod weeders and tractors, the heavy, massive power machinery by means of which solitary farmers now handle a thousand acres or more of wheat land. I come up toward Main Street on the short side street leading to the post office, and just short of the corner I find myself looking in a half-curtained window at an apple-green ceiling and part of a bare apple-green wall. It is a tiny shack, no more than a dozen feet wide and twenty long—such a shack as used to house Milo Grubb's barber shop or Jakey Klein's butcher shop. It may even *be* Jakey Klein's, moved to a new location; for an instant my hallucinating senses bring me the taint of the high beef scraps, or the liver heat-stuck to its brown paper, that we used to bum from Jakey for fishbait. But now the sign above the doorway reads "Farm Wives' Rest Home."

Weather-beaten, warped, the paint flaking off its shiplap, its windows flyspecked and with alluvial fans of dust in the corners of the frames, its partly seen interior poisonous with bilious calcimine, it hardly suggests rest. Behind it a path leads to a privy on whose front someone has painted, evidently with a finger dipped in lamp black, the legend "Ladies." The wind has cornered candy-bar wrappers and gum wrappers in the doorway and whirls them, lifts them, lets them fall into a pile, stirs them up again. I stand bemused, with grit in my teeth and dust in my eyes, thinking that here is quintessential Whitemud. Here is a human institution, born of a compassionate and humane impulse, and tailored to a felt need, falling so far short of its intention that it would draw a snicker from anyone who didn't stop to think first. If he thought first, he might elect to honor the impulse, rather than scorn the result, however shoddy.

For the snickerer should remember that in all of Whitemud, which even yet is without plumbing, there is not a service station with a toilet to which a woman from the country can take a desperate child. There is not a park where a tired woman can sit down, not a public library where she can wait out the hours of heat and tedium while her husband buys feed or seed or gopher poison or a part for his tractor, or sprawls around the Grain Growers elevator gassing with friends, or visits the licensed premises of the hotel. If a farm woman has friends in town, she can indulge in that country pastime called "the visit." But if she is from far out, and shy, she may sit a long time in the pickup parked on Main Street, reading a woman's magazine from the drugstore or frowning down on a headache. Hamlin Garland did that rural unfortunate tenderly in the story called "A Day's Pleasure," and Sinclair Lewis's stepmother spent a lot of her time promoting just such a place as this Farm Wives' Rest Home in the town that would become Gopher Prairie. It took Whitemud about forty years to do as much as it now has done for the comfort of country women. It is little enough—a superannuated false-front shack, a little calcimine, some discarded chairs, an old cot, some magazines, and a privy out behind. But it is the most humane institution in all that village, and it is purely native, the answer to a local need. If it is given up as soon as the town gets plumbing and a well-equipped service station, well and good. What matters is that it exists now to acknowledge a community responsibility; that it exists minimal and ugly only suggests, at least to one brought up on the pragmatic meliorism of the frontier, that it can be improved, and will be.

In the end, I decide not to fault Whitemud for not being what only centuries of growth and the accidents of wealth and human genius could make it. Let it be, at least for a good long while, a seedbed, as good a place to be a boy and as unsatisfying a place to be a man as one could well imagine. Unless North American tourists discover the beauty of the geometric earth and the enormous sky brimming with weather, and learn the passion of loneliness and the mystery of a prairie wind, Whitemud is going to have too little to work with; it will remain marginal or submarginal in its community and cultural life.

Nevertheless, with its occasional impulse to the humane. Nevertheless, with its occasional Corky Jones. And therefore not unhopeful. Give it a thousand years.

Acknowledgments

Remembering is by no means a lonesome occupation. Remembering for this book, I have had the pleasure of help from a good many old Saskatchewan friends, particularly Corky Jones and Bill Anderson. They are entitled to blame me if in spite of their help I have remembered wrong, or if I have occasionally warped fact a little in order to reach for the fictional or poetic truth that I would rank a little above history. I have benefited from the assistance of the Stanford University Library staff, from that of Lewis H. Thomas of Regina College, and from that of Will Ready, now of the Marquette University Library. Merle Curti of the University of Wisconsin, Thomas Presley of the University of Washington, Thomas O'Dea of the University of Utah, and the late Alfred Kroeber have warmed me with their interest and their suggestions. The book was begun on a grant from the Wenner-Gren Foundation for Anthropological Research, and completed on a fellowship to the Center for Advanced Studies in the Behavioral Sciences. To both these organizations, and to the staff of the latter, especially Phyllis Ellis, I make my sincere thanks.